About Island Press

Since 1984, the nonprofit organization Island Press has been stimulating, shaping, and communicating ideas that are essential for solving environmental problems worldwide. With more than 1,000 titles in print and some 30 new releases each year, we are the nation's leading publisher on environmental issues. We identify innovative thinkers and emerging trends in the environmental field. We work with world-renowned experts and authors to develop cross-disciplinary solutions to environmental challenges.

Island Press designs and executes educational campaigns, in conjunction with our authors, to communicate their critical messages in print, in person, and online using the latest technologies, innovative programs, and the media. Our goal is to reach targeted audiences—scientists, policy makers, environmental advocates, urban planners, the media, and concerned citizens—with information that can be used to create the framework for long-term ecological health and human well-being.

Island Press gratefully acknowledges major support from The Bobolink Foundation, Caldera Foundation, The Curtis and Edith Munson Foundation, The Forrest C. and Frances H. Lattner Foundation, The JPB Foundation, The Kresge Foundation, The Summit Charitable Foundation, Inc., and many other generous organizations and individuals.

Protecting Pollinators

Protecting Pollinators

How to Save the Creatures That Feed Our World

Jodi Helmer

Washington | Covelo | London

Library of Congress Control Number: 2018959605

All photographs by the author.

All Island Press books are printed on environmentally responsible materials.

Manufactured in the United States of America
10 9 8 7 6 5 4 3 2 1

Keywords:
Monarch butterfly, bats, honeybees, migration, native plants, invasive species, pesticides, farming, gardens, endangered species, seed libraries, climate change

For Charlotte, Sadie, Sam, and Farrah,
who deserve to grow up in a world where
nature is abundant and protected.

Contents

Introduction

On a sweltering afternoon last June, I stood over a beehive, removing one frame after another, looking for signs of life. Small hive beetles (*Aethina tumida*) had decimated the colony: they burrowed into the combs and ate the brood and pollen; their excrement contaminated the honey and covered each frame in a thick slime. The honeybees (*Apis mellifera*) either died or absconded, leaving us with a hive filled with invasive beetles and no bees.

I had done a routine inspection less than a week earlier and noticed the hive was queenless. (A hive can lose the queen for a number of reasons, including disease; she can also be killed by other bees in the colony or by a predator during her mating flight. Once the hive is without its queen, it is vulnerable and a new queen needs to be installed ASAP.)

As soon as I noticed the issue, I called my beekeeping mentor, Bee (yes, that's her real name), and she agreed to bring three new hives—one to merge with our queenless hive to get it "queen right," and two others so we could compare colonies and have additional bees to boost weak hives in case something like this happened again.

Before we could install the new hives, we did a second inspection of our original hive. Although just a few days had passed between inspections, by the time Bee arrived, the small hive beetles had taken over, killing the hive and forcing me to start over. Again.

Our first hive was a gift for my husband, Jerry, who loved the idea of producing local honey in our backyard. I was initially nervous around the stinging insects and preferred watching from afar, but I quickly became fascinated with the strong social networks in colonies and the complexity of the lives the bees led inside the small wooden box.

To learn to be a responsible beekeeper, I read countless books, attended "bee school" through the local county extension office, and connected with a patient and knowledgeable mentor. Jerry and I did hive inspections together, relying on each other to maximize our powers of observation and to troubleshoot problems—and there were a lot of problems, from small hive beetles to bees that swarmed before we could split the hive. Nevertheless, we persisted.

Learning about the threats facing all pollinators made me want to help—and a big part of that was becoming a better beekeeper and ensuring that I was doing all I could to make our hives thrive. On that blazing-hot afternoon in June, I promised three new hives filled with healthy bees that I would do my best to protect them.

The more I learned about honeybees, the more I learned about other pollinators. I started noticing sweat bees (*Lasioglossum* spp.) hovering over the clover in our yard and carpenter bees (*Xylocopinae*) burrowing into the wood in our barn to build their nests; I watched hummingbirds alight at the feeders filled with red nectar that hung in the garden; and I noticed that none of the butterflies flittering to and fro were monarchs (*Danaus plexippus*).

Watching the pollinators all around me got me thinking back to elementary school lessons on pollination. I have only the fuzziest recollections of labeling the male and female plant parts, printing "stamen" and "pistil" in careful block letters next to line drawings of flowers; and using fat black and orange crayons to color a picture of a monarch butterfly that was later hung on the classroom wall. I don't remember hearing stories about the migratory journeys of the iconic eastern monarchs that travel up to 100 miles a day to make the trek from their northern ranges to sunny Mexico, where they spend their winters hibernating in *oyamel* fir trees; or learning about the important role that pollinators played in getting my favorite foods to the table. Maybe I would have paid more attention if my teacher had explained that we needed pollinators to have chocolate!

Researching *Protecting Pollinators* helped me understand that a lot of us have forgotten the role that pollinators play in our ecosystem. When I mentioned this project, people responded with: "So, you're writing a book about bees?"

Well, sort of. In writing this book, I wanted to go back to basics. Before we can understand what is happening with pollinators and what is being done—or what can be done—to protect them, we first need to be reminded of what pollination is, who does the work, and why it matters.

Pretty creatures like honeybees and monarch butterflies have become the faces of pollination; less-attractive pollinators like hoverflies (Syrphidae) or hawk moths (Sphingidae) are almost never part of the conversation because it's hard to get children—and adults—excited about hard-to-identify insects that lack colorful anatomies and enchanting stories of long migratory journeys. So those childhood coloring pages are often filled with monarch butterflies, honeybees, and hummingbirds, which remain the most well-studied and well-understood pollinators.

Monarch expert Karen Oberhauser believes familiarity brings certain pollinators more fame. She told me, "I give a lot of talks about monarchs to the public, and so many people have stories about the interactions they've had with monarchs throughout their lives . . . and that familiarity breeds this real passion for monarchs."

No one remembers an interaction with a hoverfly, so it gets erased from our consciousness along with thousands of other less-iconic pollinator species that need our help. All pollinators are facing extreme threats—habitat loss, invasive species, pesticides, and climate change. Thanks to an increasing awareness of the impacts on pollinators, people do want to help, but they have no idea where to start—and sometimes their "helpful" gestures end up doing more harm than good.

When Island Press published *The Forgotten Pollinators* in 1997, Colony Collapse Disorder, varroa mites, neonicotinoids, and climate change were not part of the lexicon and news about the pollinator crisis was not making headlines. But authors Stephen L. Buchmann and Gary Paul Nabhan were aware of the trends affecting pollinators. Even then, there was a flicker of recognition that pollinators were struggling and we needed to do something to save them. *The Forgotten Pollinators* made the case that pollinators play an important role in our ecosystem by providing services that are essential in maintaining the stability of our food and fiber supplies.

In the first chapter, "Silent Springs and Fruitless Falls," Nabhan writes:

> It has been well over thirty years since Rachel Carson predicted a silent spring, one devoid of the chorus of insect-feeding birds, one where "no bees droned among the blossoms." That prophecy was heard far and wide, and perhaps more than any other of the last half century, it changed the way farmers, wildlife managers, and policymakers perceived "environmental protection." Yet Rachel Carson also predicted fruitless falls, autumns in which "there was no pollination and there would be no fruit."
>
> Carson suggested that fruitless falls would become more commonplace in the American countryside for two reasons. First, she said, "a bee may carry poisonous nectar back to its hive and presently produce poisonous honey." This prediction proved

> true, and considerable efforts have been made to reduce domestic honeybee poisonings by herbicides and pesticides. However, the same effort has not been diligently extended to protect wild pollinators from toxic chemical exposures, direct and indirect, on farms and wildlands. Second, she observed that "many herbs, shrubs, and trees of forests depend upon native insects for their reproduction; without these plants, many wild animals and range stock would find little food. Now clean cultivation and the chemical destruction of hedgerows and weeds are eliminating the last sanctuaries of these pollinating insects and breaking the threads that bind life to life."
>
> Of all of Carson's commentaries, this is perhaps the one that has been least heeded or understood: that habitats are being fragmented by physical destruction and chemical disruption of their biota. . . . Once again, Carson's superlative intuitions were right on track and eerily futuristic.

Pollinators are still struggling. Since those words were written more than twenty years ago, the rusty-patched bumblebee (*Bombus affinis*) made headlines—and history—in 2017 when it became the first bumblebee species in the continental United States to be placed on the endangered species list. During the same two decades, monarch populations have plummeted to record lows, and Colony Collapse Disorder has seen honeybees abandoning their hives with no apparent cause. But awareness of the issue is now greater than ever before. Today, farmers, gardeners, businesses, nonprofits, and eaters alike are stepping up to save the creatures that feed our world, planting habitats filled with native species, avoiding chemicals, participating in citizen science projects, and spreading the word that pollinators are in trouble and we need to take action to save them. Pollinators may be in peril, but they are no longer forgotten.

CHAPTER 1

Bees and Beyond

WHEN BEES ALIGHT ON FLOWERS, something magical happens. Minute grains of pollen stick to their bodies while they gather nectar and, as the bees buzz about, moving from flower to flower, pollen grains are deposited on new flowers, triggering pollination. Though the entire process lasts mere seconds, our ecosystem depends on it.

Honeybees are credited with much of the work. Headlines like "Honey Bee Extinction Will Change Life as We Know It," "The Plight of the Honeybee," and "The World's Food Supply Could Feel the Sting of Declining Bee Populations" perpetuate the idea that bees—and honeybees in particular—are the primary pollinators of global food crops. Honeybees *are* important pollinators; American beekeepers crisscross the nation every year, transporting billions of honeybees to pollinate crops ranging from apples and cucumbers to pumpkins and sunflowers. Upwards of 60 percent of commercial beekeepers in the United States travel to California between February and March to place hives among the trees in 1.3 million acres of almond orchards; apiarists bring hives from as far afield as Texas and Florida. But honeybees don't deserve all of the credit for pollinating our favorite flora.

Worldwide, 200,000 different species tackle the task of pollination: vertebrates such as birds, bats, and small mammals make up a small percentage of the global pollinator population, while invertebrates such as flies, butterflies, beetles, moths, and, of course, bees make up the rest. The more widely recognized pollinators like monarch butterflies and honeybees tend to get the most attention. To wit, the honeybee is the face of the Cheerios brand and the star of the blockbuster animated film *Bee Movie*; monarch butterflies, with their striking orange, black, and white markings and their courageous migrations to reach overwintering grounds in milder climates, are emblazoned on the Non-GMO Project label and immortalized in coloring books and even tattoos.

While certain pollinators have been thrust into the spotlight, most of the 11,000 species of moths native to the United States fly under the radar, unrecognized despite being important pollinators. Consider the hawk moth (Sphingidae spp.). Thanks to their drab brown coloring, hawk moths are unimpressive at first glance, but looks can be deceiving. Their long, narrow wings make them fast and nimble in flight, and their tongues, which can measure up to fourteen inches long (the longest of all moth or butterfly species), make hawk moths adept at gathering nectar from flowers that would be off limits to other, less well-endowed pollinators. Because their larvae are green hornworms or tobacco worms, hawk moths are considered crop pests and often blasted with pesticides. The practice has devastated their populations, much to the relief of farmers and gardeners, but also to the detriment of rare plants like queen of the night cactus (*Epiphyllum oxypetalum*) and trumpet flower (*Datura* spp.) that depend on the long-tongued pollinator for reproduction. So, even as the unfortunate-looking hawk moth faces chemical attacks that threaten its survival, the race is on to protect prettier species like monarch butterflies and honeybees.

Box 1-1
Plant Sex

Pollination is simply the name for plant sex: plants need pollen to produce fruit, seeds, and new plants. For that to happen, pollen from the stamen, the male part of the flower, must be transferred to the pistil, the female part of the plant. The pistil is made up of the style, stigma, ovary, and ovules: the stigma receives the pollen, which travels down the style and into the ovary. After a flower is pollinated, the petals fall off; the ovaries become fruit and the ovules become seeds.

Self-pollination: Plants like orchids, peas, sunflowers, beans, and eggplants self-pollinate. Their male and female parts are located close together, making it easier for the flowers to move pollen from the stamen to the pistil. These plants can self-pollinate or be cross-pollinated (see below).

Thanks to "selfing," rare plant species can still reproduce well even when there are few individual plants. This reproductive assurance benefits rare species and ensures their survival even if pollinators disappear from the landscape. Self-pollination also makes it possible for introduced species to invade new landscapes. In at least one study, invasive species of thistles were more likely to self-pollinate than the rarer native species of the same genus.

Wind pollination: Most agricultural crops, including grains like wheat, rice, corn, rye, barley, and oats, are wind pollinated; the breeze picks up nearly weightless grains of pollen and carries them from one flower to another. Plants that are pollinated in this way have lots of miniscule pollen grains but seldom have nectar.

Wind-pollinated plants seem to chase away animal pollinators; when these plants are growing in a landscape, pollinators are less attracted to those that depend on insects to reproduce. For one insect-pollinated plant species, red dead-nettle (*Lamium purpureum*), a study found that nearby wind-pollinated species reduced the amount of its nectar. The results led researchers to argue that future studies of plant–pollinator interactions should take all plant communities into consideration, not just species that rely on animal pollinators.

Cross-pollination: For pollination to occur in plants like cucumbers, carrots, melons, onions, squash, and cauliflower, pollinators must move pollen from one flower to another. Cross-pollination only occurs between two plants of the same species; pollen from a rosebush cannot pollinate a peony.

Buzz pollination: When bees grab onto a flower and flex their flight muscles, the flower vibrates, releasing pollen in a process called *buzz pollination* or *sonication*. Plants that are buzz pollinated, like tomatoes, eggplants, and potatoes, often have tubular anthers with narrow openings at one end; the pollen is small and too tightly packed to be accessible to all pollinators.

Issues with honeybees first came to light in 2006 when beekeepers started recording greater than normal colony losses with no apparent cause. These widespread hive abandonments were later attributed to Colony Collapse Disorder, or CCD. The colonies that succumbed to CCD, called "spring swindle disease" in historic literature, appeared healthy in the weeks leading up to the collapse. Without warning, the bees disappeared, leaving behind hives full of honey, pollen, bee bread, and capped brood. There was no evidence of dead adult bees—they simply abandoned the hive. Despite being responsible for 30-plus percent of colony losses—with beekeepers in some states attributing 90 percent of their losses to CCD—no specific causes have been identified, but several have been investigated. The first comprehensive survey of CCD losses evaluated sixty-one potential factors, from pesticides to pathogens like European foulbrood, varroa mites, and *Nosema* fungus, and found that no single stressor stood out as the sole cause of hive abandonment. (The study did show that CCD-affected colonies did have more pathogens and more types of pathogens than unaffected colonies.) Several other studies have since reached the same conclusions, attributing CCD to multiple stressors rather than a single cause.

Around the same time CCD was first identified, farmers began importing honeybees for the first time since 1922. Congress had passed the Honey Bee Act of 1922 in the hopes of preventing the import of hives with tracheal mites (*Acarapis woodi*). The mites, first reported in the United Kingdom in 1921, live in the tracheal tubes of honeybees and feed on their blood before burrowing through the tracheal tube walls and creating crusty lesions on the breathing tubes. In the earliest stages of infestation, colonies are largely unaffected. Bees traveling between hives (or between apiaries) can transfer the parasite. Tracheal mites affect flight efficiency, cause wing and abdominal deformities, and shorten lifespan. If more than 30 percent of the honeybees in a colony are infected, tracheal mites can be fatal to the entire colony. Fumigating the hive with menthol crystals, a crystalline alcohol extracted from peppermint oil, is the accepted method for controlling tracheal mites. Despite the congressional action, tracheal mites eventually did make their way to the United States. A commercial beekeeper in Texas reported the first infestation in 1984; the mites spread to seventeen states within a year.

News of CCD led Congress to change the terms of the Honey Bee Act of 1922, allowing the import of honeybees for the first time in a generation. Honeybees are native to Europe, not North America, so importing the species used to be commonplace. Farmers imported the iconic pollinators from Australia and New Zealand to help bridge the gap between winter losses and the early pollination season, particularly for the pollination of almond orchards in California.

The combined news of CCD and the appearance of tracheal mites led to some Armageddon-like predictions. With the number of US-managed honeybee colonies hovering around 2.5 million—down from 6 million in 1947—a 2012 report from the United States Department of Agriculture (USDA) warned that "the survivorship of honeybee colonies is too low for us to be confident in our ability to meet the pollination demands of U.S. agricultural crops. . . . We are one poor weather event or high winter bee loss away from a pollination disaster." Predictions were made that a honeybee crisis could lead to a tenfold increase in food prices.

Though the number of honeybee colonies has dropped by more than half over the last 70 years—declines have been blamed on a host of factors, including habitat loss, pesticide use, and climate change—nevertheless the bees have started to bounce back from CCD. During the 2017–2018 winter season, commercial beekeepers lost 26.4 percent of their hives (acceptable winter losses were 20.6 percent for the same time period), but it's not all good news for the little buzzers. These fragile creatures face serious risks to their survival. In addition to the essential role that honeybees play in agricultural production and maintaining biodiversity, scientists depend on honeybees to better understand changes in the ecosystem, including threats to general pollinator populations. In fact, most American scientific work on pollinators has focused on honeybees, though they are not native to the United States. Some research has been done on native managed species, including bumblebees and orchard bees, because, like honeybees, their populations are easy to manipulate so that their individual behaviors can be studied. The 2006 publication of the honeybee genome gave researchers another reason to focus their pollinator research on *A. mellifera*: sequencing the honeybee genome helped scientists understand complex biological processes that had evolved over millions of years. Christina Grozinger, director of the Center for Pollinator Research at Penn State University, explains, "There are a lot of really specific questions that you can ask with [honeybees]. You can do more-detailed experiments and more correlational research with honeybees than other bee species that are not as well understood or easy to rear. It's a model system that you can work with really well."

Honeybees are also studied extensively because of their ubiquity in agriculture. In the United States alone, more than 150 food crops require pollinators to produce fruits, seeds, and nuts; pollinators contribute up to $577 billion to annual global food production. Honeybees are the preferred pollinators because their hives can be transported between and set into agricultural fields and orchards.

While honeybees remain in the spotlight, they cannot do the job of pollination alone. Hummingbirds, bats, moths, flies, and thousands of other creatures make up the motley crew of pollinators that allow for effective and stable pollination. Diversity is more important than abundance of a single species, even a managed species like the honeybee. In fact, a 2016 meta-analysis reviewed thirty-nine studies and found that insects other than bees were also efficient pollinators, providing more than two-thirds of visits to crop flowers. Compared to honeybees, non-bee pollinators performed fewer than 50 percent of total flower visits but

Figure 1-1: Honeybees devote their lives to gathering pollen and nectar, which they transport back to the hive.

a higher number of flower visits and, as a result, their pollination services were on par with bees overall. The findings led researchers to suggest that shifting from a bee-only perspective was needed to get accurate assessments of crop pollinator biodiversity and the economic value of pollination. The researchers also noted that new studies should also consider the services provided by other types of "currently overlooked" but important pollinators.

"Much of the discussion and debate around pollinators and pollinator health over the past ten years has really been fueled by the honeybee; the honeybee has gotten a lot of attention," says Eric Lee-Mader, pollinator program co-director for the Xerces Society, a nonprofit focused on the conservation of invertebrates essential for biological di-

Box 1-2

The Rusty-Patched Bumblebee Made History

In 2017, the rusty-patched bumblebee made headlines—and history—when it was the first bumblebee species in the continental United States to be placed on the endangered species list.

Populations of the native bees, named for the rust-colored patch found on the backs of workers and males, have declined almost 91 percent since the late 1990s due to habitat loss, pesticide use, and climate change. Once abundant in twenty-eight states, their range has shrunk to thirteen states (Illinois, Indiana, Iowa, Maine, Maryland, Massachusetts, Minnesota, North Carolina, Ohio, Pennsylvania, Tennessee, Virginia, and Wisconsin) and the Canadian province of Ontario.

Rusty-patched bumblebees live in colonies with a single queen and female workers, nesting in the ground, often in abandoned rodent nests. Like other bumblebees, the species specializes in buzz pollination; vibrating flowers to shake out pollen makes the rusty-patched bumblebees more effective pollinators than honeybees when it comes to helping crops like apples and cranberries.

Plummeting populations led the US Fish and Wildlife Service to take action. The agency's successful proposal to have the rusty-patched bumblebee included on the endangered species list could help keep the species from going extinct.

Commenting on the decision, Sarina Jepsen, director at the Xerces Society and deputy chair of the bumblebee specialist group for the International Union for Conservation of Nature, told CNN, "Now that the Fish and Wildlife Service has listed the rusty-patched bumblebee as endangered, it stands a chance of surviving the many threats it faces."

Being included on the endangered species list makes it a federal crime to harm or kill the bees. Those federal protections were tested when the Illinois Department of Transportation approved a federal highway project that would destroy rusty-patched bumblebee habitat. In October 2017, the Center for Biological Diversity filed a formal notice of intent to sue the Federal Highway Administration and the Illinois DOT for failing to prevent harm to the endangered species.

The Center alleged that the rusty-patched bumblebee had been sighted in undeveloped land that was slated to be bulldozed for the road project and toll bridge, and both the federal and state agencies failed to assess the potential effects of construction on the bee (as required by law).

In a statement, Stephanie Parent, senior attorney at the Center for Biological Diversity, said, "The Endangered Species Act is 99 percent effective at protecting our most imperiled wildlife, but it can only work when its mandates are followed. Since these agencies have ignored the bees' presence, we've got no choice but to take legal action to force officials to protect these important little [insects]."

versity and ecosystem health. "But, out of the whole range of pollinator issues . . . other pollinators seem to be faring worse."

Although we know that ants, butterflies, birds, beetles, bats, flies, moths, and wasps are important pollinators, there is a dearth of information about their populations and how each might be faring in an ever-changing landscape. Even native bees—the local cousins to the imported (nonnative) European honeybees—are not well understood.

More than 4,000 species of native bees, from carpenter bees and mason bees to bumblebees and wool-carder bees, have been identified in North America. The Center for Biological Diversity released a landmark report in 2017 that showed more than half the species with sufficient data to assess were declining, and almost one in four face the risk of extinction. Bee species without enough data to determine their current population statuses are also believed to be in peril.

A 2015 "bee map" that tracked the status of wild bee populations reported similarly discouraging findings. The map listed 139 counties across the United States where bee populations were so diminished that pollination demands couldn't be met. The affected areas, including California, the Pacific Northwest, and the Great Plains, were major agricultural production areas. The most dramatic shortfalls were found in areas with high concentrations of specialty crops like apples and berries that are especially reliant on pollinators. The researchers concluded that if wild (unmanaged) bees had adequate habitat, they could contribute to the long-term stability of crop pollination and should be integrated as either a complement or an alternative to managed bees.

Jane Ogilvie, a research fellow at the Rocky Mountain Biological Laboratory in Colorado, attributes the lack of research on native bees to their behaviors: the often-solitary species fly long distances and forage over wide swaths of the landscape, making them difficult to track in long-term or controlled experiments. Ogilvie notes, "Until we get some sort of handle on what governs the population sizes of wild bees, we're not going to know at all how to manage threats to them."

Box 1-3
Raise Your Glass to Pollinating Bats

Without bats, drinks like margaritas, palomas, and tequila sunrises would disappear from cocktail menus.

Tequila is made from distilling the juices squeezed from agave (known in Mexico as *maguey*); long-nosed bats (*Leptonycteris* spp.) are their main pollinators. The miniature mammals plunge their tongues into the tubular flowers that open at night, feasting on the nectar.

Agave is such an important source of nectar that the bats migrate between the United States and Mexico following the cactus blooms. The lesser long-nosed bat (*L. yerbabuenae)* lives in the tropics from El Salvador to Mexico, migrating to the southern parts of Arizona and New Mexico during the summer; the Mexican long-nosed bat (*L. nivalis*) inhabits woodlands and forests between central Mexico and Texas. In exchange for the free meal, long-nosed bats cross-pollinate agave, transferring pollen grains from one plant to another during their evening feeding frenzies. Their coevolution means that bats and agave depend on each other for survival.

The US Fish and Wildlife Service added *L. yerbabuenae* and *L. nivalis* to the endangered species list in the 1980s. The disappearance of long-nosed bats would have a ripple effect: the same plants that depend on these species for reproduction also provide food and shelter for other insects and animals, including bees, moths, and hummingbirds; agave populations would also plummet. Shrinking bat colonies would be bad news for the survival of agave plants.

New data showing that the global tequila market is expected to hit $9 billion by 2021 might seem like good news for bats—a bump in tequila production means more agave plants—but increased commercial production of agave has had the opposite effect: rather than cultivating agave using traditional and sustainable methods (that bats depend on), producers find it easier and less expensive to use cloned agave that doesn't require natural pollination; stalks are cut before flowers bloom, leaving no pollen for bats. (This practice is also bad for agave. Artificial pollination leads to losses in genetic diversity, making agave more susceptible to disease and climate change. Allowing bats to pollinate the plants leads to agave that is healthier and more diverse.)

A nonprofit called the Tequila Interchange Project, a coalition of bartenders, scientists, and tequila enthusiasts, launched in 2010 with a goal of making tequila production more sustainable, helping both agave and bats. One of their initiatives: promoting bat-friendly tequila and mescal launched by brands like

Box 1-3 *continued*

Tequila Ocho, Siete Leguas, and Tequila Tapatio. The producers behind these brands allow 5 percent of the agave plants (about 200 plants per hectare) on their farms to flower, providing a nectar buffet for bats. As part of the 2016 pilot project, five brands released 300,000 bottles of bat-friendly tequila.

The efforts are helping increase the numbers of long-nosed bats. The populations, estimated to be around 1,000 when the bats were first added to the endangered species list, are now hovering around 200,000 in seventy-five different roosts, which means that the lesser long-nosed bats are no longer fighting for survival. Mexico removed the bats from their endangered species list in 2015, and the United States proposed doing the same in 2017. If the proposal goes through, it would be the first time a bat species was ever delisted.

In a statement about the proposed removal of the lesser long-nosed bat from the US endangered species list, Jim deVos, assistant director of wildlife management at the Arizona Game and Fish Department, said, "Many entities in both the US and Mexico have worked tirelessly toward recovery, and this announcement stands as testimony that dedicated efforts and sound management practices can lead to recovery of endangered species."

That's the kind of news worth toasting. *¡Salud!*

Managing threats is imperative. Both the diversity and occurrence of wild pollinators are declining, and some species have also become less abundant. A recent assessment called the Red List of Threatened Species, published by the International Union for Conservation of Nature, found that 16.5 percent of vertebrate pollinators like hummingbirds and bats are threatened with global extinction. (The number of species at risk of global extinction almost doubled—hitting 30 percent—for island inhabitants.) No global Red List exists for insect pollinators, but both regional and national assessments indicate those species are in trouble, too. Those assessments showed that populations declined 37 percent for certain species of bees and 31 percent for certain species of butterflies. In North America, the population of monarch butterflies (*Danaus plexippus*) declined 84% between 1996 and 2015.

Nine percent of bee and butterfly species are threatened. The rusty-patched bumblebee made history in 2017 when it became the first bumblebee species in the continental United States to be placed on the endangered species list. When pollinator populations decline—or disappear altogether—the effects are felt throughout the ecosystem.

"There is this argument, and I think it's a legitimate argument, that pollinators are sort of this critical linchpin in terrestrial ecology, [so] it should give us pause to consider that pollinators are increasingly in trouble," says Lee-Mader. "The extremely old evolutionary partnership between plants and pollinators makes them extremely important to the perpetuation of all life on earth."

Almost 90 percent of flowering plants and 75 percent of food crops depend on pollinators; the volume of pollinator-dependent food crops has increased 300 percent over the past five decades, making the global food supply more reliant on the birds and bees (and other pollinators) than ever.

Agricultural crops could be hand-pollinated. In China, where lack of habitat and excessive pesticide use have been blamed for mass bee die-offs, some farmers were forced to use paintbrushes and pots of pollen to hand-pollinate each bloom in apple and pear orchards. Critics warn that while the practice will facilitate reproduction, it is not practical: there are too few humans worldwide to manage the task. Hand-pollination is also not cost-effective: an MIT study estimated that it would cost between $5,715 and $7,135 to pollinate a one-hectare (2.5-acre) apple orchard. Based on these figures, it would cost between $409 million and $511 million to hand-pollinate the 179,146 acres of apple trees in Washington State. The result would be skyrocketing food costs and, potentially, the disappearance of certain fruit crops from store shelves.

Mini-drones have also been tested as artificial pollinators. But like the human pollen painters, so-called robot bees cannot make up for significant pollinator declines. In fact, a 2017 *Newsweek* article called the drones "comically inept," noting, "All of these drones are so far wildly expensive, ineffective, and would be dangerous to real bees." More importantly, technology cannot do the work pollinators have evolved to do, which includes detecting whether a plant has already been visited.

Outside of agriculture, up to 95 percent of the plant species found in natural habitats depend on animal pollination. Moreover, pollinators ensure the reproduction of fruits, nuts, and seeds that are essential food sources for herbivores like deer and wild turkeys. Just as pollinators impact the environment, the reverse is also true: a changing environment affects pollinators.

"We typically talk about the perfect storm of habitat loss, pesticide use, diseases and parasites, and those three decline factors tend to be closely linked to one another and they tend to have synergistic effects," says Lee-Mader. "There's a tangled web of different issues now that seem to be more acutely felt than we've ever seen in the history of the planet. We know, for example, that bees have fewer sources of flower nectar and flower pollen; [that] those bees having less diverse diets tend to have less robust immune systems . . . ; and, we think, based on a pretty ample body of research, that pesticide use can also suppress immune systems and make bees more susceptible to parasites and diseases. These things are all linked together. Climate and invasive species are also likely to have significant impacts."

It sounds hopeless, but Lee-Mader believes there is a silver lining: awareness of the issues has led to significant work being undertaken to understand the threats pollinators face and what needs to happen to address them. He notes, "There is more pollinator conservation work going on now than ever before."

To ease the pressure on pollinator populations, the Obama administration introduced the Pollinator Partnership Action Plan in 2016. The goals were ambitious: create robust public–private partnerships to reduce honeybee overwintering colony losses to no more than 15 percent

Figure 1-2: A beekeeper in San Diego, California, inspects his hives for signs of problems.

Box 1-4

Are High-Tech Drones the Next-Generation Pollinators?

The news that bees are in trouble has led to several experimental efforts to determine whether high-tech methods have the potential to supplement—or even replace—bee pollinators. Drones have emerged as a popular option.

Several researchers have created robot bees. Even Walmart is in on the action. In 2018, the retail giant filed a patent for an autonomous robot bee along with patents for six drone-based farming innovations. Though the designs are varied—some have textured bodies to help collect pollen grains; others have flapping wings—all were designed to achieve artificial pollination. Meanwhile, a NASA team was awarded $125,000 to develop "Marsbees," a swarm of robot bees designed to buzz around Mars and gather data from the atmosphere.

When Harvard introduced the first robot bees in 2014, researchers predicted that the high-tech pollinators could be used to pollinate fields of crops in the next decade. In one iteration, bee-sized drones were retrofitted with gel-coated horsehair bristles that mimic the fuzz-coated bodies of bees and generate a light electric charge to attract pollen grains. In trials, researchers kept the device, about the size of a hummingbird, aloft via remote control and maneuvered it until the bristles brushed the stamen of wild lilies (*Lilium japonicum*). The 2017 experiment marked the first successful demonstration of artificial robotic pollination. But "success" with drone pollination is much less successful than insect pollination. The research showed that although the gel allowed pollen to stick to the bristles on the robo-bee, the drone picked up just 41 percent of the pollen in the flowers and managed to pollinate those flowers on just over half of its attempts.

Drone bees might be innovative, but the artificial pollinators are not apt to replace bees for widespread pollination. Critics warn that robot bees are expensive to build, cannot pollinate without an operator at the controls, and pose threats to actual bees. In this experiment, the drone pollinated a large flower and might not be as adept at collecting and spreading pollen in smaller flowers; the process of pollinating entire crops would be time-consuming and cost-prohibitive.

So although technological innovation is generating a lot of buzz, significant questions remain about the widespread application of artificial pollination. Still, the race to build the ultimate pollinating drone continues.

within ten years; increase the eastern population of monarch butterflies to cover fifteen acres in their overwintering grounds in Mexico; and restore or enhance seven million acres of pollinator habitat in the next five years. The plan acknowledged the enormity of the task, noting that it will require an "all hands on deck" approach to include commitments from the federal, state, local, and tribal governments, the private sector, nonprofit organizations, academic institutions, and the general public.

The current administration, however, could thwart efforts to protect pollinators. When he took office, President Trump issued a legislative freeze that delayed adding the rusty patched bumblebee to the endangered species list; signed a proclamation to shrink the Bears Ears and Grand Staircase-Escalante National Monuments in Utah by a total of 1.9 million acres, putting important pollinator habitat at risk; and promised to build a border wall between the United States and Mexico that would bulldoze pollinator habitat and restrict access to essential nectar and pollen resources.

Secretary of Agriculture Sonny Purdue provided a glimmer of hope in 2017 when he signed a proclamation declaring one week in June as National Pollinator Week, noting,

> Most farmers and consumers have no better friends and few harder workers than the honeybee, as more than one-third of all US crop production requires insect pollination. But our honeybee population has been losing ground at an alarming rate. The problem represents a diverse mix of challenges requiring a wide range of solutions. And at USDA we are leading the way in research to help out our pollinator friends.

Purdue pointed to joint efforts of the USDA and the US Environmental Protection Agency (EPA) to create a National Pollinator Health Strategy.

But these efforts began under the Obama administration, and the new administration has done little to further them. In fact, the EPA has been widely criticized for failing to protect pollinators. In 2017, the agency published a set of draft risk assessments on three neonicotinoid pesticides (clothianidin, thiamethoxam, and dinotefuran) that stated, "Most approved uses do not pose significant risks to bee colonies. However, spray applications to a few crops, such as cucumbers, berries, and cotton, may pose risks to bees that come in direct contact with residue." On the same day, the agency released a second report, "Policy to Mitigate the Acute Risk to Bees from Pesticide Products," that acknowledged the impact of insecticides on bee populations. But a disclaimer included with the report noted, "This policy is not a regulation or an order and, therefore, does not legally compel changes to pesticide product registrations." The contradictions led Lori Ann Burd, director of the environmental health program at the Center for Biological Diversity, to tell the *Guardian*, "It's outrageous that, on the same day the EPA acknowledged these dangerous pesticides are killing bees, it also reversed course on mandating restrictions on their use."

Lee-Mader of the Xerces Society admits that the pendulum has swung far in the direction of pollinator decline and believes that it's going to take a lot of work to swing the pendulum back toward pollinator health: "I don't think we're there yet. If we look at the status of pollinators both domestically and globally, the picture is still pretty grim. We are still faced with some really problematic trends."

Fortunately, researchers, corporations, nonprofits, and individuals are taking action, directing funds to pollinator protection, establishing and restoring pollinator habitats, educating the public about pollinator health, and researching the threats, their implications, and possible solutions to safeguard fragile populations. Their help is needed urgently. As the Center for Biological Diversity notes, "Without these tiny, tireless creatures our world would be a less colorful and interesting place."

Box 1-5
A Presidential Plea to Protect Pollinators

Former First Lady Michelle Obama planted the first-ever pollinator garden on the South Lawn. The garden was filled with native nectar- and pollen-producing plants as well as two species of milkweed—swamp milkweed (*Asclepias incarnata*) and butterfly weed (*A. tuberosa*). Each was planted near the White House Kitchen Garden in 2014 to support pollination and raise awareness of the threats facing pollinators.

During the sixth annual White House kitchen garden planting event, Mrs. Obama told the schoolchildren in attendance that the plants would help bees and butterflies, explaining, "A pollinator garden helps to encourage the production of bees and monarch butterflies. They pollinate the plants, they help the plants grow. They're dying because of disease—we don't even know why some beehives are just totally disappearing."

In 2017, a spokesperson told CNN that the Trump administration would preserve the gardens that the Obamas built and tended on White House grounds. Several months later, "Second Lady" Karen Pence unveiled a beehive on the grounds of her Washington, DC, home. In a statement, she explained, "All types of pollinators, such as bees, butterflies, birds, and bats, are critical to providing our nation's food, fiber, fuel. and medicine. . . . The bees at the Vice President's Residence will provide an added bonus to the vegetable and flower gardens by making them well pollinated and taste even better at harvest."

Box 1-6
Pollinators in Peril

Congress created the Endangered Species Act in 1973 to help threatened and endangered species recover. To date, the following seventy-two pollinators have been added to the list:

Mammals

- Lesser long-nosed bat (*Leptonycteris curasoae yerbabuenae*)
- Little Mariana fruit bat (*Pteropus tokudae*)
- Mariana fruit bat (*Pteropus mariannus mariannus*)

Birds

- Akeke'e or Kaua'i 'akepa (*Loxops caeruleirostris*)
- 'Akiapola'au (*Hemignathus wilsoni*)

Box 1-6 *continued*

Birds (continued)

- ʻAkikiki (*Oreomystis bairdi*)
- ʻAkohekohe or crested honeycreeper (*Palmeria dolei*)
- ʻAlala or Hawaiʻian crow (*Corvus hawaiiensis*)
- Bridled white-eye (*Zosterops conspicillatus conspicullatus*)
- Hawaiʻi ʻakepa (*Loxops coccineus*)
- Hawaiʻi creeper (*Loxops mana*)
- ʻIʻiwi (*Drepanis coccinea*)
- Kauaʻi ʻakialoa (*Akaloa stejnegeri*)
- Kauaʻi nukupuʻu (*Hemignathus hanapepe*)
- Kauaʻi ʻoʻo (*Moho braccatus*)
- Maʻomaʻo or mao (*Gymnomyza samoensis*)
- Maui ʻakepa (*Loxops ochraceus*)
- Maui nukupuʻu (*Hemignathus affinis*)
- Maui parrotbill (*Pseudonestor xanthophrys*)
- Molokaʻi creeper or kakawahie (*Paroreomyza flammea*)
- Oʻahu ʻalauahio or Oʻahu creeper (*Paroreomyza maculata*)
- ʻOʻu (*Psittirostra psittacea*)
- Palila (*Loxioides bailleui*)
- Poʻouli (*Melamprosops phaeosoma*)
- Rota bridled white-eye (*Zosterops rotensis*)

Bees

- Anthricinan yellow-faced bee (*Hylaeus anthracinus*)
- Assimulans yellow-faced bee (*Hylaeus assimulans*)
- Easy yellow-faced bee (*Hylaeus facilis*)
- Hawaiʻian yellow-faced bee (*Hylaeus kuakea*)
- Hawaiʻian yellow-faced bee (*Hylaeus longiceps*)
- Hawaiʻian yellow-faced bee (*Hylaeus mana*)
- Hilaris yellow-faced bee (*Hylaeus hilaris*)
- Rusty-patched bumblebee (*Bombus affinis*)

Butterflies, Skippers, and Moths

- Bartram's hairstreak butterfly (*Strymon acis bartrami*)
- Bay checkerspot (*Euphydryas editha bayensis*)
- Behren's Silverspot (*Speyeria zerene behrensii*)
- Blackburn's sphinx moth (*Manduca blackburni*)
- Callippe silverspot (*Speyeria callippe callippe*)

continued

Box 1-6 *continued*

Butterflies, Skippers, and Moths (continued)

- Carson wandering skipper (*Pseudocopaeodes eunus obscurus*)
- Cassius blue (*Leptotes cassius theonus*)
- Ceraunus blue (*Hemiargus ceraunus antibubastus*)
- Dakota skipper (*Hesperia dacotae*)
- El Segundo blue (*Euphilotes battoides allyni*)
- Fender's blue (*Icaricia icarioides fenderi*)
- Florida leafwing (*Anaea troglodyta floridalis*)
- Karner blue (*Lycaeides melissa samuelis*)
- Kern primrose sphinx moth (*Euproserpinus euterpe*)
- Laguna Mountains skipper (*Pyrgus ruralis lagunae*)
- Lange's metalmark (*Apodemia mormo lange*)
- Lotis blue (*Lycaeides argyrognomon lotis*)
- Mariana eight-spot butterfly (*Hypolimnas octocula mariannensis*)
- Mariana wandering butterfly (*Vagrans egistina*)
- Miami blue (*Cyclargus thomasi bethunebakeri*)
- Misson blue (*Icaricia icarioides missionensis*)
- Mitchell's satyr (*Neonympha mitchellii mitchellii*)
- Mount Charleston blue (*Plebejus shasta charlestonensis*)
- Myrtle's silverspot (*Speyeria zerene myrtleae*)
- Nickerbean blue (*Cyclargus ammon*)
- Oregon silverspot (*Speyeria zerene hippolyta*)
- Palos Verde blue (*Glaucopsyche lygdamus palosverdesensis*)
- Pawnee montane skipper (*Hesperia leonardus montana*)
- Poweshiek skipperling (*Oarisma poweshiek*)
- Quino checkerspot (*Euphydryas editha quino*)
- San Bruno elfin (*Callophrys mossii bayensis*)
- Schaus swallowtail (*Heraclides aristodemus ponceanus*)
- Smith's blue (*Euphilotes enoptes smithi*)
- St. Francis' satyr (*Neonympha mitchellii francisci*)
- Taylor's checkerspot (*Euphydryas editha taylori*)
- Uncompahgre fritillary (*Boloria acrocnema*)

Other Insects

- Delhi Sands flower-loving fly (*Rhaphiomidas terminatus abdominalis*)
- Valley elderberry longhorn beetle (*Desmocerus californicus dimorphus*)

CHAPTER 2

No Place Like Home

At the Lady Bird Johnson Wildflower Center, horticulturalist Leslie Uppinghouse treks from one garden to the next, her tennis shoes crunching on the gravel. As she moves through the woodland garden, the seed silo garden, and the West Texas mountain collection garden, she points out plants like blue false indigo (*Baptisia australis*), coral honeysuckle (*Lonicera sempervirens*), Mexican plum (*Prunus mexicana*), and hop tree (*Ptelea trifoliata*).

Although the site, spanning 284 acres in the middle of sprawling urban developments in Austin, Texas, was established to showcase native plants found within different eco-regions across the state, it's turned into more than just a home for flora and fauna. The 800 species of Texas native plants planted throughout the Lady Bird Johnson Wildflower Center teem with pollinators that come to the garden to seek shelter, lay eggs, collect pollen, or feed on nectar.

"Part of the criteria we use [when choosing plants] is: What is the benefit to pollinators? We don't put in things that don't have a purpose,"

Uppinghouse says. “We talk a lot about nectar plants [because monarchs travel through Texas during their southern migration], so nectar plants help monarchs—but other pollinators, too. We have ten species of bumblebees here in Texas and I have seen at least six out of ten, which is a really wide variety. This entire place is a lovely habitat for pollinators.”

Lady Bird Johnson founded the Wildflower Center in 1982, before neonicotinoids and GMOs were part of the lexicon, before populations of monarch butterflies reached record lows, and before the rusty-patched bumblebee was added to the endangered species list.

Today swaths of concrete surround the gardens on all sides. Ribbons of asphalt that make up the MoPac Expressway run alongside its western edge and a tangle of narrow streets winding through the suburban neighborhoods border the remainder of the perimeter. The Wildflower Center stands out, island-like, an oasis for the pollinators that are running out of places to call home.

Lady Bird Johnson, a passionate naturalist, once declared, “Too often we have bartered away not only the land, but the very air and water . . . under the bright guise of progress. And in our unconcern, we have let a crisis gather which threatens health and even life itself.” It’s not hard to imagine that she would be proud that her prized native plants were providing pollinator habitat at a time when the essential species are struggling to find places to call home.

The Ann and O. J. Weber Pollinator Habitat Garden, installed in 2003, occupies a shaded spot where paths wind around islands of plantings. The garden was designed with ten different plant communities containing more than 150 different species that provide areas for pollinator eggs, larvae, pupae, and adult invertebrates. Several puddling stations—areas where colorful butterflies can alight on shallow pools of mud to sip water and take in essential minerals from the earth—are tucked into protected areas of the pollinator garden. A small insectary houses caterpillars in their larval phases of the butterfly and moth life-cycles to protect them from predators; the newly hatched butterflies are released into the garden after they have pupated.

Although there is a dedicated pollinator garden, the pollinator habitat at the Wildflower Center isn't limited to a single garden. In fact, almost all of the plantings throughout the wildflower center benefit pollinators. To wit: since volunteers started tracking pollinator sightings, a total of 1,800 insects and 93 species of butterflies have been recorded in the gardens. Records showed species ranging from common pollinators like salt marsh skippers (*Panoquina panoquin*) and pipevine swallowtails (*Battus philenor*) to rare sightings of cecropia moths (*Hyalophora cecropia*).

Uppinghouse perks up when reminiscing about sightings of cecropia in the pollinator garden. On a bleak February morning, she points out the Mexican plum tree where she spotted caterpillars and, later, chrysalis. The cecropia is the largest native moth in North America, with a wing span upwards of six inches. Their bodies—red with white collars and white bands on the abdomen—stand out against their dark brown wings, which are accented with red bands and white crescent spots.

"When the moths are still caterpillars, we see them on the Mexican plum and, if you listen closely, you can actually hear them eating," Uppinghouse says.

In the area devoted to theme gardens, Uppinghouse points out her favorite place to spot pollinators: a pyramid bush (*Melochia tomentosa*). In the hot afternoon sun, she often plants herself on the edge of the raised bed where the bushy perennial, with its gray-green leaves and tiny star-shaped pink flowers, is rooted. She explains, "I love visiting in late afternoon and counting how many different bees are buzzing around the plant."

Despite the lush landscape, Uppinghouse worries that the gardens might not be enough. "I look around and I'm so proud of all we're doing to provide resources for pollinators, but it feels like a small effort when there is such a huge need."

Sanctuary City

At the tip of Manhattan, across the harbor from the Statue of Liberty and Ellis Island, a popular public park provides refuge for tired and huddled masses of pollinators. The Battery (known to most New Yorkers as Battery Park) encompasses twenty-five acres and includes the Castle Garden Emigrant Depot, where eight million immigrants were welcomed into New York between 1855 and 1890 (before the Ellis Island Immigrant Inspection Station was built) as well as an urban farm and gardens. It's also home to a bee sanctuary called BeeVillage.

Like the immigrants who landed in New York a century ago, honeybees are foreigners that now call the United States home. European colonists brought the bees in during the 1700s—perhaps some arrived at ports in New York. The connection between the nonnative bees and the first waves of immigrants provides docents at the Battery Conservancy opportunities to talk about the risks facing these insect immigrants, such as environmental and climate change. With more than four million visitors buzzing about the Battery every year, there are opportunities to spread the message far and wide.

"The Battery . . . created a biodiverse habitat that not only attracts people but also bees, birds, and butterflies," notes Honeybee Conservancy director Guillermo Fernandez. "The honeybees have become an educational magnet and an engaging attraction."

To further draw attention to the hives, volunteer beekeepers from the Honeybee Conservancy designed each of the three hives to resemble iconic New York architecture: one hive resembles a tenement apartment building and another was transformed to look like the John Bowne House, a historic home that dates back to 1661, making it the oldest home in Queens. Pollinator gardens surround the apiary to provide plenty of habitat for the bees. Bees help pollinate the flowers, which include asters, blueberries, and spicebush.

Box 2-1
Habitat Affects Honey Flavor

What is the difference between clover honey, sourwood honey, and tupelo honey? The honey-making process is the same—bees collect nectar and pollen, bring it back to the hive, and turn it into honey—but the source of that pollen and nectar affects the color, flavor, and aroma of the honey; each varietal is a product of the bees' habitat. In other words, honey, like wine, has terroir. California bees that harvest nectar from avocado blossoms produce honey with a rich, buttery flavor, while bees that forage from orange groves in Florida make light, sweet orange-blossom honey. Rainfall, temperature, and other environmental conditions can also affect honey flavor from year to year.

There are 300 varieties of honey in the United States alone. Some varieties can only be produced in certain areas of the world. Tupelo honey is made when bees consume nectar of the tupelo gum tree, which only grows in the swamps along the Chipola and Apalachicola Rivers of the Florida Panhandle. Bees that ingest pollen from sourwood trees in the Blue Ridge and Allegheny mountains of northern Georgia and western North Carolina produce sourwood honey. Even honey labeled "wildflower" or "clover" tastes different, depending on where the wildflowers and clover grow, according to C. Marina Marchese, beekeeper and coauthor *The Honey Connoisseur*. "Wildflower honey from California is different from wildflower honey from Texas and wildflower honey from Connecticut," she says.

The diversity is so great that the Honey and Pollination Center at the Robert Mondavi Institute at the University of California, Davis, developed the Honey Flavor Wheel. The concept, based on the Wine Aroma Wheel, features ninety-nine terms used to describe the flavor of honey, ranging from *lemon*, *bergamot*, and *caramel* to *leather*, *spicy*, and *cat pee* (yes, really).

To understand the diversity and complexity of honey, tasting is essential. Marchese founded the American Honey Tasting Society to showcase the range of honey flavors and share information about how habitat gives honey its terroir. Meaderies, specialty food stores, and farmer's markets often host honey tastings, and the protocol is similar to wine tasting: honey is poured into wine glasses, and its aroma, color, texture, and flavor are explored. Marchese notes that the experience often convinces self-proclaimed honey haters to change their minds. "To truly understand the diversity, you have to taste honey side by side," she says.

As with wine, though, for many of us it can often be hard to choose a favorite honey. But when you take care of bees year-round, the various flavors they produce taste equally sweet.

BeeVillage also provides nesting sites for solitary bees and has earned designation as a certified Monarch Waystation, welcoming migrating butterflies to stop to rest or nest in the lush gardens surrounding the labyrinth.

Honeybees are also welcome to take refuge in hives at the Cathedral Church of St. John the Divine in Upper Manhattan. The church is home to a second BeeVillage, where two hives are set among the gardens. One of the queens is called the Divine Queen. Thanks to shrinking habitats, creating bee sanctuaries is more important than ever.

Habitat Loss Threatens Survival

Honeybees are not the only pollinators in need of sanctuary. Butterflies, bats, birds, and many other species can't make their homes in cornfields or between the blades of grass in suburban lawns; the habitats taking over our landscape are inadequate for species to nest, rest, and feed, leaving pollinators struggling—and often failing—to adapt to shrinking habitats.

While scant global data exists about the sheer number of acres lost to development and deforestation, a report issued by the Environmental Working Group—*Plowed Under: How Crop Subsidies Contribute to Massive Habitat Losses*—tracked the transition of once-wild spaces to agricultural production. The findings: between 2008 and 2011, more than 23 million acres of grassland, scrubland, and wetlands were converted to row crops such as corn and cotton, with the greatest losses occurring in the Midwest and the Great Plains. Some data show that these kinds of changes to land use might have a more immediate impact on pollinator health than even climate change.

In California, as much as 90 percent of vernal pool habitat (shallow areas prone to intermittent or seasonal flooding) has been lost over the last two decades. As the habitats vanish, so do several of the floral species growing in the area. One of those flowers, the yellow carpet

(*Blennosperma nanum*), is disappearing altogether from the landscape. Its brilliant yellow petals are the sole floral host for its namesake native bee, the yellow carpet solitary bee (*Andrena blennospematis*).

Yellow carpet solitary bees, native to California, are distinct from honeybees in both their appearance and behavior. Their tiny bodies are olive green with pale stripes on their abdomens and, as their name suggests, the gorgeous creatures live solo, not in colonies. Once found in eleven counties in the central part of the state, the bees are now facing extinction, having been spotted in just one California county over the last decade. Habitat loss is implicated in their demise. As the Center for Biological Diversity explains, "This beautiful bee's life is so intertwined with the life of the flower it depends on, they share the same name. . . . The bees' fate is completely tied to its specialized flower and therefore [to] the health and survival of the pockets of the California vernal pool ecosystems where they live."

The sunflower leafcutter bee (*Eumegachile pugnata*) faces a similar fate. The largest of all native leafcutter bees in North America, it relies on sunflowers as the main source of pollen for its brood. As swaths of sunflowers are replaced with monocultures of wheat and corn, the sunflower leafcutter bee has lost habitat across its range, which spans from the Great Plains to Arizona. Several of the states that the native bee calls home, including Nebraska, Texas, and South Dakota, have some of the highest agricultural conversion rates in the nation. The bee's already-shrinking population is projected to decline more than 80 percent.

Commercial-scale agriculture also contributed to a 21 percent decline in the number of milkweed plants between 1995 and 2013. Milkweed is the only food source that monarch caterpillars consume; without it, the species cannot survive. The bulk of the milkweed losses occurred in the central breeding region in the United States. More than 70 percent of milkweed in these areas is in farming regions; the shrinking availability of the essential plant could increase competition among larvae for food and among adults for nesting sites to lay eggs. If milkweed losses continue, a model predicts monarchs will experience an additional 14 percent decline.

Researcher Ryan Norris, a professor at the University of Guelph in Ontario, noted, "Our work provides the first evidence that monarch butterfly numbers in eastern North America are most sensitive to changes in the availability of milkweed on breeding grounds, particularly in the Corn Belt region of the United States."

Conventional agriculture is taking a toll on pollinators, according to Eric Lee-Mader of the Xerces Society. Farmers are stepping up to be part of the solution. "Farmers all over the country who are enrolling in pollinator conservation practices," says Lee-Mader.

Wayne Fredericks is one of those farmers. Fredericks grows corn and soybeans on 975 acres in Osage, Iowa. In 2014, he planted several patches of pollinator habitat on his farms. Now, almost seven acres of colorful wildflowers like sunflowers (*Helianthus*), black-eyed Susan (*Rudbeckia hirta*), yellow cup plants (*Silphium perfoliatum*), and purple coneflowers (*Echinacea purpurea*) stand out against vast expanses of row crops. Fredericks loves nothing more than looking out the window of his farmhouse at the riotous patches of color dotting the landscape on his farm.

"All of the habitats are visible from our house and the roadsides that we travel," he says. "We thought it was something positive we could do [for pollinators], and there was the appeal of the visual aspect. We've seen a lot of bees and a tremendous amount of red admiral [butterflies] (*Vanessa atalanta*)—those were just thick in the landscape last season. We love showing it off."

Planting pollinator habitat also made economic sense. "In many of these places that didn't fit our machinery perfectly, we'd have overlaps [which meant going over the same spot more than once] and, when that happens, we have additional input costs—more seed and spray—so we can have negative profits in those areas. It made obvious economic sense [to plant pollinator habitat in those areas]," Fredericks says.

Fredericks made the decision to convert a portion of his farmland to pollinator habitat after using a computer application called AgSolver to run a profit scenario, which revealed that certain areas—behind wind breaks, or close to streams, or too small and oddly shaped to fit equipment—were not generating a profit. Enrolling in a Conservation Reserve Program, an initiative offered through the USDA Farm Service Agency to provide cash incentives to farmers to increase pollinator habitat, allowed Fredericks to cover the cost of planting habitat and generate nominal annual income on otherwise unproductive areas of farmland.

The habitats grow more robust with each season, and pollinator visits have increased around the farm. Fredericks admits monarchs are still elusive, though: "I think it's going to be a slow return, but the only way we're going to get them to return at all is to reestablish habitat."

The potential to help flagging monarch populations and other struggling pollinators is a passion for Fredericks, who sits on the boards of the American Soybean Association, the Iowa Soybean Association, and the Monarch Collaborative, a group of national organizations representing farmers, ranchers, landowners, and agricultural companies, and he's encouraging other farmers to follow suit. He often has groups of other farmers take tours of his farm, and the pollinator habitats are one of the first features he shows off.

"The whole idea is that we can have both productive agriculture [and] monarch conservation," he says. "We're trying to create some room in the conservation part of the [2019] Farm Bill for an increase in acres for pollinator habitat, and we're trying to raise awareness [among farmers] that pollinator habitat doesn't have to be planted on productive pieces of farmland. We all have acres here and there that are in grass, [and] through an effective program, we could convert some of that over to pollinator patches."

Working with farmers to convert acreage to pollinator habitat is essential, according to Lee-Mader. At the Xerces Society, he manages a team of ecologists working with farmers to plant pollinator habitats on more than 300,000 acres of farmland (an additional 600,000 acres of pollinator habitats have been established over the last decade, including tens of thousands of acres located on agricultural land).

"There is more pollinator conservation work going on now than ever before," says Lee-Mader. "I think the bulk of the work happening is happening in agriculture, which is where we need it first and foremost. Agriculture is one of the major pressure points on pollinator health, so we need to engage farmers to be part of the solution."

These flowering hedgerows, insectary strips, native-plant field borders, and cover crops benefit pollinators and farmers alike. A report published by the Nature Conservancy suggested that planting one acre of native pollinator habitat per twenty-five acres of farmland could actually serve as a form of crop insurance by increasing yields and improving crop quality. Additional research revealed that planting wildflowers surrounding fruit, vegetable, nut, and seed crops provides nectar and pollen to attract native pollinators and could increase crop production.

Planting cover crops, a practice that fell out of favor around the 1950s with the widespread use of chemical pesticides and fertilizers designed to do the same jobs, adds organic matter and nitrogen to the soil, suppresses weeds, improves soil structure, reduces erosion, and attracts beneficial insects to reduce pest populations. Planting legumes, vetches, and grasses between tree rows, along fence lines and orchard borders, and in fallow areas provides forage for bees. The benefit to honeybee colonies, which are transported long distances to pollinate crops such as almond orchards, led the nonprofit Project *Apis m.* (named for *Apis mellifera*), to start distributing free cover-crop seed mixes for almond growers. Well-nourished colonies are healthier and stronger, allowing them to fend off pests and cope with major stresses to the hive, such as pesticides and transportation.

Despite fears that providing additional forage will lead bees to spend less time gathering—and spreading—pollen from almond blooms, Project *Apis m.* notes that bees are more attracted to the blooms because of the sheer quantity of high-protein pollen available for the taking. Moreover, research found that growing a variety of flowers improved pollination rates for nearby crops. In hives with pollen from limited sources (such as almond orchards that lacked additional habitat for pollen collection), the larvae became poor foragers as adults.

For Cascadian Farm, an eleven-acre organic farm in the Upper Skagit Valley in Washington State that produces fruits and vegetables for well-known brands of cereal, granola bars, frozen fruit, and fruit spreads, investing in pollinator habitats also provided a significant return on investment. For years, the farm relied on commercial beekeepers to transport hives so that bees could pollinate the five varieties of blueberries (Spartan, Toro, Bluecrop, Patriot, and Jersey) grown on the farm. Cascadian Farm needed five hives per acre during the bloom period—about fifty-five hives per season—for pollination. In 2014, the former farm manager forgot to rent hives and the blueberries still flowered and set fruit. The farm has not rented hives since. "As I understand it," says site director Ashley Minnerath, "[the farm manager] started renting hives because an agronomist suggested renting hives as an insurance policy in case our native pollinators didn't come through, but the one year we had no hives, pollination was just fine."

Minnerath credits the farmscape for supporting enough native creatures to pollinate the crops. Patches of native plants like elderberry (*Sambucus nigra*), salmonberry (*Rubus spectabilis*), and thimbleberry (*Rubus parviflorus*) separate the small plots of blueberries, and wildflowers were planted between rows of raspberries in a new one-acre test plot in order to attract pollinators. Cascadian Home Farm also established a quarter-acre wildflower meadow near its farm store last spring. The colorful meadow was planted with late-blooming flowers to provide forage for native bees; honeybees—probably visitors from hives on a neighboring property—are often spotted gathering nectar in the meadow. The flow-

Box 2-2
Pollinator Strips Might Not Work

Concerns over disappearing habitat have led to campaigns encouraging farmers to sow strips of habitat around agricultural land to ensure that pollinators have access to nectar and nesting sites.

To test the effect of these pollinator strips, researchers at the Centre for Environmental and Climate Research at Lund University in Sweden compared pollinator visits at small-scale agricultural landscapes with those on intensely farmed cropland by placing pots planted with wild strawberries or field beans in the borders surrounding both landscapes. The plants in small-scale farming settings were better pollinated than plants located in field borders surrounding arable cropland. Researchers also investigated how flower strips affected pollinator visits in both settings. Pollination increased in arable fields adjacent to pollinator strips, but there was no effect on pollination of the strawberries and field beans just a few hundred meters from the strips. In small-scale farming landscapes, the habitat strips actually reduced pollination of the potted plants, which researchers suspected was a result of increased floral competition.

Researcher Lina Herbertsson explained that wild bees manage better in landscapes with a lot of field borders *and* other untouched environments. In the absence of pristine habitat, including areas of intensely farmed land, habitat strips only help pollinators in the immediate vicinity but still leave vast expanses of pollinator-unfriendly habitat. "If we want to increase pollination in varied agricultural landscapes," Herbertsson concluded, "it seems to be a better strategy to restore and maintain pastures and meadows and to manage field borders in a way that favors the local flora, rather than adding sown strips of flowering plants."

The takeaway: the same measures could have different impacts in different landscapes. For this reason, efforts to increase biodiversity must take the surrounding environment into account to achieve the desired result.

ers also attract beneficial insects to help control crop pests and allow the farm to honor its commitment to organic production.

Providing habitat for native bees is essential, according to Minnerath, who explains that without appropriate flowers, the species might disappear. She adds, "It doesn't make sense to rely on one resource [honeybees] when we have 4,000 species of native bees."

Eschewing rented hives and relying on native pollinators might seem risky. Minnerath admits that the "all or nothing" approach could impact the crops, explaining, "You get better yields and bigger berries when you have great pollination, and I wonder if we're losing some of that by not bringing in pollinators." But research shows that the opposite might be true: scientists at the University of Michigan have estimated costs between $400 and $800 per acre to establish pollinator habitat and found that higher yields of blueberries helped recoup those costs in under four years.

Buzzing about Bee Better Certification

Consumers concerned about pollinators have a new option for choosing foods that help protect fragile species. "Just like issues like Fair Trade or the Non-GMO Project or Rainforest Alliance that have resulted in formal certification systems, there is now this new emerging certification for pollinator conservation for farms," explains Lee-Mader of the Xerces Society.

In 2017, the Xerces Society launched a program called Bee Better Certified. Farmers agree to follow strict standards, including setting aside at least 5 percent of their land to habitat; providing nesting sites such as undisturbed ground and butterfly host plants; implementing a comprehensive pest-management strategy that includes nonchemical practices as first-line strategies and limiting or eliminating high-risk pesticides; and caring for managed colonies of bumblebees. Oregon Tilth, a third-party organic certifier, ensures that farmers adhere to standards.

"It ends up being, I think, sort of a model system for incorporating pollinator conservation into agriculture," Lee-Mader says. Farmers who earn certification can add the Bee Better Certified label to their products. In addition to incentivizing farmers to prioritize pollinator conservation, the distinctive black-and-white label helps consumers make informed purchasing decisions.

The Xerces Society designed the program for both large- and small-farm operations that produce crops ranging from almonds and apples

Box 2-3
A Cotton-Pickin' Boost for Pollinators

Farmers who want to improve cotton yields should add pollinator habitat. Researchers at the University of Texas at Austin found that the greater the area of natural habitat near cotton crops, the more diverse the pollinators that visit cotton plants. Increasing pollinator diversity within 800 feet of cotton fields can boost production up to 18 percent, according to the study published in the journal *Agriculture, Ecosystems, and the Environment*.

Cotton plants produce large flowers that develop into the iconic white-fiber bolls for which the plant is known. The cotton bloom often fails to coincide with the most active times for honeybees, which are among the most common pollinators in cotton fields; attracting a diversity of pollinators increases pollen distribution and efficiency, significantly increasing cotton yields.

Texas farmers are responsible for an estimated 25 percent of total US cotton production. Planting wildflowers between rows of cotton or on the edges of cotton fields, introducing flowering crops into the crop rotation, and reducing pesticide spraying during daylight hours can all have positive impacts on pollinator diversity and crop yields. Cotton growers who add pollinator habitat can increase annual revenues upwards of $108 per acre; at this rate, cotton farms in the South Texas region alone could generate an additional $1 million on an annual basis.

Senior author Shalene Jha, assistant professor of integrative biology at UT Austin, believes the research is proof that pollinator protection and profitable agriculture can go hand in hand. "We've shown that there are multiple benefits to biodiversity," she explains. "With the right management, cotton farmers can have higher crop yields and support native plants and animals."

Box 2-4

Could the Farm Bill Help Pollinators?

In 2008, Congress passed two bills that prioritized pollinator conservation: the Pollinator Habitat Protection Act (S. 1494), which included pollinators in conservation programs; and the Pollinator Protection Act (S. 1694), which allocated resources to studying honeybees, including potential causes of Colony Collapse Disorder. Both were included in the US Farm Bill.

The Farm Bill is a massive piece of legislation governing programs ranging from farm credit and rural development to nutrition assistance; it also includes agricultural conservation. Allocating federal funding to habitat conservation on private lands provides incentives to farmers to create wildlife corridors, restore wetlands, and plant pollinator habitats. To date, around 50 million acres are enrolled in at least one Farm Bill conservation program.

In advance of the upcoming Farm Bill, set to be released in 2019, fifty wildlife groups, seed companies, and other conservation organizations are urging Congress to include provisions that encourage farms to plant native species. The Natives First Coalition spearheaded the so-called native-plant standard to give funding preference to conservation projects that incorporate native plants, which provide superior food and habitat for pollinators.

The Conservation Reserve Program (CRP) is a government-administered land-conservation program that makes annual rental payments to farmers in exchange for taking eco-sensitive areas out of production and planting species that improve environmental conditions; certain sections of the CRP require farmers to plant native grasses. Other sections require introduced (nonnative) species.

Adding a native-plant standard to the next Farm Bill could be a boon for pollinators, especially if a proposed CRP expansion is also approved. The House Agriculture Committee drafted legislation that would increase the limit on CRP enrollments from its current cap of 24 million acres to 30 million acres. (The cap was reduced from 32 million acres to 24 million acres in the 2014 Farm Bill. Wildlife groups argue that the reduction eliminated critical habitat.)

Expanding the CRP is expensive—as much as $997 million over ten years, according to some estimates—but maintaining the current cap on enrolled acreage comes at a great cost to pollinators that depend on suitable habitat for their survival.

to vegetables and wine grapes sold as both fresh produce and processed foods such as nut butters and freezer items. The label can be used on products sold at supermarkets or direct to consumers through farmers markets and CSA programs.

Sran Family Orchards was the first farm to become Bee Better Certified. The California almond growers have created 24 acres of permanent pollinator habitat and 116 acres of flowering cover crops between rows of almond trees across ten orchards in Fresno and Madera Counties. Lee-Mader notes that "dozens" of additional farms are going through the certification process. The still-to-be-named applicants include one of the largest berry farms in the Pacific Northwest, a 7,000-acre grain and oilseed operation in Montana, and the largest vegetable producer in Iowa.

"At some point, I hope that the program achieves some kind of critical mass," says Mader. "[The certification] provides farms with some way to differentiate themselves in the marketplace . . . and provides consumers with assurance that the ingredients in their foods are coming from farms that are doing something significant and meaningful [for pollinators]."

Stitching Together a Patchwork of Habitats

Although establishing pollinator habitats on individual farms is important, stitching together a critical mass of safe, appropriate places for fragile species to find food, shelter, and nesting sites is essential.

It's not just that habitats are disappearing; the distance between them is increasing, making it harder for pollinators to make long treks. Fragmentation, which breaks up continuous stretches of habitat, might be as devastating to pollinators as losing their homes altogether—but the effects are under-studied.

Research shows that bats that roost in tree cavities are more vulnerable to fragmentation than cave-roosting species; some species of bats decline in response to fragmentation, but others thrive. The abundance of pollinator species is lower in fragmented habitats, which might lead to lower fruit- and seed-setting in smaller habitats, limiting pollination.

Habitat fragmentation is especially troublesome for monarch butterflies. The featherweight pollinators travel up to 100 miles per day during their annual migration from eastern North America to the Sierra Madre mountain range in Mexico or from western North America to California. During the arduous trek to their overwintering sites, the iconic black, orange, and white butterflies depend on roosting sites. Illegal logging in the Monarch Biosphere Reserve, the area in central Mexico where millions of migrating butterflies spend the winter, has led to deforestation that exposes monarchs to wind and cold temperatures, leading to their death.

In a statement about the impact of deforestation on monarch populations, Chip Taylor, professor of ecology and evolutionary biology at the University of Kansas, said, “It’s so truly spectacular, one of the most awe-inspiring phenomena that nature presents to us. There is no way to describe the sight of 25 million monarchs per acre—or the sensation of standing in a snowstorm of orange as the butterflies cascade off the fir trees. To lose something like this migration is to diminish all of us.”

Patches of pollinator habitat aren’t just important for migrating butterflies; the plantings also provide places to feed and nest for the species that stick closer to home. Stitching together a patchwork of habitats was one of the goals of creating the North Carolina Butterfly Highway.

With the bells from the light-rail crossing ringing in the background, Angel Hjarding, director of pollinator and wildlife habitat programs for the North Carolina Wildlife Federation, dressed in a gauzy butterfly-printed scarf, points out the pollinator plants at First Ward Park in downtown Charlotte, North Carolina. When the Charlotte-Mecklenburg Parks and Recreation department established the four-acre park on the site of a former parking lot, the raised beds were filled with traditional landscape plants like fescue grass (*Festuca*), Bermuda grass (*Cynodon dactylon*) and bush clover (*Lespedeza bicolor*) that, while popular, provided no value to pollinators. "The commercial landscape industry never stops to ask, 'Who's eating this?' We need to start thinking about how we address the needs of pollinators in urban areas, and habitat is one important option," explains Hjarding.

In 2017, Hjarding suggested using grant funds to replace 3,000 square feet of "useless" plants in First Ward Park with alternatives like milkweed and mountain mint (*Pycnanthemum muticum*) that provide nectar and habitat for butterflies and other pollinators. The pilot project turned into a flagship public site on the North Carolina Butterfly Highway.

Now, walking along the paved path between raised beds and the great lawn as traffic whizzes past, Hjarding explains the need for the collection of pollinator habitats that make up the Butterfly Highway: Charlotte added more than 15,000 residents in 2016, making it one of the fastest-growing cities in the nation, and development has kept pace. In June 2017, more than 2,000 new residential units were under construction in the downtown area alone. Exploding development means less pollinator habitat and longer distances between available habitats.

By planting "pollinator patches" in Charlotte—and throughout North Carolina—Hjarding hoped to provide a network for fragile populations to congregate. She recruited fifty households in five neighborhoods to kick-start the North Carolina Butterfly Highway in 2015. The project has grown to include 1,700 patches of habitat at parks, government buildings, community centers, and residential yards. (Around the same time when Hjarding launched the North Carolina Butterfly Highway, former Charlotte mayor Jennifer Roberts signed the Mayor's Monarch Pledge, creating a new landscape ordinance that required at least 50 percent of all new trees, shrubs, and ground cover planted as part of city projects in Charlotte to be native plants.)

The Butterfly Highway moniker is a bit misleading, Hjarding admits: unlike roadside habitat projects, the North Carolina Butterfly Highway isn't connected with an actual road. Instead, it's a series of interconnected habitats that help pollinators travel from one place to another, creating a path of habitat. The original participants decided to call it the Butterfly Highway—but it's not just for butterflies.

Hjarding explains, "I asked, 'What about the Bee Highway or the Pollinator Highway?' and their response was 'No bees in my neighborhood!' and 'What's a pollinator?'—but people love butterflies. It triggered memories for them. People said, 'I remember seeing butterflies in my childhood, but now I don't see them as much,' so there was a cultural connection."

That connection helped Hjarding recruit participants eager to plant pollinator habitat on their properties. The habitats range from small raised beds filled with nectar plants in residential yards and apartment complexes to more ambitious projects like the plantings at First Ward Park.

"Are these small-patch habitats important? Yes. Can we save pollinators by putting in these pit stops on balconies and in backyard gardens? Probably not. But these small patches in combination with land conservancies and even our game lands are all about not altering the landscape into development . . . and the other part of this that's important is creating connectivity in the landscape to address habitat fragmentation."

Andrea DeLong-Amaya, director of horticulture for the Lady Bird Johnson Wildflower Center, encourages homeowners to think of their yards as individual squares in a patchwork of pollinator habitats. "I think about whether each little square is fracturing habitats or connecting habitats," she says. "If every little yard is connected to every other little yard, homeowners can provide pockets of habitat, because if we're going to replace [existing habitats] with homes, then those homes have to fill in the gaps. If everybody participates, it will work."

Figure 2-1: A lush garden with a diversity of nectar sources provides excellent habitat for pollinators.

Box 2-5
Fireflies Are Burning Out

Childhood memories of chasing fireflies after dark might soon be a forgotten pastime.

Fireflies (Coleoptera: Lampyridae)—also called lightning bugs—glow like Christmas lights because of a chemical reaction: a compound called luciferan in their abdomens mixes with oxygen, calcium, and adenosine triphosphate to produce light. More than 2,000 species of these illuminated pollinators use their bioluminescent backsides to attract mates, scare predators, and claim their territories. Firefly populations are in decline as a result of habitat loss.

There is little data about their populations. Researchers at Michigan State University studied the eastern firefly (*Photinus pyralis*) in ten communities between 2004 and 2015 and found the twinkling fireflies (which aren't flies at all—they're beetles) prefer undisturbed habitats like fields. A study published in the *Journal of Insect Conservation* noted negative correlations between urbanization and lightning bug abundance.

In addition to eliminating nesting sites and nectar sources, development also increases light pollution. While it's unclear how artificial illumination affects fireflies, studies have linked increases in light pollution to decreases in firefly populations. Most species of fireflies start flashing between twelve and sixteen minutes after sunset. Fireflies tend to increase their flight altitude as light levels decline, suggesting that the species is sensitive to slight changes in ambient light. Research published in the *Coleopterists Bulletin*, the journal of the Coleopterists Society, examined the impact of artificial night light on fireflies at six sites in Maryland. The number of flashes per minute were recorded under natural moonlit conditions; artificial light was added on subsequent nights. The light was more intense than a full moon but less intense than a streetlight. The presence of artificial light was linked with significant declines in flash frequencies, with the number of flashes per minute declining 50 percent. If artificial lights make it harder for fireflies to spot each other's glowing backsides, it can disrupt mating and, in turn, cause population declines.

Would a Border Wall Harm Pollinators?

President Trump campaigned on the promise of building a 700-mile border wall to stop migrants from crossing into the United States from Mexico. Conservationists are concerned that the border wall would also become a barrier to pollinators.

The proposed location of the border wall cuts through areas of essential pollinator habitat, stripping out miles of vegetation and fragmenting habitat. At eighteen feet high, the wall would make it impossible for butterflies and some bats to cross, separating them from the plants they depend on for survival. Making matters worse, the lights required to illuminate the wall could attract—and burn—insect pollinators.

Little research exists to evaluate the ecosystem impacts of a border wall. One study estimated that 134 mammals, 178 reptiles, and 57 amphibian species live within thirty miles of the proposed border wall; no pollinator counts were conducted. Study co-author Jesse Lasky, assistant professor of biology at Pennsylvania State University, notes that the region of southeast Arizona and southwest New Mexico, where the research was conducted, is one of the centers of biodiversity in the nation. The section of the wall that would run through the Santa Ana National Wildlife Refuge—home to butterflies like the cloudless sulphur (*Phoebis sennae*), giant swallowtail (*Papilio cresphontes*), and gray hairstreak (*Strymon melinus*), as well as nine species of hummingbirds, including the rufous hummingbird (*Selasphorus rufus*)—will be built without an environmental impact study.

Even though his research was conducted on mammals, reptiles, and amphibians, Lasky notes that "There is a lot of evidence that animals that fly can also have their movements disrupted by barriers like this and the destruction of their natural habitat. Flying creatures are pretty restricted in terms of the heights they'll fly and how far they'll venture away from natural vegetation. Because the border patrol wants lots of visibility along the barriers, they often destroy native vegetation in very wide strips and install stadium lighting and roads along the barriers, so they've been building essentially a no man's land between the two layers of fence that's totally devoid of any vegetation."

Lasky explains that stripping the landscape of vegetation to build a wall can be done without any assessment of the possible impacts on the environment because of the Real ID Act, a law created after September 11, 2001, to help protect the nation's borders. "For a regulatory law, it's really quite extreme; I don't know of anything else like it," he says. "It's pretty glaring to me as a case where we might not have very good assessments of potential risks for such a large-scale [project], but because of this law, the border wall isn't subject to the same kinds of provisions that other construction projects would be. . . . If we were treating it like a normal project, I'd probably still be very concerned about the prospect of larger border barriers for animal movements, but at least we'd have more studies to put some actual numbers on the kinds of risks they pose."

Conservation groups like the Sierra Club, the Center for Biological Diversity, and Defenders of Wildlife are pushing back against the proposed wall. In December 2017, the Texas-based National Butterfly Center, a project of the North American Butterfly Association and home to 100 species of butterflies, filed a lawsuit against the Department of Homeland Security to require the Trump Administration to conduct assessments before building a wall through the sanctuary.

Investing in Habitat Restoration

Restoring habitat is expensive, and encouraging participation often requires outside funding to bring projects to fruition. Government-backed cost-sharing programs are helping rebuild pollinator habitats.

In 2015, the US Department of Agriculture's Natural Resources Conservation Service committed $4 million in technical and financial assistance to help plant milkweed and nectar plants along field borders and pastures. The funding targeted farmers in ten states—Illinois, Indiana, Iowa, Kansas, Minnesota, Missouri, Ohio, Oklahoma, Texas, and Wisconsin—critical areas for monarch migration where milkweed was plentiful in the Midwest before the proliferation of commercial-scale farming. Additional support was made available nationwide through the Conservation Stewardship Program.

Private companies have also stepped up to support pollinators. Bayer created a Feed a Bee program in 2015, handing out seed packets in the hopes of planting 50 million wildflowers to expand forage areas in all fifty states.

"It's neat to see how excited people are," says Sarah Myers, apiarist and outreach coordinator for Bayer CropScience. "People might not want to keep bees, but they want to help pollinators, and [doing that is] as easy as planting a flower. If one person does it, it might not make a big impact, but it can have a ripple effect."

Last year, Feed a Bee expanded to include pollinator habitat grants and, to date, the agribusiness giant has partnered with 112 organizations in 37 states and planted more than three billion wildflowers. Ripple effect indeed. Häagen-Dazs, WhiteWave (makers of Silk Almond Milk), Boeing, Greif Corporation, Toyota, and Burt's Bees have all invested in pollinator habitats.

Food manufacturing giant General Mills committed more than $4 million to establish pollinator habitats. A significant portion of the funding was allocated to planting flowers on its partner farms that produce ingredients like fruits, almonds, and oats used in products ranging from cereal and granola bars to pasta sauce. The commitment includes: 11,300 acres of pollinator habitat on 160,000 acres of organic and conventional supplier farms by 2020; five miles of hedgerow and wildflower strips on the ranch that supplies almonds for Lärabar products; and an additional 20 acres of habitat planted on 500 acres of organic farmland operated by two organic dairy farms that supply milk to the Annie's brand.

The investment makes good business sense, according to Beth Robinson-Martin who oversees organic sourcing for General Mills and leads its Pollinator Council. "You really have to think that it's bad for business," she says, "if the bees die, the plants die, and you have no product, [so investing in habitat] is good for the pollinators and good for the farmers—but it's really good for our business, too."

Protecting habitat also feels good. Robinson-Martin admits to tearing up when she thinks back to the first time she saw border plantings on the fringes of one of the farms growing tomatoes for the Muir Glen brand during a visit to Williams, California, in 2006. She remembers seeing the hedgerow, which stretched for more than half a mile along the side of the road, teeming with bees and butterflies. "I was standing out there—the pollinator habitat was about two years old at the time—and just looking at the difference on both sides of the road," she explains. "On one side was this beautiful, lush pollinator habitat and all of these insects, and on the other side—nothing. I don't know who [the land across the street] belonged to, but it was just a field of dirt with nothing on it. It was like a wasteland on one side, and on the other side: life, with all of these five-foot-tall flowers and hummingbirds and monarch caterpillars, which I hadn't seen since I was a kid—just a gorgeous, green, beautiful, almost-mile-long hedgerow. It was like seeing the difference between our post-apocalyptic future and this beautiful biodiverse home. It was moving to see these spaces come to life and see what a difference habitat could make for pollinators."

Pollinators Are Moving to Bee City USA

A nonprofit based in Asheville, North Carolina, came up with a creative plan to entice pollinators to move into local neighborhoods: establish Bee City USA.

The program encourages communities to create public–private partnerships to raise awareness of the importance of pollinators and provide sustainable habitats filled with native plants and maintained with minimal use of pesticides. The "open source" model allows cities to adopt the program to meet the unique needs of their communities (and their pollinator populations), and adapt it to work in public and private spaces ranging from parks, schools, and libraries to neighborhood associations—all with a goal of making the world safer for pollinators, one city at a time.

To date, sixty-six cities in twenty-four states, including Eureka Springs, Arkansas, Ann Arbor, Michigan, Carson City, Nevada, and Boone, North Carolina, have earned the designation Bee City USA. Bee City Canada launched in 2016 and has registered ten cities so far. Interest from universities led to the creation of "Bee Campuses" to recognize institutions for their pollinator protection efforts. There are thirty-seven (and counting) registered Bee Campuses across the nation.

The goal is not to have communities undertake large fundraising efforts to develop beautiful gardens. Instead, Bee City USA encourages cities to work with their existing resources, noting: "Pollinators don't need showplaces; they need food (pollen and nectar) and places to mate, nest, and overwinter."

Awareness campaigns emphasize the importance of suitable pollinator habitat, urging communities to remove invasive species and use alternatives to toxic pesticides. They also call public attention to seasonal changes and the need to pitch in to ensure the survival of essential pollinator species.

Want to plant a pollinator garden? Head to the library. In addition to housing collections of books to help choose the best plants and identify the pollinators that alight on the colorful petals in search of nectar, some libraries also operate "seed libraries" that allow cardholders to check out seeds for their gardens.

Unlike library patrons who borrow books, those borrowing seeds aren't expected to return them (although gardeners are welcome to collect seeds and donate them back to the libraries to keep the collection

Figure 2-2: The Desert Botanical Garden in Phoenix, Arizona, is home to several unusual pollinator-friendly plants, including these "stinky" cactus-like carrion plants.

growing). The native-plant seeds are designed to attract a range of pollinators.

Stetson University in DeLand, Florida, offers several native wildflowers, including bee balm (*Monarda punctate*), ironweed (*Vernonia angustifolia*), and partridge pea (*Chamaecrista fasciculate*). The Vancouver (British Columbia) Public Library operates seed libraries at four of its urban branches. The Ramsey Library at the University of North Carolina Asheville started a seed library in 2018.

Barb Svenson, collection and resource management librarian at the Ramsey Library, envisioned the seed library as a community resource that could increase pollinator habitats across the city of Asheville. With the help of a library colleague, Wendy Mullis, she collected seeds from campus pollinator gardens. The pair cleaned and dried twelve varieties of seeds, including asters and echinacea, and offered them to the public free of charge. The project was a hit. "We had a great response from the campus and the community at large," Svenson says. "We've had several people asking when we'll do it again."

Sponsor-A-Hive, Save a Bee

Beekeeping is expensive. The initial startup costs—beehives, tools, and packages of bees—means that organizations such as schools, nature centers, and food banks interested in using beehives as teaching tools often cannot afford to start programs.

To help advance bee conservation, the Honeybee Conservancy has launched a Sponsor-A-Hive program. Organizations receive equipment as well as honeybees, mason bees, or leafcutter bees.

The Honeybee Conservancy calls bee houses "science classes in a box" that inspire about science, environment, agriculture, and pollination. The bees are often incorporated into school gardens, pollinator patches, and wildlife habitats, where their presence helps pollinate flowers and vegetables and bolster bee populations.

"Beekeeping is an expensive undertaking and we feel that people should be able to be involved, regardless of their income level," says Honeybee Conservancy's Fernandez. "Sponsor-A-Hive advances bee conservation and empowers underserved communities with bees and the education and tools needed to support local agriculture."

Since its 2016 inception, the nonprofit has provided bee houses to partner organizations (after they undergo a rigorous application process) in 165 cities. The recipients become passionate stewards for bees, helping raise awareness of the threats facing important pollinators and how their communities can help.

CHAPTER 3

Taming Toxics

In the Bee Lab at the Ohio State University, Reed Johnson, an assistant professor, pulls a frame of late-stage capped brood from a beehive and places it in an incubator, waiting for adult bees to emerge. Each day, as bees hatch, Johnson gently brushes them off the frame and into a screened wooden box, marking each with their "birthdays" and feeding them with a sugar-water solution.

When the bees are three days old, the screened box is placed in a styrofoam cooler rigged with a hose from a carbon dioxide tank. Johnson uses the odorless gas to knock out the bees so he can dose them with pesticides. The doses are applied to the thorax using a micro-applicator that resembles a caulking gun; each group of bees receives a different dose. Bees are assessed one, two, and three days following the pesticide application. The goal is to determine the lethal dose.

"Lethal dose" tests are the foundation of all pesticide research. Johnson notes that the tests he conducts in the Bee Lab are the same as the tests that companies like Bayer and Syngenta must conduct (through third party labs) before their products hit the market. The results show the level at which pesticides are lethal to bees. "We try to simulate what bees would be experiencing [in the field], to see how much pesticide is in the pollen the bees consume, but no one knows the answers to those questions," Johnson explains. "We can make some guesses, and people have measured some concentrations, but the real question is, 'How does relating your laboratory results to field exposure?' That's always a challenge."

Measuring fatalities is just one area of pesticide research. Other tests focus on the "sublethal" effects, which don't kill bees but impact their physiology and behavior, according to Christina Grozinger at Penn State.

When honeybees leave their hives to forage, collecting sweet nectar from the colorful blooms of flowers like clover and dandelions, pollen sticks to their bodies and gets carried back to the hive. If bees visit plants that were sprayed with pesticides or hit by drift when nearby plants were sprayed, those chemicals return to the hive, too. In a 2010 study, researchers took samples of beebread, pollen, brood nest wax, and beeswax foundation, as well as adult bees and brood from beehives in twenty-three states and one Canadian province. Samples were taken from both healthy colonies and those diagnosed with Colony Collapse Disorder to test for 200 different chemicals, including miticides, insecticides, fungicides, and herbicides. The 749 samples were found to contain 118 different pesticides and metabolites.

"That sort of raised the alarm that bees . . . forage very broadly and on a lot of agricultural crops, so they bring back a lot of chemicals to the hive," Grozinger says.

Neonicotinoids are at the heart of the debate about the impact of pesticides on pollinators. The chemicals, related to nicotine—the word *neonicotinoid* means "new nicotine-like" insecticides—are systemic insecticides used to control sap-and root-feeding insects like aphids and grubs.

Rather than remaining on the surface where it's applied, a neonicotinoid pesticide is absorbed by plants and transported to the leaves, flow-

Box 3-1

The Pests Decimating Honeybee Colonies

The words *varroa mite* make beekeepers shudder in their veils. The mites first appeared in the United States in the 1980s and fast became a major pest, decimating honeybee colonies. During the 2016–17 winter season, beekeepers lost an estimated 33.2 percent of their hives.

Varroa mites (*Varroa destructor*) attack both bees and brood, using their jaws to attach their small, reddish-brown, flattened oval bodies to the thorax and abdomens of bees, sucking their blood. The pests attack both adult bees and developing brood, causing weakness or deformities like missing legs and wings. Left untreated, mite populations will explode and kill entire colonies. It's been called "the world's most devastating pest of Western honeybees."

Infestation starts in bee brood. A female mite enters the brood cell before it's capped and sealed in with the larvae, on which the mite lays eggs. (Beekeepers often first notice an infestation by looking for dark mites on the white pupae of drone cells.) By the time an adult bee emerges from the cell, several mite eggs have hatched and matured and begun to seek out new bee hosts. The pests spread like wildfire, both within hives and also between colonies via drifting workers and drones.

Varroa transmits viruses that are deadly to honeybees, and European honeybees have no innate immunity to the viruses carried by the pests. In the 1990s, beekeepers were concerned when mites attacked one in five bees; now, one in three bees is affected. Until the mites became widespread, most of the viruses that affected honeybees were considered harmless, but proliferation of the pests has changed that: as the mites have become more common, the viruses have become more virulent. Most of the new honeybee viruses that have been discovered are associated with varroa mites; the mites act as vectors, helping viruses spread throughout colonies. One of those new diseases is *Varroa destructor* virus-1, which causes high rates of overwintering colony losses. In 2016, researchers tested hives in 603 apiaries and found varroa mites in 66 percent of colonies; pest assessments in 2010 found varroa mites in fewer than 3 percent of colonies, pointing to a rapid and widespread increase in the infestations.

Chemical treatments are the sole option for killing mites in affected colonies. Several different pesticides are used, including sticky strips coated with tau-fluvalinate and amitraz; a slow-release gel called thymol; and formic acid pads that release fatal fumes. All of these treatments will kill varroa mites without harming bees. With the exception of formic acid, none of these chemical treatments can be used during the honey flow.

continued

Box 3-1 *continued*

Losses are decreasing. The 2016–17 winter losses were almost 6 percent lower than the previous year, and overall losses were the second-lowest recorded in the past seven years—but that doesn't mean varroa mites are no longer an issue. In fact, concerns over the problematic parasites led scientists at Bayer to begin exploring alternative treatments.

Drawing inspiration from old-school flea and tick collars, researchers created a small plastic strip with holes attached to the hive entrance. Bees must go through this "varroa gate" to enter or leave the hive; the strip is embedded with a mite-killing chemical that can be transferred to bees entering and exiting the hive for several weeks. One of the researchers on the project, Gudrun Koeniger, wrote about the importance of the varroa gate, explaining, "We have learned over the past few decades that no single weapon is effective in controlling mites. We need an integrated approach to mite control." Koeniger hopes the varroa gate will be an important tool in the battle against the destructive parasites and help save honeybees from infestations and death.

Researchers are still fine-tuning the chemical formulation and application rate and performing field tests. The problem, according to Bayer's Myers, is the efficacy of the active ingredient.

"It wasn't working here," she explains. "So we're having to look at different [active ingredients]. The mode of action is still something we want to pursue. . . . We do have [active ingredients] that we're screening and testing, and, at some point . . . we hope that we can see it as a new solution for beekeepers."

ers, roots, and stems, where it remains for several weeks to protect crops like corn, cotton, sugar beets, soybeans, and canola during the growing season. The so-called neonic can be applied to foliage or soil, or used as a seed treatment (coated seeds are dipped in pesticide).

Imidacloprid was the first neonic to become available in the 1990s. Since then, several additional variations, including acetamiprid, clothianidin, dinotefuran, nitenpyram, thiacloprid, and thiamethoxam, have hit the market, making neonicotinoids the most common class of insecticides in the world. Neonics are used on at least 140 crops in 120 countries, including an estimated 80 to 95 percent of corn and almost half of all soybeans planted in the United States—covering a total area about the size of California. The concentration of pesticides applied to seeds has increased. When coated seeds were first introduced, neonicotinoid levels ranged from 0.25–0.5 mg per seed (for thiamethoxam and clothianidin); now, 0.5 mg per seed is the default rate among most seed companies and several companies offer seed treatments with 1.25 mg of neonicotinoid per seed, leading entomologist Christian Krupke to tell NPR, "The level of use is way out of step with the level of [pest] threat in most fields."

Several studies have implicated the popular pesticides in pollinator decline. Pollinators might ingest the pesticides while collecting nectar from the flowers of treated plants or eating insects exposed to the pesticides; direct exposure is also possible if pollinators are foraging when neonicotinoids are applied. The chemicals remain on plants and in the soil long after their initial application and might leach into groundwater or run off into other bodies of water, extending the timeframe for possible contamination.

The pesticides are systemic: neonicotinoids get taken up in the soil and move around the whole plant, which protects against insects but also gets into the pollen and nectar. Each time pollinators visit a treated plant, their meal of the plant's pollen and nectar also includes a dose of the pesticide. Ecotoxicologist Vera Krischik at the University of Minnesota has conducted research showing that neonicotinoids sprayed on plants in greenhouses remain in the pollen for long periods; ten weeks after the initial application, there is still enough residue to kill a bee.

"There is an old statement that says, 'The dose is the poison,'" Krischik explains. "When you drink two cups of coffee a day, you're fine; but if you drink 280 cups of coffee a day, you're not fine. It's the same with plants. When you put a neonicotinoid on as a seed treatment, corn gets 1.36 milligrams, but when you put it in a nursery plant in a three-gallon pot, you apply 300 milligrams. By the time the corn plant grows, after a month or two, there are no neonics left. It's left in the soil but completely diluted by the plant's growth. There are different formulations you apply to different crops . . . but basically, the more you apply, the more persistent [the pesticide] is going to be."

Not all neonic exposures are fatal. The pesticides effect neurons, which mean they can cause brain damage in pollinators. According to one study, acute doses did not significantly affect bumblebees, but chronic "field-realistic" exposure levels were linked with slower learning and impaired short-term memory, which could hurt both individual bees and their colonies. Exposure has also been linked to a scrambled sense of direction that may make it difficult for foraging bees to return to their hives and communicate the location of nectar-rich forage to their colonies. Additional studies reported impacts on the queen ranging from damage to the ovaries that limited reproduction to dramatic queen losses, causing hives to collapse.

Although research has concentrated on bees, the pesticides also appear to harm other pollinators. A study on clothianidin and milkweed plants suggested that the pesticide could stress monarch populations, reducing the size of larvae and increasing mortality. And in 2017, Canadian scientists released the results of the first research to assess the effects of neonicotinoids on hummingbirds.

Plummeting populations of rufous hummingbirds (*Selasphorus rufus*) led Christine Bishop, research scientist with Environment and Climate Change Canada, to question whether the avian pollinators fared better in agricultural areas or natural habitats.

Rufous hummingbirds—named for the reddish-brown (rufous) coloring on their faces— measure less than 3.5 inches in length and weigh between two and five grams. The petite pollinators have been called the feistiest hummingbirds because of their tendencies to attack other hummingbirds seeking out nectar at flowers and feeders. Their tenacious behavior isn't limited to their own species; rufous hummingbirds will direct their aggression toward species weighing twice as much. The rufous hummingbird prefers nectar from flowers as colorful as their plumage; the nimble pollinators seek out plants with tubular flowers, such as Columbine (*Aquilegi*a), Indian paintbrush (*Castilleja*), and larkspur (*Delphinium*), using their superior flight skills to move from one flower to the next at remarkable speeds. Though nectar makes up the bulk of their diet, they also nosh on insects for protein; gnats and aphids are among their favorites. The rufous hummingbird has a more extensive breeding range than other species and has been spotted from Alaska to Mexico, breeding in open areas, including mountainsides, and nesting along the West Coast, traveling more than 2,000 miles to overwinter in warmer climates. Their populations have declined 60 percent since 1970.

Climate change and habitat loss hurt populations; an overabundance of deer might also be to blame, since they feast on several of the same plants hummingbirds depend on for nectar. Bishop led the first team of researchers to see if pesticides were a factor. The decision was made during a conversation with another researcher about what was driving population declines. "She said, 'When you're banding hummingbirds, they often pee and poop while you handle them. Maybe we can [use those samples] to look at pesticide exposures in the birds as well,'" Bishop recalls.

Feeders were placed at two sites in British Columbia: blueberry fields in the Fraser Valley that are routinely sprayed with insecticides, including neonicotinoids, and areas of Vancouver Island far from agricultural land. Researchers looked at samples from rufous hummingbirds and Anna's hummingbird (*Calypte anna*), a medium-sized species with iridescent emerald green feathers and a bright rose-colored throat that lives along the Pacific Coast. Unlike the rufous hummingbird, populations of Anna's hummingbirds have increased; their range has expanded farther north and east.

When either species alighted on the feeder, a screen dropped to trap the birds so researchers could collect samples. Since the excreta, which

Bishop describes as "a golden pearl of pee and tiny pinhead-sized fecal pellets," was insufficient to measure exposures in individual birds, researchers pooled the samples from both species to get enough volume.

The results showed high levels of three neonicotinoids (thiamethoxam, clothianidin, and imidacloprid) in the urine collected from hummingbirds in the blueberry fields; samples collected on Vancouver Island did not contain detectable levels.

"We think that exposure is primarily from the crop . . . but blueberries only bloom for three weeks of the year, so that can't be their only food source, and we don't know where else they're getting the neonicotinoids. . . . It's still an ongoing research question, trying to figure out exactly where the sources are for the birds. What we know now is that we have high concentrations of neonicotinoids in urine."

The findings are complex. Mixing urine samples from two species—one that is thriving and another experiencing decline—makes it impossible to tell precisely what impact the pesticides are having on either of the species. Neonics were not detected in fecal matter—samples did show piperonyl butoxide, a compound applied with the pesticides to make them more toxic to insects. The chemical could impair the birds' liver function, making it harder for hummingbirds to detoxify the pesticides. Even if both species showed similar pesticide exposure, Bishop notes, "Rufous hummingbirds might be really sensitive to these [pesticides] versus another species. Even though they are all hummingbirds, they can have different physiologies."

The results showed that hummingbirds living in agricultural areas were exposed to pesticides, but what exactly that means remains unclear. "It's just the first step in looking at whether or not we can even measure pesticide in the birds and [their levels of exposure]," Bishop explains.

Bishop is continuing the research and hopes that with more samples and additional analyses she'll be able to paint a fuller picture of what impact pesticides might have on hummingbird health and populations.

Box 3-2
Harmful Herbicides

Neonicotinoids might dominate the conversation about chemicals and pollinators, but the impacts of herbicides must be explored, too. Mass losses of milkweed—the sole source of food for monarch larvae—are linked to herbicide applications.

Thanks to the introduction of herbicide-resistant crops such as Roundup Ready corn and soybeans, farmers can spray broad-spectrum weed killers like glyphosate (sold under the trade name Roundup) on their fields, sparing the crops while killing the weeds. But the applications kill milkweed, too. Researchers have estimated an 81 percent decline in monarch populations and a 58 percent decline in milkweed in the Midwest, an essential breeding ground for monarchs, between 1999 and 2010. Over the last two decades, the number of milkweed plants growing in natural areas has increased while these essential host plants have all but disappeared from agricultural areas—indicating that agricultural herbicides might be to blame for losses.

Researchers at Michigan State University studied monarch populations between 1994 and 2003, the period when farmers in the Midwest started spraying herbicides on a large scale. They found that when glyphosate use went up, monarch populations went down. The results are the first empirical evidence of a connection between the herbicides and pollinator decline.

Despite the studies linking pollinator deaths to widespread use of glyphosate, the herbicide is regarded as the safest of the synthetic herbicides. Dicamba, sold under trade names like Diablo, Oracle, and Vanquish, is, by contrast, considered the most dangerous because it tends to drift away from the application site. Applied to the soil to kill weeds before crops are planted, dicamba is found in more than 1,100 products. Researchers at Penn State applied sublethal doses of dicamba to common boneset (*Eupatorium perfoliatum*), a native plant that attracts pollinators, and found that "drift-level doses" reduced flowering and led to fewer pollinator species visiting the plants.

Concerns about drift prompted the EPA to issue a proposal requiring a buffer zone in all directions to protect wildlife habitat. But the agency reversed its decision when Monsanto, the agrochemical company that manufactures dicamba, countered with its own research claiming drift distances were exaggerated in other studies. Now the buffer zone is limited to applications on the parts of a field located downwind from wildlife habitats. The protections were

continued

Box 3-2 *continued*

loosened around the same time that research found that dicamba drift had damaged more than 3.6 million acres of soybeans.

Dicamba use has only grown with the introduction of Monsanto-manufactured dicamba-tolerant crops. Roundup Ready 2 Xtend, soybean seeds bio-engineered for tolerance to both dicamba and glyphosate, received approval for commercial planting in November 2016.

In a report titled "A Menace to Monarchs," the Center for Biological Diversity claims that 60 million acres of monarch habitat in the Midwest will be doused with dicamba by 2019, escalating the threat to struggling monarch populations. Their research shows that herbicide drift associated with the increased use of dicamba will endanger an additional nine million acres of monarch habitat, posing an even greater risk to milkweed and monarch populations than glyphosate.

In the meantime, it's getting harder to spot these adorable little birds as their populations remain in peril.

The slew of studies linking neonicotinoids to pollinator decline led to several restrictions—and a few outright bans—on the popular pesticides. In 2013, the European Union banned the use of three neonicotinoids—imidacloprid, clothianidin, and thiamethoxam—on flowering field crops such as corn, sunflower, and rapeseed, citing risks to managed bee colonies as well as wild bees. In 2018, the ban was expanded to include *all* field crops. Sixteen countries, including the United Kingdom, France, and Germany voted in favor of expanding the ban. Outdoor use of the pesticides is now forbidden in the European Union; greenhouse applications are still permitted because bees are not expected to be exposed in greenhouse settings. "With hindsight, [the European Food Safety Authority] appears to agree that the [initial approval procedure for neonicotinoids] was not thought through at the time," ecologist David Goulson of the University of Stirling in the United Kingdom told *Science* magazine.

Bayer, however, called the EU bans "a bad deal for Europe," claiming that the European Food Safety Authority risk-assessment findings are "outside the current mainstream science on bee health" as conducted by organizations like the EPA. The neonic manufacturer warns that the bans will not help bees and, in fact, could do more harm. Without neonicotinoids to control crop pests, Bayer claims, farmers might resort to spraying a greater volume of chemicals or turning to older, less effective methods of pest control.

Health Canada has also announced changes in the regulation of clothianidin and thiamethoxam, issuing nationwide bans of the use of the chemicals on orchard trees and strawberries, restricting their use on berries and legumes, and introducing new labeling requirements for seed treatments. The province of Ontario similarly implemented new rules aimed at reducing the number of acres planted with neonicotinoid-treated corn and soybean seeds by 80 percent by 2017. The new rules helped ensure that neonicotinoid-treated corn and soybean seeds are used only when there was a demonstrated pest problem. Winter cereal crops, plants grown in greenhouses, and certain crops sprayed post-flowering are exempt from the ban. Because these bans are so recent, no peer-reviewed data has yet been conducted to evaluate their effect on bee populations.

Agrochemical producers have challenged the bans, arguing that lab studies showing negative effects were based on neonicotinoid concentrations that far exceed those found in the nectar and pollen of plants treated in the field. On its website, neonicotinoid manufacturer Bayer argues: "While many laboratory studies and other studies applying artificial exposure conditions described sublethal and other effects [of exposure to the pesticide], no adverse effects to bee colonies were ever observed in field studies at field-realistic exposure conditions." CropLife America, a national trade association representing pesticide manufacturers and distributors, noted that ongoing research and field studies have consistently found no adverse effects on bee colonies when pesticides are applied according to label directions.

Penn State's Grozinger acknowledges that proponents of pesticides "love bringing up field data" because it's so difficult to draw clear conclusions from "field-realistic" data. Indeed, field studies paint a complicated picture of the effect of the pesticides.

Still, most studies continue to find that neonics are damaging to populations of insect pollinators. For example, research published in the journal *Nature* described a study in which nectar laced with three common neonicotinoids—imidacloprid, thiamethoxam, and clothianidin—was offered to wild buff-tailed bumblebees (*Bombus terrestris*). The buff-tailed bumblebee, named after the buff color on the tail of the queens (workers have white tails with a faint buff-colored stripe between their tails and abdomens), is the largest bumblebee species and nests in colonies of up to 600 bees. Found in lowland areas in the United Kingdom, these bees are among the first to emerge in the spring to seek out pollen and nectar. Their single-minded focus on foraging earned the buff-tailed bumblebee the nickname "nectar robber" because they bite holes at the base of flowers and suck out the nectar if the flowers are too deep for their tongues. The *Nature* research found that the bees preferred sucrose solutions laced with neonics over sucrose alone. The findings held true when the neonic-laced nectar was offered to honeybees. Based on the 2015 findings, the researchers noted, "Our data indicate that bees cannot taste neonicotinoids and are not repelled by them. Instead, bees preferred solutions containing [neonicotinoids], even though the consumption of these pesticides caused them to eat less food overall. This work shows that bees cannot control their exposure to neonicotinoids in food and . . . treating flowering crops . . . presents a sizeable hazard to foraging bees."

In 2017, researchers conducted the largest field research to date on the impact of neonics on bees. Scientists monitored honeybees and two species of wild bees—red mason bees (*Osmia bicornis*) and buff-tailed bumblebees, also known as large earth bumblebees—at thirty-three sites in the United Kingdom, Germany, and Hungary.

The red mason bee has been hailed as "an extraordinary pollinator" that is between 120 and 200 times more efficient than the honeybee.

Although these native bees are endangered, their services are in high demand. Commercial fruit growers often rent the bees when their trees flower, hanging nests and cocoons (which look like dirty cotton wool) in their orchards so the bees will emerge and begin pollinating.

As part of the field trial, both red mason bees and large earth bumblebees were placed near canola fields. Some of the fields had canola grown from seeds treated with neonicotinoids and a fungicide; others were planted with canola treated with fungicides but not neonicotinoids. In the United Kingdom and Hungary, bees feeding on canola treated with neonics struggled with reproduction, and fewer colonies survived the winter. The bees placed in canola fields in Germany fared better in canola fields treated with neonics, producing more eggs and more larvae. Fewer colonies placed in treated fields survived the winter, but the results were not statistically significant.

Researchers believe the discrepancies are related to the local environment, including plant diversity. The bees in the United Kingdom and Hungary collected up to 50 percent of their pollen from canola; just 10 percent of the pollen collected in Germany was from canola. The bees in Germany also had fewer parasites than the bees at the other sites, leading the researchers to posit that bees weakened by disease are more vulnerable to pesticide exposure. Researchers received some funding from neonic manufacturers Bayer and Syngenta, but they insisted that the pesticide manufacturers had no influence over their findings.

Joe Milone, a PhD student at North Carolina State University, believes current pesticide research often fails to take a holistic look at all of the stressors impacting honeybee health, noting that few studies look at the impacts of multiple compounds or interactions such as parasites, and how those combinations of stressors could take their toll on a hive.

"You really have to look at this issue holistically," he says. "These stressors don't occur in a vacuum; there are several different interactions happening at once, and the more we understand the web of interactions, the better we'll be able to optimize our agricultural toolset."

Milone is part of a research team at NC State that is investigating the effects of pesticides on honeybee health. He's using federal pesticide residue data to mimic realistic exposures in hives by contaminating honeycomb and pollen supplements, and then seeing what happens to reproduction. Though he's researching pesticides, Milone admits that "their environment consists of chemical exposures and biological exposures, [and] everything in their environment works together to have an effect. The more we understand all of the different interactions happening at once, the better we'll be able to optimize our [response]."

As agrochemical manufacturers and researchers continue to spar, the debate has led to new efforts to find solutions. Bayer and Syngenta, the largest neonicotinoid manufacturers in the world, stepped up efforts (and earmarked millions of dollars) to expand bee habitats and promote bee health. In 2014, Bayer opened a Bee Care Center in North Carolina.

An oversized yellow metal sculpture of a bee welcomes visitors to the Bee Care Center. The LEED Silver–certified glass-walled building is part science museum, part research lab. Bayer CropScience invested $2.4 million to build the 6,000-square foot facility behind its North American headquarters in Raleigh, North Carolina. Inside, curated displays filled with colorful models and posters explain honeybee biology, the role of bees in agriculture, and the threats to bee health.

A *New York Times* article about the opening of a sister facility on a Bayer campus in Monheim, Germany, in 2013, points out, "There is, of course, a slight caveat to all this buzzy good will. Bayer is one of the major producers of a type of pesticide that the European Union has linked to the large-scale die-offs of honeybee populations in North America and Western Europe. . . . Not everyone believes Bayer cares about bees." The title of an article published in the *Atlantic Monthly—"Bayer Wants You to Know It Doesn't Kill Bees. Bayer Loves Bees. Come to Bayer's Bee Care Center and learn how Bayer-made pesticides—which were banned by the European Union for killing bees—are perfectly harmless."*—also points to the

Figure 3-1: The Bayer Bee Care Center in Raleigh, North Carolina, welcomes visitors interested in learning more about pollinators.

skepticism surrounding the Bee Care Center. Indeed, Bayer generated €46.8 billion ($56.9 billion USD) in sales in 2016, and neonicotinoids are a major contributor to their bottom line.

Beekeeper Sarah Myers, who accepted a role as outreach coordinator for the Bayer Bee Care Center in 2014, is aware of the criticisms but insists that the issue of pesticides and bee health is not black and white. The issues plaguing bees, she says, would not go away if Bayer (and other pesticide manufacturers) simply stopped making neonicotinoids.

"It might help some," she says. "Pesticide exposures, misapplications—those things happen. But [eliminating pesticides] is not going to take care of all of our problems with bees. We have forage problems. We have pests. We have diseases. We have management issues. . . . It's much more complicated than just pesticides, [and] what we're hoping to do here is open up the conversation."

On tours, some of that conversation happens over a microphone linking visitors to researchers working in a small lab located behind a glass wall in the Bee Care Center. Entomologist Kim Huntzinger hunched over a small plastic cutting board, a pair of tweezers in one gloved hand and a small scalpel in another. With one deft movement, she sliced the abdomens from dead honeybees and slipped them into a plastic bag; the specimens will be crushed and viewed under the microscope to look for the presence of a deadly parasitical fungus of the *Nosema* genus. At the other end of the table, entomologist Ana Cabrera peered into the plexiglas window on one side of a box containing a bumblebee colony, watching as the insects climbed across tightly packed cells that resembled handfuls of corn puffs cereal glued together to form a mound. Behind her, a rolling plastic cart stacked with several more nests awaited inspection. Bayer is in the midst of a research project aimed at devising field tests to determine how pesticide applications impact bumblebee colonies. Cabrera explains: "Unlike honeybees that you can do testing on year in and year out, how do you devise a field test on a species when their seasonality is maybe six or eight weeks? For us to be able to devise a study to be able to test [pesticides] in the field, we have to understand the biology of bumblebees."

The glass wall and microphones at the Bee Care Center were designed to promote transparency about ongoing research. But Myers admits that much of the research, including testing of the controversial neonicotinoids, happens offsite—so visitors hoping to ask tough questions about the research are out of luck.

Neonicotinoids were embraced for their effectiveness in controlling destructive crop pests like aphids and grubs that had developed resistance to other insecticides. Not long after entering—and dominating—the market, the next-generation products replaced older insecticides.

Figure 3-2: At the Bayer Bee Care Center in Raleigh, North Carolina, melittologist and research associate Kim Huntzinger searches for the queen in a bumblebee colony.

Box 3-3
Neonics Not Welcome

In 2016, Maryland became the first state to ban neonicotinoids. Governor Larry J. Hogan Jr. allowed S.B. 198/H.B. 211 to become law, prompted by concerns that the pesticides contribute to pollinator deaths. The ban is aimed at curtailing consumer use; certified applicators, farmers, and veterinarians are exempt. Violators can be hit with a $250 fine. The original legislation included language that would have mandated labeling of treated plants and seeds, but that provision did not make it into the final bill.

Minnesota promptly followed suit, enacting restrictions on neonic use later in 2016. The executive order, titled "Directing Steps to Reverse Pollinator Decline and Restore Pollinator Health in Minnesota," requires verification of need prior to use, increased inspections and enforcement of labeling requirements, and promotion of best-management practices. The restrictions are only relevant to neonic sprays; treated seeds aren't considered pesticides and cannot be included under the executive order. The Minnesota Department of Agriculture is working to have seeds classified as pesticides so that they would be included in the restrictions.

Box 3-4
White-Nose Syndrome and Pesticides

Bats diagnosed with white-nose syndrome (WNS) look like they've had their ears, noses, and wings dipped in powdered sugar—but the white fuzz is sinister, not sweet. A nonnative fungus, *Pseudogymnoascus destructans*, causes WNS. The fungus thrives in cold, humid environments like the caves where bats cluster during hibernation. Bats with WNS exhibit odd behaviors during hibernation, including long arousals from torpor, the resting state when their core temperatures and metabolic rates drop to conserve fat reserves for flying around during the day in subzero temperatures. Bats with WNS often have damage and scarring to their wing membranes, impairing flight, as well as lower body weight and signs of starvation and dehydration.

The first cases of WNS were diagnosed in Albany, New York, in 2006. Since then, the disease has decimated bat populations, killing at least seven million bats. Cases of WNS have been confirmed in twenty-eight states and five Canadian provinces; most confirmed cases are in the Northeast, the Midwest,

Box 3-4 *continued*

and the South. (In 2016, a bat with WNS was found in Washington State—1,300 miles from the closest known cases of the disease.) To date, all fatalities have occurred in vesper bats (that is, so-called evening bats or common bats, members of the largest family of bat species). Research suggests that one species, the little brown bat (*Myotis lucifugus*), has a 99 percent chance of extinction by 2026 due to WNS.

The fatalities have been blamed on a number of factors: an infectious parasite, environments that allow the *P. destructans* fungus to thrive, and susceptible hosts with reduced immune responses during hibernation. Pesticides have also been implicated as a possible cause for WNS.

The disease emerged as a serious threat to bat populations around the same time as the initial widespread use of neonicotinoids and herbicides containing glyphosate. Researchers have compared the bats' abnormal behavior to the disorientation described in CCD honeybees, which causes bees to delay foraging and eventually abandon the hive.

Pesticides target the same beetles, moths, spiders, and other insects that bats feast on. Since the insectivores consume up to one-third of their body weight in insects every day over the course of their thirty-year lifespan, bats are vulnerable to bioaccumulation of pesticides. Bats might also be exposed to pesticides during application. Farmers tend to spray during the evening hours, when temperatures fall and bees are less active—the same time, however, that bats are moving about. *P. destructans* could be an opportunistic fungus that takes advantage of immune systems weakened by pesticides.

European bats diagnosed with WNS survive, and the disease doesn't appear to have a negative impact on their health; in the United States, the fungus causes mass die-offs, with mortality rates hitting 100 percent in some caves.

Scientists are struggling to understand WNS and develop solutions to prevent it from rendering certain species of vesper bats extinct. Several federal and state agencies have closed caves on public lands to tourism in order to prevent the unintentional spread of the disease. Current research includes testing fungus-free artificial hibernation sites; using live bacteria or fungi to control the fungus that causes WNS; and tracking individual bats to explore differences in survival.

All 300 species of vesper bats are insectivores. Although WNS doesn't appear to affect pollinators or migrating species, there are concerns that this might change if the disease evolves.

Most of the current research focuses on grower-applied pesticides. In fact, neonicotinoid-coated seeds are excluded from government pesticide research data because the chemicals are applied before the seeds reach growers, leaving significant gaps in data about their impacts.

At Penn State, Grozinger has read the research on pesticides and pollinator health and, while she thinks the studies are important, she wants to see the conversation shift from fatal concentrations and rates of exposure to more global questions about pesticide use. "When we talk about the impacts on bees," she explains, "it becomes like this rabbit hole where we start to ask, 'But what is going on and at what concentration? What if we feed them this or that?' and it gets complex, which leads to, 'Let's get more data; we have to do more studies. I think [the conversation] needs to shift to what extent we need them."

Grozinger points to research conducted by colleagues at Penn State that explored the impact of neonic-coated seeds on crop yields. Their 2014 study found that thiamethoxam-based seed treatments decreased insect predators, which led to an increase in slugs—and that in turn harmed soybean fields, reducing crop densities by 19 percent and yields by 5 percent. Additional research, published in 2017, turned up similar results with researchers noting neonicotinoid applications showed no benefits to yields in corn crops; and, in 2016, the EPA released a statement claiming that the seed treatments "provide little or no overall benefits to soybean production in most situations."

"I think the key [message]," says Grozinger, "is that if growers actually had the choice . . . they wouldn't be putting these things in the field because they get no benefit from it. Overall, we will see improvements with biodiversity if the neonic seed treatments are taken out of use."

Researchers exploring the link between pesticides and pollinator decline are getting a lot of support from growers, according to Grozinger. "People are trying to come up with strategies to use pesticides in ways that are less problematic for bees. There can be little tweaks to the system that can improve things, where you can still use pesticides for pest control, but you minimize the effect on pollinators."

Rather than taking a hard stand on neonics, Fredericks, the Iowa farmer, embraces compromise. "We can have productive agriculture along with [pollinator] conservation," he says. "The message that I want to get across is that if you want participation from farmers and farm groups, there has to be a middle road."

During spring and summer planting seasons, Fredericks hops onto his four-wheeler and rides around his 975-acre farm with a tank filled with herbicide to kill the noxious weeds that pop up along the edges of the fields and threaten to intermingle with the crops. Milkweed (*Asclepias*) that monarchs depend on grows wild along those same fencerows and hedgerows. Fredericks watches out for milkweed and does his best to avoid it—and encourages others to do the same.

"I'm aware of where my habitats are and where the beehives are. We go online and find those and try to follow the rules as best we can. I'm not worried about spraying right up next to habitat if my wind direction is favorable," he adds. "We realize that, yes, we're probably going to kill some bees or butterflies during that two-or three-day window [when we're spraying], but you have three or more months of the whole year when that habitat has been beneficial for the species. So, we feel that it's better to get a whole lot more acres of habitat . . . not having a cooperative relationship with agriculture, you don't get many acres of habitat at all. I think you end up with a whole lot less effective habitat being a purist than you do being cooperative."

Many farmers do consider their impact on pollinators. At the Ohio State University, Johnson, who focuses on pesticide use in almond orchards, notes that there is a strong push to shift to nighttime applications because bees don't forage after dark. Timing, he explains, can have a profound effect on pesticide exposure. "I think there's a long-term trend toward increased pollinator safety [and] that is how the problem is going to be solved: it will be unallowable to apply pesticides in ways in which bees are likely to be exposed to them. The pesticides aren't going to go away; the way they're applied is going to change."

Pesticides might not be disappearing, but they are changing. In the last ten years, the EPA has registered many new insecticides that have limited uses on different pests. Products with active ingredients like pyrethrins, acephate (organophosphate), permethrin, and birenthrin are recommended alternatives to neonics. Krischik, the ecotoxicologist, believes targeted pesticides that tackle specific issues like the growth rates of larvae or mite infestations should be used instead of chemicals that target a much broader range of insects. Integrated pest management (IPM) could also help reduce the use of neonicotinoids and prove beneficial to pollinators. IPM principles, based on field experiments and peer-reviewed research, advocate pesticide treatment only when the level of pests reaches a predetermined threshold; IPM also advocates rotating crops, changing sowing dates, and trying nonchemical options.

Because pesticides will remain the first line of defense for some farmers, companies have started making efforts to develop more sustainable products. Ortho vowed to remove neonicotinoids from their outdoor products. In 2016, the manufacturer eliminated imidacloprid, clothianidin, and dinotefuran; the full transition to neonic-free products is expected to be complete in 2021. The company, which manufactures products like Scotts Miracle Grow, explained, "This change does not reflect our opinion on the science, which is still being debated. Rather, as the industry leader, this move reflects our commitment to helping homeowners feel comfortable in knowing that our products are safe for their family and the environment when used as directed."

Consumer demand for pollinator-friendly pest control might have had something to do with the decision. A similar wave of public pressure coincided with the 2018 total ban on neonics in the European Union. The environmental activist group Avaaz secured more than five million signatures on its petition to prohibit the pesticides, writing, "We call on you to immediately ban the use of neonicotinoid pesticides. The catastrophic demise of bee colonies could put our whole food chain in danger. If you act urgently with precaution now, we could save bees from extinction." Avaaz vowed to take the fight to ban neonicotinoids worldwide, targeting the United States and Canada.

Krischik believes there are parallels between neonicotinoids and DDT (dichloro-diphenyl-trichloroethane), the first modern synthetic pesticide. Developed in the 1940s to combat insect-borne diseases like malaria, DDT was also effective at controlling crop pests. In the late 1950s, the USDA (the federal agency responsible for pesticide regulation before the formation of the EPA) started limiting its use because a growing body of evidence showed that the pesticide damaged the environment. It was banned in 1972, but without the support of the USDA. Instead, Krischik credits charismatic, well-funded, politically savvy New Yorkers for pushing the government to prohibit the pesticide. But she isn't sure that a similar all-out ban on neonicotinoids is necessarily called for now. Instead, she describes the issue as "complicated" and argues that the controversial chemicals should be restricted, but still allowed, in cases where they benefit crops. Moreover, Krischik doubts that a ban would ever take effect in the United States.

"Is the paradigm [that we witnessed with DDT] going to happen again? I'd love to give you an overwhelming, 'Yes, America is great and we're going to fix it,' but I can't say that. Our pesticide industry is a very strong lobbyist group. That's the issue here in America."

Box 3-5

Could Crop Insurance Promote Pesticide Use?

Farming is risky business. To hedge against natural disasters like floods or droughts, farmers purchase crop insurance. In 2017, the policies covered 130 different crops spread across 311 million acres—about the size of California, Texas, and New York combined—with a total value of more than $106 billion. Farmers spent upwards of $3.7 billion for crop insurance protection.

Several studies have attempted to measure the potential environmental consequences of the coverage, with some researchers arguing that crop insurance leads farmers to take more risks. For example, knowing that crop failure is covered might make farmers more apt to plant on land vulnerable to erosion or to specialize in fewer crops.

Research has also explored the impact of crop insurance on pesticide application rates. The results were mixed, with some studies finding that farmers with crop insurance spent 21 percent more on pesticides than uninsured farms while others reported that farm insurance reduced chemical inputs. Other data found that crop mix could affect inputs: corn growers applied more pesticides and fertilizers, while soybean farmers applied less.

In the event of a claim, adjusters will ask about the insecticide program a farmer follows, making notes about the chemicals used and dates applied.

Penn State's Christina Grozinger believes that some farmers might be reluctant to use uncoated seeds due to concerns that doing so might void their crop insurance coverage. "You have to follow certain protocols to show that you were fully managing your crops; if you don't do that, you can't get crop insurance," she explains. "That is something that has to be reconsidered so that [coated seeds] don't become insurance policies that makes farmers think, 'I have to treat because if I don't and something bad happens, I can't recover my losses.'"

In an ironic twist, crop insurance doesn't provide protection for organic crops that can't be certified because they were hit by pesticide residues from neighboring farms. Pesticide drift is not insurable.

CHAPTER 4

The Need for Native Plants

Ask Lora Morandin about the importance of native plants and she'll describe a scene in Yolo County, California. Hailed as one of the most productive farm regions on Earth, thousands of acres of tomatoes and lettuce dominate the landscape.

In 2009, Morandin, acting research and Canadian program director for Pollinator Partnership Canada, designed an experiment to learn how bees react to native versus exotic plants. She compared four mature hedgerows with four new hedgerow sites. The mature hedgerows were planted in 1996 with perennial shrubs and grasses in an effort to attract pollinators and reduce insect pests. The new hedgerows, with a mix of native shrubs and forbs (broad-leafed flowering plants), were established between 2007 and 2008 to boost native bee populations. Timed aerial netting allowed Morandin and colleagues to collect bees from flowers, identify species, and estimate the size of local bee populations. At mature hedgerow sites, researchers walked along the site and checked each flower for the presence of bees. Samples were taken three times between April and August.

A total of twenty-three native bee species were netted on flowers at new hedgerow sites; seven species were only observed on exotic plants and seven species were only observed on native plants. At mature hedgerow sites, thirty species of native bees were identified; twenty-three bee species were only observed on native plants and one bee species was only observed on exotic plants. California buckwheat (*Eriogonum fasciculatum*), salvia (*Salvia* spp.), California poppy (*Eschscholzia californica*), California coffeeberry (*Rhamnus californica*), and Great Valley gumplant (*Grindelia camporum*) were the most preferred native species. In short, native bees preferred native plants.

"It's a pretty common finding that native plants attract a more diverse community of pollinators," Morandin says. "Pollinators often evolve alongside native plants over thousands of years; a lot of pollinators specialize on some of the native plants and, if they don't have plants from a certain plant family or genus or sometimes even this specific species of plants, they can't survive."

The co-dependent relationship between monarchs and milkweed is one of the most iconic examples of the essential role native species play in pollinator survival. Although the tissues in the leaves of these tender perennials contain toxic chemicals called cardenolides that can trigger heart failure in vertebrate predators, monarchs have evolved to become cardenolide-tolerant. Not only will the toxins not harm the butterflies, they depend on them for survival. Monarchs lay their eggs on milkweed leaves to protect them from predators, and their caterpillars munch on the milkweed leaves after hatching, ingesting the chemicals and, in turn, become unappetizing to predators. Without native milkweed, monarchs are in grave danger.

While native plants are best for pollinators, not all nonnative plants are problems. Some nonnative species—also called introduced species—don't spread on their own or outcompete native plants and pollinators. In contrast, invasive species, which are nonnative—or alien—to an eco-

Box 4-1
Venus Flytraps Control Their Appetites for Survival

The snapping jaws of a Venus flytrap (*Dionaea muscipula*) will close around beetles, ants, and crickets, but the carnivorous plant controls its appetite when it comes to pollinators. To understand why, researchers at North Carolina State University located plants at several sites around the flytrap's limited native range in Wilmington, North Carolina, and monitored visitors during its five-week flowering season. Out of 100 insects that visited the flower, green sweat bees (*Augochlorella gratiosa*), checkered beetles (*Trichodes apivorus*), and notch-tipped flower longhorn beetles (*Typocerus sinuatus*) were the only common visitors carrying pollen. Despite being seen on the Venus flytraps often, these species were never found in the traps.

"It's important to recognize that the flytrap isn't distinguishing pollinators from non-pollinators, [but] pollinators and non-pollinators are responding to characteristics of different parts of the plant," explains study co-author Clyde Sorenson, professor of entomology at NC State. "Put another way, the flytrap can't tell a bee from a spider, but bees can apparently distinguish a flower from a trap."

The flytrap appears to have evolved to support its pollinators: the flowers are located on the tops of stalks that grow eight to twelve inches above the traps, allowing flying pollinators to access the flowers without getting caught in the traps; most of the prey devoured by the flytrap do not fly and end up walking or crawling into the traps. The team continues to research reasons for the insects' different responses, but Sorenson offers a couple of explanations, including that flowers are physically separated from traps and that attractants like color and odor are different in the flowers versus the traps.

"Understanding these relationships can be important to the conservation of this remarkable plant, which is threatened by habitat conversion, fire suppression and, most insidiously, poaching," Sorenson says. "Even though this is one of the most famous plants in the world, we are only really just beginning to understand its ecology and biology."

system are called *invasive* for their likelihood to cause economic or environmental harm. The worst invasive plants are referred to as noxious weeds. The USDA maintains both federal and state noxious-weed lists, which include nectar plants such as yellow star-thistle (*Centaurea solstitialis* L.).

But the impact of invasive—even noxious—species depends on the context. In some environments, the introduction of alien species is deemed a "beneficial invasion" because these interlopers can offer ecosystem benefits, including helping devastated regions rebound from natural disasters and damage by humans. In a study published in *Conservation Biology*, researchers claimed, "We predict the proportion of nonnative species that are viewed as benign or even desirable will slowly increase over time." However, species that are benign in one environment can be fatal in others. Invasive species can be so problematic that a 1999 executive order established the National Invasive Species Council to control them and restore ecosystems.

Dramatic increases in the number of both established and new invasive populations have been noted worldwide and are believed to be the second-greatest threat to biodiversity after habitat loss. Invasive species can also contribute to habitat loss themselves. Because they grow and spread quickly and have a knack for adapting to a range of conditions, invasives often choke out native species, creating monocultures. Less plant diversity means less and lower-quality habitat for wildlife, including pollinators. In fact, the presence of invasive plants in a habitat is one of the criteria in Endangered Species Act listings. An estimated 42 percent of species on the threatened or endangered species list landed there because invasive plants and animals affected their environments. When an invasive plant species takes over, it can change the way animals feed and forage, and make pollinators less efficient.

And when invasive species dominate a landscape, they create a ripple effect: many invasive plants have shallow root structures that fail to bind the soils, increasing the likelihood of erosion. Invasive species can also create dense cover in forest understories, preventing sunlight from reaching seedlings or saplings, slowing growth, and causing trees to die. The trees that do survive are at greater risk of succumbing to wildfires because vines like English ivy (*Hedera helix* L.), sweet autumn virgin's bower (*Clematis terniflora* DC), and Japanese honeysuckle (*Lonicera japonica*) climb trees, wrapping trunks with their vines and creating a path for fire to reach tree canopies. Entire forests can be wiped out. In fact, invasive species are responsible for an estimated $120 billion in annual damages in the United States alone.

Native plants restore ecosystems. Many have deeper root structures that extend into the earth, helping to bind soils and reduce erosion; these same root systems also keep sediment out of streams, improving water quality. Native plants evolved in specific regions and are better adapted to local growing conditions such as temperature ranges and the amount of rainfall; the low-maintenance plants also require far less water than

Box 4-2
Identifying Invasive Species

Invasive species represent significant threats to biodiversity and ecosystems, but data on the locations and density of the invaders is scant. In 2017, the Global Register of Introduced and Invasive Species (GRIIS) was launched to provide country-specific checklists of invasive species. Data for an estimated 1,100 species in twenty countries has been added; the environmental impacts are known for just 20 percent of these species.

GRIIS, developed with the Global Invasive Alien Species Information Partnership as part of the Convention on Biological Diversity, aims to establish open-source national and global baselines of invasive species to help countries prioritize the worst invaders and allow for long-term monitoring. Access to accurate identification of problematic species, including their ranges and potential environmental impacts, can help with risk assessments and inform policies designed to combat invasive species. The database can also be used to monitor the success of eradication efforts.

While national checklists might never be complete or 100 percent accurate, they do provide a simple method for collecting data. The website, www.griis.org, does not include invasive species in the United States—yet. The goal is to expand the database to include additional countries and further expand the usefulness of the data.

their invasive counterparts. Long-lived native species, including oaks and maples, store greenhouse-gas emissions such as carbon dioxide, helping combat climate change. Native plants provide nectar for pollinators (plus shelter and nuts, seeds, and fruit for other forms of wildlife), and several pollinators, including butterflies and moths such as the monarch, pipevine swallowtail (*Battus philenor*), and atala (*Eumaeus atala* Poey), are dependent on specific native-plant species.

Pipevine swallowtails are showstoppers. Despite an unimpressive undercarriage of dark-colored wings with bright orange spots and blue markings, these large butterflies have a "notice me" vibe in flight thanks to the shocking iridescent blue or blue-green coloring on the upper surface of their hindwings. The butterflies, native to Florida, got their name for their relationship with native flowering vines called pipevines. The vines, members of the *Aristolochia* genus, give off a toxic chemical that pipeline swallowtail caterpillars are immune to but their predators are not. The butterflies depend on these caterpillar-hosts to protect them; as adults, pipevine swallowtails feed on nectar from a range of plants in their native habitats along the West Coast, as well as in the South and the southwestern United States.

The atala butterfly, with its deep black wings with rows of iridescent turquoise spots and a bright red abdomen, is found only in South Florida. Its host plant, the coontie palm (*Zamia pumila*), was wiped out in the 1900s, decimating populations of the butterflies. Though the species is still considered rare, awareness of its decline has led to the planting of coontie gardens that have helped the atala rebound. (The coontie is important, too. Not an actual palm at all, the drought-tolerant native is the only cycad—a class of ancient plants—native to North America.)

Pollinators often co-evolve with native plants. Their physiologies match such that both benefit from the nectar and pollen. Aggressive growth of invasive species can choke out those valuable native plants, leading to the loss of essential resources. Moreover, the flowers of non-

Figure 4-1: Cheddar pinks (*Dianthus gratianopolitanus*), "Feuerhexe" ("Firewitch"), are colorful perennials that attracts pollinators.

native plants might have structures that are inaccessible to pollinators, making it impossible to reach nectar. Nasturtium (*Tropaeolum majus* L.), colorful annuals native from Mexico to South America, have spurs that block short-tongued bees from reaching the nectar; French marigold (*Tagetes patula* L.), aromatic annuals native to Mexico and Central America, are also impenetrable to pollinators.

Even when pollinators can get hold of nectar from invasive species, there can still be trouble. Invasive species might have nectar with a different composition of sugar or amino acids, which can lead to poor nutrition; the morphology of the flowers might be different, too, which can mean less efficient feeding.

"You can see a good number of pollinators on some of these invasive plants, but these plants don't bloom from early spring to late summer," Morandin says. "A diversity of native plants provides a succession of [blooms], so pollinators have ongoing access to resources."

Christopher Kaiser-Bunbury, senior lecturer in ecology and conservation at the University of Exeter, also points out that the more native species there are in a habitat, the more options pollinator have for forage; if a invasive species dominates a landscape, it provides only a single source of nectar. Multiple nectar sources, on the other hand, help boost both plant and pollinator populations. "If one pollinator species disappears, another species kicks in. So we have sort of an insurance that the service is still provided," says Kaiser-Bunbury. "It's better for the plants, but it also means that the feeding niches of individual pollinators are broadened because pollinators aren't reliant on one or two or three species [of plants], but maybe on four or five or six. That's extremely exciting because it means that by restoring our native-plant communities, we strengthen the robustness and resilience of pollinator communities."

In the absence of native plants, invasive species can threaten pollinator survival. In forests in the eastern and midwestern United States, invasive garlic mustard (*Alliaria petiolata*) chokes out the native mustard species, toothwort (*Cardamine* spp.), which provides the main source of food for caterpillars of the West Virginia white butterfly (*Pieris virginiensis*). When the butterflies lay their eggs on the foliage of the invasive mustard species, toxins in the leaves prevent the eggs from hatching, further threatening the already-rare butterfly.

Even when both native and invasive species are present, pollinators might choose to visit invasive species. The consequence of that choice is not black and white. Some pollinator species take advantage of the additional flowers and successfully incorporate invasive plants into their diets. The results of a European study, published in the journal *Nature* compared the amino acid composition of pollen from three native plant species, purple loosestrife (*Lythrum salicaria*), Scotch heather (*Calluna vulgaris*) and red clover (*Trifolium pretense*), and two invasive plant species, butterfly bush (*Buddleia davidii*) and Himalayan balsam (*Impatiens glandulifera*). Both purple loosestrife and Scotch heather are considered invasive species in the U.S. but are native to the European region where the research was conducted; all of the native and invasive species in the study are common in the diets of pollinators in Europe and the research revealed that all five species provided accessible pollen resources for the buff-tailed bumble bee (*Bombus terrestris*). Although *T. pratense* provided the highest level of nutrients, the amino acid content of the pollen was similar in both invasive and native species, leading researchers to conclude that invasives could help feed the bumblebees.

In addition to fighting for survival in habitats where invasive plant species dominate, native pollinators also face competition from introduced pollinator species. The presence of both native and nonnative pollinators in an environment can create rivalries over nesting sites and flowers, spread pathogens and parasites, mix genes, and disrupt native pollination networks.

Some invasive pollinators were introduced to farms on purpose, with little consideration of the consequences. The most infamous example is the European honeybee (*Apis mellifera*), which a beekeeper introduced

Figure 4-2: A bumblebee lands on a purple coneflower (*Echinacea purpurea*) in search of nectar and pollen.

Box 4-3
Ten Pollinator-Friendly Native Plants

When selecting plants for the garden, remember that native species make the best host and nectar plants for pollinators. Choose a range of species with different bloom times to provide resources from spring until fall, and plant flowers in clumps at least three feet wide to make them more visible to pollinators.

The Xerces Society publishes regional plant lists for pollinators, providing examples of annuals, perennials, and biennials in all colors of the rainbow. The recommendations include:

- Wild lupine (*Lupinus perennis*) is native to the Great Lakes region. The perennial, which produces blue flowers, is a larval host plant for several species of butterflies, including the endangered Karner blue butterfly (*Lycaeides melissa samuelis*).
- Purple giant hyssop (*Agastache scrophulariifolia*) grows up to six feet tall and provides nectar-rich purple flowers for pollinators. It's native to the Great Lakes region.
- In the Southeast, wild bergamot (*Monarda stulosa*) is a native herbaceous perennial with pink or lavender flowers that attracts butterflies and hummingbirds.
- The white blooms on the perennial calico aster (*Symphyotrichum lateriorum*) provide shallow nectaries that attract a diversity of insect pollinators in the Northeast.
- Golden Alexanders (*Zizia aurea*) are native to the Midwest. Their showy yellow flowers attract bees; the perennial is also a host plant for black swallowtails (*Papilio polyxenes*).
- Lemon beebalm (*Monarda citriodora*) can be grown as an annual, biennial, or perennial in the Southern Plains region. The showy purple flowers on the low-growing plant attract hawk moths, hummingbirds, and long-tongued bees such as bumblebees.
- As its name suggests, the California poppy (*Eschscholzia californica*) is native to California. The orange flowers have a long bloom time, making them a favorite for a diversity of bees.
- Redbud (*Cercis orbiculata*) is also native to California. The perennial shrub produces clusters of pink or red blossoms; their nectar attracts bees.
- Long-tongued bees such as mason bees and bumblebees love nectar from the yellow flowers on the Oregon grape (*Mahonia aquifolium*). The perennial shrub is native to California and the Maritime Northwest.
- Riverbank lupine (*Lupinus rivularis*) serves as a host plant for several butterflies. The plant, native to the Northwest, grows as an annual, biennial, and perennial.

Box 4-4

Doggy Detective Keeps Bees Safe

The newest apiary inspector at the Maryland Department of Agriculture has four legs, golden fur, and a powerful sniffer. Mack, a two-year-old yellow Labrador retriever, joined the team in 2015 to help his mom, chief apiary inspector Cybil Preston, inspect beehives for American foulbrood (AFB), a highly contagious bacterial disease that gives off a distinct odor. AFB is listed as an invasive species in the Center for Agriculture and Biosciences database. The international nonprofit included it because the bacterium responsible for the disease, *Paenibacillus larvae*, can produce over one billion spores per infected larva, and the spores resist both heat and chemical treatments. Once it infects honeybee brood, it will eventually kill the colony.

"Maryland has a thriving beekeeping industry, and most of our beekeepers have thousands of hives that travel from state to state for pollination," explains Preston. "It's our job to make sure that infected hives don't cross state lines."

The Maryland Department of Agriculture has had a "bee dog" on staff since 1982 and is believed to be the only state agency in the nation using a dog to detect AFB. Mack is the fifth dog to hold the position. His predecessor, a black Lab named Klinker, retired in 2014. "The program is a unique asset to our department and we didn't want to let it go," Preston says.

To keep a dog on staff, Preston set out to find and train a new canine apiary inspector. A member of her local beekeeping group told her about Mack. The dog was living in a garage and needed a new home. Mack proved to be a quick learner. Preston taught the dog basic commands and then partnered with the team at the Maryland Department of Public Safety and Correctional Services, where Mack completed a fourteen-week training program and earned certification as a detection dog.

In the field, Mack works from November to April. When temperatures are cooler, the bees are less active, making Mack less apt to get stung. He moves from beehive to beehive, sniffing each one for the distinct odor of AFB infestation. If he smells AFB in a hive, he sits to alert Preston that a manual inspection is needed. Using his nose, Mack can inspect 100 hives in forty-five minutes. Preston must open each hive to perform a visual inspection, which slows her down; she can inspect ten hives in the same amount of time. "If we want to be efficient," Preston says, "we need a dog."

Box 4-4 *continued*

Last year, Maryland state inspectors checked 2,200 hives and found thirteen cases of AFB. Preston believes that the dogs help keep the disease in check. One hundred percent of the hives that Klinker, the former detection dog, alerted on, tested positive for AFB.

Hive inspections are the first line of defense in preventing the spread of AFB. When the disease is confirmed, the antibiotic Terramycin can be used to control the symptoms, but it doesn't destroy the spores; hives infected with AFB are frequently destroyed. In Maryland, having a canine apiary inspector is an economical option for performing more inspections and improving detection. The bonus to having a dog on the team: it brings important attention to control the spread of the deadly disease.

"A lot of beekeepers . . . hear about the dog and call us out to inspect their hives," Preston explains. "These kinds of relationships are essential for keeping instances of AFB down."

to Santa Cruz Island, California. The beekeeper eventually abandoned the project, but the bees still spread across the island, taking over flowers and crowding out native bees. In 1987, a project was launched to eradicate honeybees from the island. The goal was to restore native bee populations, reduce pollination of invasive weeds, and help native plants bounce back. The removal team also hoped to turn the island into a living laboratory that allowed for comparisons of pollination services in the United States.

The project spanned twenty years. The first phase involved locating and eliminating feral honeybee colonies. A total of 200 colonies were identified; four years after the original eradication efforts began, plant visitation shifted, with more native bees and fewer honeybees visiting flowers on the island. By the final phase, no honeybees were found at any of the inspection sites. Eradicating honeybees from Santa Cruz Island eliminated a competitor, helped researchers complete a survey of native bee species diversity, and increased native bee visits to both native and exotic plants. Researchers called it a "rare case" of eliminating an introduced exotic species.

Eradication of invasive pollinators species is controversial. Take, for example, European wool-carder bees (*Anthidium manicatum*). First reported in Ithaca, New York, in 1963, the invasive bees, named for nesting behavior that involves using their jaws to cut plant hairs and ball them up using a motion similar to carding wool, are said to pose serious threats to native bumblebee populations. In addition to damaging the plants, collecting plant hairs triggers chemical changes that attracts other wool-carder bees. The often-aggressive bees compete with bumblebees for nectar and pollen; males use five "spikes" on their abdomens to defend flower patches, attacking—and often killing—visiting bumblebees. As a result, native bumblebees avoid foraging for nectar and pollen when European wool-carder bees are present. As populations of wool-carder bees continue to grow, the exotic species is putting added pressure on native bee populations and could be contributing to the spread of invasive plant species. In New Zealand, more than 80 percent of the plants that wool-carder bees visited (and pollinated) were exotics, which means one invasive species could be helping another to thrive.

Lynn Kimsey, director of the Bohart Museum of Entomology at the University of California, Davis, is not among the experts who insist that invasive pollinators like wool-carder bees must be eliminated. In fact, she believes that wool-carder bees are not the terrorists some have made them out to be and that they actually pose few threats to their environment. Given their benign presence, Kimsey thinks that attempts at eradication could do more harm than good. "We might succeed in pushing species around to different locations, but we have never successfully caused the extinction of any invasive species; the ones we've driven to extinction are native species," she notes. "[To eradicate invasive pollinators] we'd have to release parasites, pathogens, or predators, and there are always unintended consequences. Biology is messy."

Messy, perhaps, but several studies show that eliminating invasive creatures, including other pollinators, benefits native species. In Hawaii, an invasive western yellow jacket (*Vespula pensylvanica*) was wreaking havoc on the ecosystem, preying on other pollinators, consuming massive amounts of floral nectar, and killing other arthropods that tried to visit its flowers. Researchers tested the impact of species eradication, removing the invasive western yellow jackets from nine-hectare (twenty-two-acre) plots over two years and monitoring changes in pollinator visits and fruit production on the native tree species ʻohiʻa lehua or Gaudich (*Metrosideros polymorpha*). Getting rid of the yellow jackets led to significant increases in visits from bee pollinators as well as fruit production; honeybees became the substitute pollinator, replacing extinct and threatened bird and bee species.

Ants clustered in the center of the salmon-colored petals of pumpkin vines might look benign, but the invasive yellow crazy ants (*Anoplolepis gracilipes*) are scaring off bees and, according to a 2017 study, hurting pollination. Researchers in India covered flower buds with nylon mesh bags to protect them from yellow crazy ants. After the flowers bloomed, the bags were removed and bees were allowed to visit flowers for fifteen minutes before the flowers were covered again. Three-quarters of the "ant-free" pumpkin flowers set fruit. Yellow crazy ants took up residence in the unprotected flowers, resulting in fewer honeybee visits. None of the ant-infested flowers set fruit and, in several cases, the ants killed the honeybees that landed on flowers.

In the absence of native pollinators, invasive species can take over the role (often to the detriment of the ecosystem), which is what happened on one island off the coast of New Zealand. New Zealand has lost a number of its native vertebrates, including most of its native pollinators; at the same time, several nonnative species have arrived on the island (through both accidental and intentional means).

Researchers compared the pollination of three native plants:

Pōhutukawa evergreen tree (*Metrosideros excelsa*), New Zealand honeysuckle (*Knightia excelsa*), and Veronica (*Veronica macrocarpa* Vahl) on two islands in New Zealand. On North Island, all of the native pollinators disappeared with the arrival of species such as invasive ship rat (*Rattus rattus*) and the silvereye (*Zosterops lateralis*), regarded as one of the most widespread birds in the island nation. (Native pollinators are still thriving on Little Barrier Island thanks to a nature reserve.) Cameras captured pollination of the flowering plants, which revealed that, in the absence of native birds and bats, invasive pollinator species stepped in.

Watching ship rats pollinating native plants surprised study co-author David Wilcove, professor of ecology, evolutionary biology, and public affairs at Princeton University. He suspects ship rats became accidental pollinators after arriving on the islands, drinking nectar, and dispersing pollen grains. After the disappearance of native pollinators from North Island, invasive species became crucial pollinators. Though the interlopers have stepped up to pollinate native plants, invasive species are less efficient in the role, according to Wilcove. "They're trying to perform a similar function and not doing it well," he says.

But even if introduced species only do a passable job, it could be risky to eliminate them. Wilcove admits, "The importance of that function, of course, is magnified by the fact that there aren't native pollinators to do the work."

Removing invasive species and restoring native plants could support native pollinators, but the scale of the problem is overwhelming. In the United States, more than eight million acres of land in the National Wildlife Refuge System are overrun with invasive plants and animals, and controlling the interlopers is expensive. One report showed that while $8.1 million was spent on eradication, an additional $107 million in proposed projects went unfunded. Thanks to the massive scale of the problem—and miniscule budgets dedicated to solving it—volunteers are key to removing invasives.

Box 4-5

Replacing Honeybees with Native Pollinators

Every spring, Wonderful Orchards places 92,000 honeybee colonies in its orchards to pollinate almonds. But declines in honeybee populations, due to parasites and colony collapse disorder, led the Shafter, California, grower to experiment with replacement pollinators.

Wonderful Orchards, the world's largest almond grower, launched a project almost two decades ago to see if native blue orchard bees (*Osmia lignaria*) could be used to pollinate the almond trees growing on its 46,000-acre operation. The goal: breed one million female blue orchard bees in twenty acres of netted cages to test their potential as their orchards' primary pollinators.

Blue orchard bees are similar in size to honeybees, but, as their name suggests, these native bees are metallic blue in color, not golden with black stripes. The solitary bees mate in early spring and make their nests in holes or hollow tubes stocked with fruit-tree pollen to feed their brood. Once each hole is filled with food and an egg, the bees seal it with a mud wall and then repeat the process. The larvae, and later the pupae, remain in their nests until the following spring, often emerging at the same time that peach and apple trees start blooming.

When it comes to pollination, blue orchard bees rule. Honeybees collect pollen on their legs, while blue orchard bees use the back-and-forth motion of their legs to get pollen to attach to the stiff hairs on their abdomens. A few hundred female blue orchard bees pollinate crops as well as a colony of 10,000 honeybees. Despite their pollen-collecting domination, blue orchard bees are rarely used for commercial pollination.

Blue orchard bees don't live in colonies, which makes it hard to keep them in one place. If farmers release the bees into their orchards, the native species often takes off. The USDA Agricultural Research Service experimented with various housing options to help the bees settle in, using smaller hives scattered throughout tart-cherry orchards. The findings showed promise: thanks to nesting activities that added new bees during the season, the return rate for bees put out into the orchards was 108 percent (meaning that the number of returning bees plus newly hatched bees exceeded that of the original population). By comparison, the retention rate in almond orchards is 40 percent.

For blue orchard bees to be viable for commercial pollination, farmers must keep their investments in the field. The bees retail for 50 cents each, costing an average of $300 per acre. The cost to rent beehives averages $40 per hive, with

continued

Box 4-5 *continued*

average stocking rates of two hives per acre. If blue orchard bees remain in the orchards, it's a one-time cost compared with annual beehive rental.

In addition to cost savings, the pollination potential of blue orchard bees is of particular interest to farmers growing cherries and pears. Honeybees prefer not to forage in pear orchards because the blossoms produce nectar that is low in sugar compared to the blossoms of other flowering plants; sweet cherries bloom early in the spring when it might be too cool for honeybees to forage. Blue orchard bees hold promise as suitable replacements.

At Wonderful Orchards, blue orchard bees weren't meant to replace honeybees. Instead, the company wondered whether the native and introduced species could be used together. Despite achieving some success in the field, the California almond grower abandoned the project in 2018. In a statement, Mark Carmel, director of corporate communications, told *Scientific American*: "We've determined that continuation of the program is not financially feasible. In addition, we were unable to consistently achieve the level of female replication needed to make the program successful."

Despite some promising initial research, it looks like honeybees won't be buzzing through the unemployment line anytime soon.

Upwards of 100 volunteers show up for the annual Honeysuckle and Invasive Species Removal Day held annually at Forest Park in St. Louis, Missouri. Teams have been dispatched into the 1,300-acre urban park for the past two decades to tame aggressive species like honeysuckle (*Lonicera*).

Volunteers established the annual event in the 1980s after noticing declines in bird populations as honeysuckle started dominating the forest. The public showed up *en masse* for the first event, toting chainsaws and machetes. Since then, they have been ripping out honeysuckle and reclaiming the park for native plants and the species that depend on them.

Japanese honeysuckle (*Lonicera japonica*) was brought to New York as a fragrant ornamental vine in 1806 and quickly established itself. Like other species of invasive honeysuckle, Japanese honeysuckle is opportunistic. It spreads via underground rhizomes and aboveground stolons, rooting everywhere the nodes touch the soil and forming dense, impenetrable layers in the forest understory. The vines, which can grow up to sixteen feet long, also tangle themselves around trees and shrubs, competing for sunlight before choking them out and creating an impenetrable monoculture. It even outcompetes native vines like trumpet honeysuckle (*Lonicera sempervirens*). Once lauded as an ideal plant for wildlife habitat and erosion control, Japanese honeysuckle is now considered "one of the most menacing plant invaders." It's earned a spot on noxious weed lists in forty-six states and cannot be sold or imported in Connecticut, Illinois, Massachusetts, New Hampshire, or Vermont. Honeysuckle is difficult to remove because it resists biological controls, making chainsaws and machetes the main methods of eradication. Herbicides like glyphosate and triclopyr appear to work but could present problems for pollinators.

Despite hosting an annual "honeysuckle kill" for almost twenty years, Forest Park still struggles with the invasive species, according to park ecologist Amy Witt. The fast-growing vine often grows unchecked in local gardens and, thanks to its heady fragrance and pretty blossoms, homeowners are often reluctant to remove it or, in some cases, might not know the difference between the invasive and native species. Birds collect the berries and deposit seeds in the park, re-invading areas that were cleared or creating new honeysuckle infestations.

Witt calls honeysuckle removal "a short-term step to a longer-term solution," noting that effective plans must include both removing invasive species and creating an environment that thwarts honeysuckle from taking over again. In Forest Park, volunteers tackle mass removals and ecologists work to maintain areas between the so-called honeysuckle kills, tearing out invasive plants that crop up in the landscape. The park expanded its honeysuckle removal projects to include other problematic invasive species like white mulberry (*Morus alba*) and winter creeper

(*Euonymus fortunei*). In addition to yanking these species from the forest understories, the park keeps tree canopies thinned and schedules prescribed burns to help keep populations in check. But restoration takes time, and this work is part of an ongoing effort to create "resilient habitats." Resilience requires species diversity so that ecosystems can compete against pests and invasives.

Removing invasive plants from a landscape supports pollinators in several ways. One of the benefits is obvious: fewer invasives means more natives. Invasive species can grow fast and form dense thickets, making it harder for pollinators to find native flowers. Getting rid of these plants gives native species more room to breathe, more exposure to sunlight, and more access to water and nutrients. Pollinators can actually see where the flowers are and change their foraging behavior accordingly, explains the University of Exeter's Kaiser-Bunbury.

To get more insight into invasive plants and pollinators, researchers with the US Forest Service conducted several studies on the impact of ripping up acres of Chinese privet (*Ligustrum sinense*). The fast-growing shrub forms dense thickets that invade fields, fencerows, and forest understories. First introduced to the United States in 1852, the ornamental has been blamed for declines in the diversity and abundance of native plants and trees.

The Forest Service started removing Chinese privet from four riparian forests in 2002. Initially, foresters used a mulching machine, chainsaws, and machetes; the sites were later sprayed with an herbicide to prevent resprouting. Five years later, less than 1 percent of the test sites were covered with privet compared with 60 percent of untreated sites.

Scott Horn, an entomologist with the US Forest Service, was surprised at how long the benefits lasted. After the initial removal, he thought the team would have to go back every two years to keep the site clear. "It turns out that we went two years, then four years, then six years . . . and we decided to see how long we could go [before treating

Box 4-6

Adopt a Trail

Removing invasive species is hard work. Several communities have launched Adopt-a-Trail programs to honor the volunteer work crews that devote their time to clearing natural areas.

Columbia, Missouri, introduced its Adopt-a-Trail program in 2017. Volunteers participate in training sessions to learn to identify invasive species, and they commit to maintaining one-quarter-acre sections of the Columbia Trail System. In addition to removing plants like Japanese honeysuckle (a process that often involves using saws and chemicals), the city provides native flowering shrubs and trees to attract pollinators and beautify the trail. To honor the work that goes into invasive species removal, the city provides markers identifying the volunteers who maintain each section of the trail.

Community conservationist Danielle Fox called the Adopt-a-Trail program, "A great start to educate the public on invasive species," but noted it was not, in and of itself, an effective tool for managing the fast-growing species taking over parks. The trail system, she told the *Columbia Missourian*, needs a restoration plan that involves maintaining healthy habitat and taking a native-plants-only approach. In the meantime, the program provides essential manpower to clear invasive species—a monumental task that staff in the parks and recreation department could not handle on their own.

Several other cities and national parks host similar programs. The Appalachian Mountain Club oversees Adopt-a-Trail programs in multiple parks, allowing "adopters" to maintain habitats in areas such as the White Mountains of New Hampshire, the Delaware Watershed Gap National Recreation Area in New Jersey, and the Hundred-Mile Wilderness Area in Maine. In 2017, 650 volunteers dedicated 2,210 hours to clearing 122 miles of trails in Eagle County, Colorado, as part of its Adopt-a-Trail program. The inaugural year of the program was so successful that it was expanded to include public sites in several local towns and Bureau of Land Management lands; sections of eleven new trails were available for adoption.

again] because we knew one of the questions people were going to ask was how long these efforts last," he recalls. "We didn't treat again until [2018]. For the first time in twelve years, we resprayed it. Some of it had come back, but we went from 100 percent coverage of Chinese privet to less than five percent."

The results were dramatic for pollinators. Five years after the invasive ornamental was removed, privet-free sites had almost three times as many pollinator species and four times more individual pollinators than control sites. Researchers called the effort a "relatively simple method of improving pollinator habitat" that led to more bees and butterflies; it was a smart investment.

Similar benefits were reported on a remote island in the Indian Ocean. British researchers traveled to the Seychelles to look at eight separate parcels of mountaintop land: invasive species made up at least one-quarter of the plants in the one-hectare (two-and-a-half-acre) spaces. After an evaluation of all native and nonnative plants, the scientists removed almost 40,000 invasive plants. Eight months later, native plants were producing about 17 percent more flowers—leading to 23 percent more pollinator visits—in the parcels where invasive species were removed. Meanwhile, pollinator populations had rebounded more than 20 percent.

Kaiser-Bunbury was part of the research team in the Seychelles. He believes the research speaks volumes about how removing invasive species can restore native plants, explaining, "We weren't looking at how one pollinator was interacting with one plant species but how the entire community of pollinators is interacting with the community of plant species. By removing invasive species and allowing the pollinators to access their native-plant communities again, we strengthened the resilience of these [pollinator] communities toward preservation."

There is, however, a downside. While the number of pollinators and the amount of fruit growth went up, native species became more susceptible to attacks, including flower theft. Kaiser-Bunbury is taking a broader look at how removing invasive species affects the entire ecosystem. He acknowledges, "We need to pull it all together. It might be a plus for pollinators and native seed dispersal but a negative for predation and pollen robberies, which could affect reproduction of native-plant communities. We need to know more."

Relationships in the complex web of native and nonnative plants and native and nonnative pollinators are indeed delicate. One of the major goals of restoration is to repair mutually beneficial interactions between native plants and native pollinators. Sometimes that can be accomplished by stripping invasive plants from the landscape; at other times, it requires removing pests. As we've seen, invasive pollinators can displace native pollinators. Yet eradicating the interlopers can trigger unintended—and unwanted—changes in plant–pollinator interactions or leave the remaining species unable to adapt.

The eradication of honeybees from Santa Cruz Island was in some ways a major success. But the long-term picture is more complicated. Once the honeybees were gone, seven new bee species turned up on the island. One of those species, a leafcutter bee (*Megachile apicalis*) was invasive and took up residence in conjunction with the island-wide spread of another invasive species, yellow star-thistle (*Centaurea solstitialis*), earning it the nickname the "starthistle" leafcutter bee. Leafcutter bees belong to one of the largest bee families, with more than 3,900 species; all are solitary and several, including *M. apicalis*, use their jaws to cut pieces of leaves—hence their name—to build nests. Bees like the star-thistle because of its rich nectar, which has helped the invasive plant spread far and wide. Removing bees from the landscape results in significant declines of the introduced plant, but, as long as bees are present to pollinate it, the star-thistle continues spreading. Its co-dependent relationship with the leafcutter bee had led to competition between the starthistle leafcutter bee and its relative, the alfalfa leafcutter bee (*Megachile rotundata*), for nest sites in areas like California and the Pacific Northwest, where the yellow star-thistle thrives. The pollinators

Box 4-7
Eat the Invaders

Removing invasive species that are choking out native plants is an essential element of restoring pollinator habitat. Once invasive plants are removed from the landscape, tossing them in the compost pile is not the only option. Several invasive species are actually quite tasty.

Sow thistle (*Sonchus asper*), often found in pastures and orchards, is a nutritious green rich in vitamins A and C, calcium, and iron that can be added to salads or stir-fry. Watercress (*Nasturtium officianale*) grows along streams and in ditches in all lower forty-eight states. A member of the mustard family, watercress has small round leaves with a peppery flavor. Use watercress in salads or sauté the leaves and add them to an omelet. The youngest leaves on lamb's quarters (*Chenopodium album*) are the tastiest. The invasive plant grows almost anywhere, including gardens, croplands, and meadows; it even grows up through cracks in sidewalks. It tastes similar to chard or spinach, making it a flavorful addition to soups and salads.

Some critics warn that promoting the culinary uses for invasive species might help them thrive. A study published in *Conservation Letters* argued that "creating a market engenders pressure to maintain that problematic species."

But proponents of the practice contend that invaders thrive because the species have no enemies—except us, when we eat them. Though the idea of eating invasive species is not new, the concept is making a comeback. Several conservation groups, government agencies, and the media promote the practice, and a number of cookbooks have been published with field guides to identify invasive species and recipes featuring the problematic plants.

The idea of eating a species to extinction is not far-fetched. Human appetites have driven several species, including Atlantic cod, passenger pigeons, and American ginseng, to extinction or near-extinction. Campaigns that promote eating invasive species also help drive awareness of the issue. The *Conservation Letters* study notes that foodies who participate in harvest programs to learn about the culinary value of invasive species might also learn about the impacts of nonnatives and feel inspired to help with eradication—even if the species have no culinary value.

Box 4-8

Caprine Cleaning Crew

Invasive species might be "baaa-d" for the environment, but they can taste just fine—at least to goats. The four-legged eating machines have been recruited to help clear nonnative species like Japanese knotweed (*Fallopia japonica*), Japanese honeysuckle (*Lonicera japonica*), Asiatic bittersweet (*Celastrus orbiculatus*), and multiflora rose (*Rosa multiflora*). Thanks to their voracious appetites, goats can serve as a chemical-free cleaning crew.

Edgewood Park in New Haven, Connecticut, hired three goats (Cinnamon, Brooklyn, and Iris) to clear invasive species from a two-and-a-half-acre section of the park in 2018. The goats were tasked with eating 80 percent of the invasive plants during their first year of employment and will return to the park the following season to finish their "goatscaping," with the goal of devouring the few remaining invasive plants, stressing the root systems until the plants cannot regenerate.

The University of Georgia similarly hired goats to eradicate invasive species from its campus in Athens. The "UGA Chew Crew" was employed from 2011 to 2017 and had a significant impact on the landscape, replacing machines and chemicals once used to remove invasive species on campus. The landscape company that hired out the goats left town, leaving the campus without their goats; in 2018, the Office of Sustainability put out a "goats wanted" message to find a replacement Chew Crew, and they hope to have their own UGA herd in the future.

A herd of thirty goats nosh on invasive garlic mustard at Clay Cliffs Natural Area in Leland, Michigan. Although the goats don't eat garlic mustard roots, they decimate the foliage before the seeds bloom, making it harder for the fast-growing plant to spread and easier for volunteers to pull it from the soil. Goats have aggressive digestive systems and none of the seeds they ingest can germinate, so that invasive species cannot spread through goat droppings. In 2008, volunteer work crews removed 660 bags of invasive garlic mustard from one site; eight years later, the same site yielded just 60 bags, proving that the efforts are working to eradicate the species.

are helping the invasive plants thrive, and, in areas where one invasive species is supporting another, eradication requires doubling down on efforts to remove both—a feat that might be impossible.

Scientists are trying to tease out the ripple effects of removing invasive species, including the potential impact on native-plant pollination and pollinator behavior. In Maine's Acadia National Park, park rangers were concerned about the proliferation of three invasive plants—Japanese barberry (*Berberis thunbergii*), alder buckthorn (*Frangula alnus*), and purple loosestrife (*Lythrum salicaria*). These plants offered more nectar and pollen than their native counterparts, including wild raisin (*Viburnum nudum*), meadowsweet (*Spiraea alba*), and lowbush berry (*Vaccinium angustifolium*), which meant pollinators were choosing the invasive over native species. Despite the imbalance of pollinator visits, native plants did not seem to suffer; in some cases, fruit set was higher among native meadowsweet when it was grown near invasive loosestrife. Plus, native bee populations were higher at sites with invasive species.

The complex matrix of native and invasive pollinators and native and invasive plants supporting and harming each other creates a unique challenge for the ecosystem. Princeton's Wilcove believes it all boils down to context, explaining, "The identity of who is pollinating whom matters a great deal. If either native or nonnative pollinators are helping to spread weeds, then that causes problems. Conversely, we have nonnative pollinators like the honeybee that are pollinating our food, so that's a reason to be very concerned about the fate of those nonnative pollinators. It's context-dependent. We can't make general statements about all nonnative pollinators or . . . all nonnative plants."

CHAPTER 5

Lessons from a Warming Planet

AMY BOYD NEVER PLANNED TO STUDY CLIMATE CHANGE.

Boyd, a biology professor at Warren Wilson College, was researching sweet shrub (*Calycanthus floridus*), a native woodland plant that thrives in forests near her office in Asheville, North Carolina, when she noticed something was off.

Each spring, when Boyd ventured out into the forest to check bloom time of the sweet shrub, she separated the petals and watched as sap beetles (*Nitidulidae*) flowed out. As their name suggests, sap beetles are known for feeding on sap, often in the wounds of trees. The plump black beetles also nosh on flowers, fruits, and fermenting plant tissues and are attracted to sweet shrub for its pungent rotting-fruit fragrance. On the sweet shrub, Boyd noticed the beetles bedded down in the shelter of the reddish-brown petals before they unfurled. Sap beetles, the main pollinators of sweet shrub, populated the plant in significant numbers. "They would come out like clowns out of a clown car at a circus. You can't even imagine how many beetles were hiding in there!" Boyd recalls.

The same thing happened season after season: Boyd went out into the woods in mid-May, opened the sweet shrub petals, and the sap beetles flowed out. A few years ago, spring temperatures spiked and the sweet shrub bloomed three weeks earlier than normal. For the first time since Boyd started studying the native plants in 2007, she parted the petals and not a single beetle spilled forth. "What we're seeing is that when the flowers bloom later in the spring, the beetles show up," she explains, "and when the flowers bloom earlier in the spring, the beetles aren't there. As we look more globally at how the timing of spring is changing, climate change seems to be implicated."

The sweet shrub and sap beetles depend on each other but use different cues to decide when to be active and when to reproduce. Thanks to climate change, they are missing each other.

It's estimated that climate change will lead to an average temperature increase of two to four degrees Celsius before 2050. The shift might seem minimal—when summer temperatures increase from 80 to 84 degrees, we might not even notice—but the impact on pollinators could be profound.

Various models have documented patterns of climate change and how pollinators have responded. Data show that warmer temperatures have led to declines in certain pollinator populations; earlier arrivals of spring, which has advanced about 2.3 days per decade, have impacted the first flowering dates of plants and the seasonal flights of certain pollinating insects. Over the past century, the timing has advanced four days per one degree Celsius, with bumblebees advancing their spring flight times an average of two weeks between 2001 and 2007 alone. Both plants and pollinators are also shifting their locations to adapt to warming temperatures: species have shifted an average of 6.1 kilometers (3.79 miles) closer to the poles per decade. In Southern California, 90 percent of dominant plant species made a mean elevation shift of 65 meters over the past three decades, creating mismatches between geographic distribution of interacting species. Overall, it appears that insect-pollinated plants react more strongly to a warming climate than self-pollinating plants, and flowers with earlier bloom times are more sensitive than species that bloom later in the season.

In some cases, co-dependent species both emerge earlier and continue the relationship needed for their mutual survival—a process scientists refer to as a "linear advancement." While some studies suggest that pollinators might be robust enough to withstand climate disruptions, a growing body of research illustrates just the opposite. Scientists cite global warming as "one of the biggest anthropogenic disturbance factors imposed on ecosystems."

Box 5-1
Bats Help Save the Rainforest

Love biodiversity? Thank bats. In the process of gathering nectar, bats consume seeds from various tropical plant species that are later sown in different areas of the forest when the bats regurgitate or defecate. In a restored tropical rainforest in Mexico, bats and birds were responsible for 94 percent of plant species that were not introduced through conservation efforts.

The red fig-eating bat (*Stenoderma rufum*), a species of fruit-eating bat native to Puerto Rico, helped a rainforest on the island recover from the devastation of Hurricane Hugo. Other species abandoned the Luquillo Experimental Forest after the hurricane hit in 1989, but the red fig-eating bat remained, perhaps because the rare bats, once thought to be extinct, were too weak to relocate to new habitat. Although the hurricane did hurt the remaining populations, the bats were instrumental in spreading seeds of a native palm-like tree called bulletwood (*Manilkara bidentata*). In fact, the red fig-eating bat provides the only way the seeds are dispersed, giving the species a critical role in regenerating the forest.

Bats are so effective at regenerating forests that German researchers installed artificial bat roosts in deforested areas of Costa Rica to help native seed dispersal. A total of ten species of nectar-feeding bats moved in within a few weeks, including five species that became permanent residents. The bats dispersed sixty-nine different seed types, speeding up vegetation growth and providing habitat to attract additional seed dispersers such as birds.

Box 5-2
Developing Mite-Resistant Bees

With varroa mites decimating honeybee colonies—and concerns that repeated treatments with miticides could enable mites to develop resistance—researchers at the USDA Carl Hayden Bee Research Center started exploring the possibility of breeding mite-resistant bees.

Colonies of Russian honeybees appear to have lower levels of varroa infestations than European honeybees. It's believed that the Russian stock, a strain of *A. mellifera* that has been exposed to varroa since 1900, has developed a degree of genetic resistance to the mites thanks to increased grooming and removal of parasitized larvae that make it harder for mites to reproduce in the hive.

The USDA studied whether mite-resistant bees could help overcome varroa infestations. The results were disappointing: workers from infected colonies can drift into neighboring hives, taking mites with them; and foraging workers from unaffected colonies might steal honey from mite-infested colonies, bringing mites back to their hives. It appears that Russian honeybees might not be able to ward off the hitchhiking mites. A large population of foraging bees with mites renders even "mite-resistant" bees defenseless against varroa.

Climate change might make varroa infestations worse: both mite populations and the numbers of foraging bees increase in the fall. Warmer temperatures extend the season for foraging flights, allowing mites to continue migrating into colonies.

Timing Is Everything

Pollinators need plants for nectar and pollen; plants need pollinators to set fruit and reproduce. These partnerships have evolved over millions of years and the timing is precise: pollinating insects mature at the exact time nectar flow begins. Both plants and pollinators depend on climate signals to start biological responses like blooming and mating (the timing of these events is called *phenology*), but not all species use the same cues. Some rely on temperature, while others use day length. When the cues that species depend on change, the biological processes that have evolved to coincide stop matching up. In other words, if temperature increases from historic norms before day length increases, species might emerge at different times.

Climate change is leading to earlier springs, so those species that depend on temperature cues are leafing out, blooming, mating, or laying eggs earlier while those that depend on day length still come out at the same time. Regardless of the temperature, the timing of their biological responses remains the same. These "phenological mismatches" cause problems for both species.

Long-term data collected from the Rocky Mountain Biological Laboratory between 2009 and 2016 suggest that the snow is melting earlier, leading flowers to bloom sooner. This might seem like a boon to pollinators, but early access to the nectar buffet comes at a price. The sooner spring arrives, the higher the risk of frost or late-season droughts that kill off blooming plants. Flowers that bloom earlier might not bloom as long, causing nectar to plummet during a time when pollinators depend on it. Three species of bumblebees in the Colorado region—the black-notched bumblebee (*Bombus bifarius*), the yellowhead bumblebee (*Bombus flavifrons*), and the white-shouldered bumblebee (*Bombus appositus*)—are struggling to access enough nectar, which researchers attribute to climate change.

Ogilvie, the researcher at the Rocky Mountain Biological Laboratory, commented, "There isn't that much research on the topic, which is kind of impressive given how abundant bumblebees are, [but] we lack some long-term monitoring of insect populations." Ogilvie and her collaborators looked at both the number of flowers blooming in a season and the number of days flowers bloomed; they found that pollinators had fewer nectar sources and those sources had become less reliable. Bumblebee populations fell when there were fewer days of blooming. For two other species, the number of low floral days increased, suggesting climate change is having a negative effect. For the remaining species, the impacts of earlier springs are more complicated. These bees saw increases in both the number of low floral days *and* the number of good floral days, so it's unclear exactly what effect climate change will have. "You would think that climate change would have a positive effect because of the longer seasons, but it really means there are more days in a season where there aren't enough flowers for the bees," Ogilvie explains.

The total number of flowers did not fluctuate, but climate change did make the seasons longer, so bees needed to forage over longer periods of time, putting a strain on available flowers. Bumblebee colonies face a greater risk of starvation because of more days with fewer flowers. Honeybees may be better able to adapt than other pollinators because they store nectar and pollen to feed their colonies during a dearth. By contrast, bumblebees do not store food, making them more vulnerable when less nectar and pollen are available—but Ogilvie believes that bumblebees are resilient. "Bumblebees are quite intelligent," she says. "It's possible that if there are fewer flowers on a particular day, they may expand the types of flowers they're visiting. If bumblebees are able to behaviorally respond to the changes in the flowers, they might still be able to get enough food to survive."

Although the findings were striking, Ogilvie believes additional long-term monitoring of bee populations is essential to tease out the effects of climate change. Bumblebees have annual life cycles, making them slow to respond to change; the species living in higher-altitude areas (like the bumblebees studied as part of this research) might be especially susceptible to climate change because the fluctuating temperatures are more dramatic in these regions. Ogilvie plans to repeat the experiment in 2020 to see if the pattern continues.

Boyd, the biology professor at Warren Wilson College, also believes that additional research is needed to determine the impact of bloom time and pollination mismatches between the sweet shrub and sap beetles. She explains that if the beetles don't show up, it means the sweet shrub isn't pollinated. While the plants can reproduce through underground rhizomes, they cannot create new genetic diversity.

The impact on the beetles is less clear. Because sweet shrub blooms for such a short period, it's not a major food source for the beetles. Still, seeing all those beetles in the petals makes Boyd wonder whether the pollinators are using the shrub as a breeding ground. If that's the case, the phenological mismatch could hurt their populations. "When organisms evolve a dependence on each other," she says, "they can really benefit from that because they get services from one another, but it also creates a bit of precariousness."

In the best-case scenario, the changes would be mutual: both plants and pollinators would emerge at the same time—even if that timing advanced as a response to warming temperatures. While some studies show that this does happen with some species, other research has found the opposite to be true: plant and pollinator species do not react in the same way to a warming climate. In Japan, flowering plants blossomed earlier during a warm spring, but the emergence of bumblebee queens was unaffected, leading to less seed set in bumblebee-pollinated plants. In the Iberian Peninsula shared by Portugal and Spain, warmer temperatures led both the honeybee and the cabbage white butterfly (*Pieris rapae*) to emerge earlier than their preferred forage species, leaving them without access to the main nectar sources in their diets. When the plants and pollinators that depend on each other for survival get their signals crossed, it can have a profound effect on both species.

As Boyd says, "Some [species] will be more dependent on their partners than others and some may survive without them, but others are going to be in real trouble."

Rising Temperatures Raise Risks

To get an in-depth look at how climate change affects plant–pollinator interactions, scientists studied 1,420 pollinator species and 429 plant species in an area with both prairie and forest habitats in Western Illinois, finding that up to half of the local pollinators suffered from disruptions in their food supply. Specialized pollinators (species that visit only

Box 5-3

Climate Change Could Be Poisoning Monarchs

Monarchs depend on milkweed (*Asclepias*) for survival. The butterflies take advantage of the cardenolides, toxic chemicals in the leaf tissues that can trigger heart failure in vertebrate predators, to protect their eggs and larvae. Monarch caterpillars munch on the milkweed leaves after hatching, ingesting the chemicals that make them unappetizing to predators. Monarchs have evolved to become cardenolide-tolerant, but climate change appears to be changing the relationship between the butterflies and their host plants.

In 2018, researchers at Louisiana State University published a study that found climate change was triggering chemical changes in milkweed that could lead to the inadvertent poisoning of monarch caterpillars. Increased levels of cardenolide poison larvae, delay larval growth, and stunt forewings in adult butterflies. Study co-author Bret Elderd, an associate professor of biology at LSU, explained, "It's a Goldilocks situation for monarch butterflies. Too few of these chemicals in the milkweed, and the plant won't protect monarch caterpillars from being eaten, but too high a concentration of these chemicals can also hurt the monarchs, slowing caterpillar development and decreasing survival."

Native milkweed naturally produces fewer cardenolides, and the levels of those toxic chemicals appear to be less affected by rising temperatures. In contrast, the climate-related increases in cardenolides appear to be especially problematic in tropical milkweed (*A. curassavica*). Although butterflies love the hardy species—and under current conditions, monarchs that feed on tropical milkweed show higher survival rates than those feeding on native swamp milkweed (*A. incarnata*)—the nonnative species appears most prone to climate-related chemical changes, affecting the growth and survival of monarchs in the future.

Few studies have explored the impacts of climate change on species interactions, which is particularly important for plant and pollinator specialists whose interactions are tightly linked. The researchers note that "the potential for such ecological traps to emerge as temperatures increase may have far-reaching consequences."

a small number of plant species) were most apt to be left without food; but even generalists that visited a larger number of plant species had their diets significantly narrowed. The mismatches could lead to the extinction of specialized pollinators, and others could experience population declines because the diminishing number of plant species means pollinators might have to travel farther or wait longer for food.

Several pollinators have already started to feel the heat from rising temperatures: Two species of butterflies were listed as threatened on the endangered species list: the Bay checkerspot (*Euphydryas editha bayensis*) and Quino checkerspot (*Euphydryas editha quino*) have lost 80 percent of their populations in southern and low-elevation areas like Baja California because the climate has become too warm and dry for both to survive.

The Bay checkerspot is native to California and could once be seen flitting about the San Francisco Bay Area, making its home in 12,000 acres of native grasslands. The butterflies, which got their names from the telltale yellow, red, and white spots in a checkerboard pattern on their upper wings, were credited with keeping invasive species from taking over their habitats. The Quino checkerspot also has a trademark checkerboard pattern on its upper wings. Populations of these brown, yellow, and red butterflies, once found throughout California, have diminished to a mere seven known populations: six in Riverside and San Diego Counties and one near Tecate, Mexico. A draft recovery plan was created when the Quino checkerspot was added to the endangered species list in 1997, but the outlook isn't good: too little is known about the ideal habitat for the rapidly disappearing butterflies to allow conservationists to prepare a management program. The butterflies appear to be adapting by shifting to higher altitudes and choosing new host plants on which to lay their eggs. The National Academy of Sciences implicated climate change as the primary cause of the decline of both subspecies; the Quino is "the first endangered species for which climate change is officially listed as both a current threat and a factor to be considered in the plan for its recovery."

In honeybee colonies, climate change could be fatal. Honeybees spend the winter in a cluster with the goal of maintaining an in-hive temperature of 93 degrees. When the weather warms up, the bees start laying eggs and the cluster expands, but a cold snap—even if it lasts just one day—could be enough to kill off the eggs that the cluster cannot keep warm, forcing the colony to rebuild from scratch.

Rising temperatures have also created issues for hummingbirds. In the southern limits of their breeding range, the broad-tailed hummingbird (*Selasphorus platycercus*) has always arrived at the same time and its preferred flower has remained stable for decades. Near the northern limit of the breeding range, the hummingbird still arrives at the same time, but both the first flowering date and peak flowering time have shifted earlier. That means nectar is available during a narrowing window. Scientists suggest that climate change might lead some hummingbird species to shift their habitats to lower latitudes.

Most species of hummingbirds in North America are generalists, seeking out nectar in a wide range of colorful flowers, according to Geoffrey LeBaron of the National Audubon Society. These generalist species should be more adaptable to climate change than species in Latin America that depend on specialized relationships with small numbers of flowers. Even though specialized pollinators are at greater risk, generalists are far from immune to these changes.

In Colorado's Rocky Mountains, data collected over nearly forty years, from more than two million flower counts, found that sixty species of plants were flowering earlier. The shifts were not uniform, which meant patterns of flowering and abundance were no longer what pollinators had come to depend on. Researchers called the shifts a "substantial reshaping of ecological communities" related to climate change. "In the alpine meadows, it's not just one flower but all of those flowers that are coming out earlier and earlier, and hummingbirds haven't advanced their migration to keep up with that advancing bloom time," explains LeBaron. "When the hummingbirds arrive, it's not that one flower is gone, but almost all of the flowers are gone. In that first two-week period [after the flowers bloom and] before the hummingbirds get there, there are far fewer resources because all of the [flowers] are starting to fade and don't have as much nectar in them."

Relocating for Survival

In addition to rising temperatures that result in advancing bloom times, LeBaron notes that climate shifts have changed migration patterns. Species living in the eastern United States normally migrate to Central America in the winter, but, as the temperatures in their overwintering grounds rise, the hummingbirds have started returning to the Gulf Coast of the United States earlier and spending more time in the area.

The ruby-throated hummingbird (*Archilochus colubris*) is arguably the prettiest of all hummingbirds. Adult males sport a black mask, green crown, and their namesake bright-red throats that look like jaunty mufflers around their necks. (Female ruby-throated hummingbirds have white, not red, throats.) The species is as fast as it is fancy, zipping between flowers at high speeds while maintaining the ability to shift its direction and speed of flight with amazing precision. Found in forests, hedgerows, and scrub across North America, these migratory birds have changed their travel patterns as a result of climate change.

Between 1880 and 1969, the first arrivals of ruby-throated hummingbirds in the spring advanced between 11.4 and 18.2 days (depending on latitude). The shifts in migration patterns were associated with warmer winter and spring temperatures in their North American breeding grounds. During warmer winters, the hummingbirds arrived later at high latitudes; their arrivals were later at both mid and high latitudes during warmer springs, leading researchers to suggest that the species was taking longer stopovers between their wintering grounds and their breeding grounds. LeBaron suspects that the hummingbirds might need the breaks to rebound from the stresses of migration, but the extended stops around Louisiana, Texas, Mississippi, Alabama, and Florida could put hummingbirds at risk because of competition with other birds in the area. The hummingbirds often arrive in their breeding range in poor condition.

During the fall migration, species living in the western United States started showing up along the East Coast, a phenomenon LeBaron believes could be a result of upticks in severe storms that displace the hummingbirds from their homes. The Audubon Society used citizen science data to develop a forecast of how climate changes over the next twenty, fifty, and eighty years could change the hummingbirds' overwintering and breeding grounds. The projections raised concerns. "It's a little scary in terms of looking at how the climate space available for some of these birds is potentially going to rapidly change or completely change," LeBaron says.

The United Nations Food and Agriculture Organization notes that increases in global temperatures are having profound impacts on the ecosystem, and it remains unclear how pollinators will respond to climate change over the long term.

Bumblebees are among the creatures struggling to relocate to areas with cooler temperatures. In North America and Europe, bees at the edge of the northern range have failed to move farther north, while populations on the southern ends of their range are shifting to higher elevations, bringing more bumblebees together in less space. This contraction of their habitat will force the bees to compete for resources. On the southern ends of their ranges, populations are shrinking, and the bumblebees that fail to move to cooler temperatures at higher elevations will be more susceptible to a changing climate.

In contrast, bats appear to be adapting to a changing climate by moving their habitats. The nocturnal pollinators have been spotted at higher-than-normal elevations in Costa Rica; in North America, their wintering ranges continue moving northward; eastern red bats (*Lasiurus borealis*) were recorded in Saskatchewan, Canada, farther north than

Figure 5-1: Some plants bloom at night to attract nocturnal pollinators like bats.

ever before. But these moves are not necessarily good for the bats. National parks have seen significant losses of bats and high turnover—and this pattern is expected to continue. Changes in temperature could also affect hibernation times. Both insect- and nectar-eating bats would suffer if their hibernation ends before plants and insects emerge later in the season.

Bat Conservation International points to climate-change models that predict average temperatures along the Texas-Mexico border could increase by three to five degrees Fahrenheit before 2080; increases in the minimum winter temperatures could expand the range of common vampire bats (*Desmodus rotundus*) up to 100,000 square miles to locations in Mexico, Texas, Louisiana, Florida, Arizona, and California. The expanded habitat of these carnivores could have serious ecological impacts, including negative effects on other pollinating bat species.

Philip Stepanian, research scientist at the University of Oklahoma, was part of a team that used historical weather surveillance data to measure the number of Mexican free-tailed bats (*Tadarida brasiliensis*) living in Bracken Cave between 1995 and 2017. The nocturnal bats live in colonies numbering in the tens of millions, migrating to Mexico in the winter and returning to Bracken Cave, near San Antonio, to have pups in the spring. The research is believed to be the first long-term study to use radar to measure animal migration.

Researchers have tried going into the caves to count the bats or estimate their populations based on guano volume, but getting an accurate count remained challenging and, without data, it was impossible to detect changes. Weather surveillance—the same radar network that measures raindrops—proved sensitive enough to provide essential information. Stepanian was surprised at what it showed.

Colonies of Mexican free-tailed bats were expected to inhabit Bracken Cave (as well as other regions of Texas, Oklahoma, and New Mexico) during the summer, but more than two decades of weather data showed that bats remained in the cave when winter arrived. Between 1954 and 1956, no bats were found in Bracken Cave or surrounding caves during the winter; it's likely that they left Texas when the temperatures dropped. In the mid-1990s, colonies of bats were found in Bracken Cave in December and January, and the number of bats remaining in the caves during the winter months has continued to increase. Currently, an estimated 300,000 Mexican free-tailed bats spend the winter in Bracken Cave. It's unclear whether the overwintering bats had failed to migrate to Mexico or had arrived from their home ranges farther north.

The discovery that a growing number of bats remained in Bracken Cave instead of migrating to Mexico was surprising on its own. Also telling was the fact that the migrating bats returned earlier in the spring and that the date continues to advance about one-half day per year. If the trend continues, Stepanian notes, "At some point, all of these pregnant female bats from Mexico are going to start arriving in Texas."

The Mexican free-tailed bats are insectivores, not pollinators, but Stepanian thinks climate change could have similar effects on other species that are of equal concern, explaining that "bats have been doing their thing for thousands of years [and] have a well-established schedule; any change to that schedule is concerning because it's new, it's different, and we don't know exactly how it will affect them."

At this stage, Stepanian admits, the potential implications of the changes are unclear. The bats appear to be adapting, but that adaptation might be short-lived, and, if temperature shifts continue, the bats might stop migrating altogether. If bats remain in their colonies without intermingling with bats from other colonies at their joint overwintering grounds, the chances of inbreeding increase. Remaining in the same cave could also lead to an increase in the numbers of parasites and in more-virulent and more-widespread diseases. "We have what we see as a strong indicator that climate is the thing that's driving these patterns," says Stepanian, "but we want to catch it with a smoking gun . . . we'd

Box 5-4

Climate Change Helps Invasive Species Thrive

Thanks to climate change, frost ends earlier in the spring and arrives later in the fall. The extended growing season might be good news for gardeners, but it also gives invasive species more time to take over.

Invasive species are flexible and better able to adapt to their environments than native species, giving them an edge as the planet heats up. Climate change might also increase nitrogen levels in the soil, and, in some regions, those shifts will make invasive species grow faster, crowding out native species. The earlier bloom time gives invasive species more time to shade out competitors and hog additional nutrients, water, and pollination services.

Extensive research has been conducted on the impact of climate change on the growth of purple loosestrife (*Lythrum salicaria*). The wetland plant grows purple flowers on tall spikes that can produce almost three million miniscule seeds in a season. The extensive root system can send out up to fifty shoots, creating a dense web of plants that prefer habitat with wet soil. The plant was first discovered in the Great Lakes region in 1869 and was believed to have been brought over from its native Europe and Asia in the ballast of a cargo ship. Data shows that the purple loosestrife flowers bloom twenty-four days earlier than they did 100 years ago in Massachusetts.

Researchers transplanted purple loosestrife between sites in Virginia and Ontario, Canada to test the impact of a different climate zone on the invasive species. The farther from the original site the invasive wetland species moved, the fewer fruits it produced; the local plants in the northern plots bloomed almost three weeks earlier than the southern transplants, maximizing seed production in a shorter growing season and producing thirty-seven times more fruit. The purple loosestrife transplanted in the south produced one-quarter the number of seeds of their local counterparts. The results led the researchers to conclude that the plants adapted to different climates as it migrated and evolved to new sites in short periods of time.

Climate scientist Bethany Bradley believes a warming planet will accelerate the spread of invasive species. "Invasive plant species are well suited to thriving in novel environments because of their ability to beat out competitors for resources," she told the Union of Concerned Scientists. "So it stands to reason that the more we disrupt the climate, the more these plants might be able to expand their reach."

like to start looking at other bat colonies to see whether the same things are happening in other locations."

Monitoring Matters

Assessing the impact of climate change on pollinators is challenging: temperature shifts are subtle—a few degrees or fractions of degrees over years—which means data has to be collected over long periods to tease out possible patterns.

British researchers did just that, combing through data from Kew Gardens and natural history museums in London dating back to 1848 for specimens of early spider orchid (*Ophrys sphegodes*) and the buffish mining bee (*Andrena nigroaenea*). The results were startling.

With its chartreuse petals and dark reddish-brown velvet-like lip, the orchid resembles a female buffish mining bee and emits the same sex pheromones to lure the male buffish mining bees for pseudocopulation. Pollination depends on males emerging earlier than females and orchids flowering before the females emerge. The two species coevolved such that the orchid blooms at the same time the bee emerges, but climate change has created a mismatch between the species.

Each one-degree (Celsius) increase in spring temperatures caused the orchid to bloom six days earlier. In addition to fast-forwarding the bloom time, the same temperature increase changed the dates the bees emerged: the female miner bees appeared fifteen days earlier and the males followed six days later—or nine days ahead of their normal schedule. Because the females were already buzzing about, the males were less apt to visit the orchids for pseudocopulation and so the chance of pollination decreased, which could lead to extinction. Karen Robbirt of the Royal Botanic Gardens called it "the first clear example, supported by long-term data, of the potential for climate change to disrupt critical [pollination] relationships between species."

Blaming climate change for population declines could oversimplify complex relationships between pollinators and the environment. For starters, the populations of most species show significant year-over-year fluctuations, so, even if rising temperatures hurt their chances of survival and reproduction, other environmental conditions could be at play, too.

Adaptation might be possible for some species. Monarchs, for one, appear to have adjusted to changing conditions in certain environments. The butterflies have been transported to New Zealand, Australia, Portugal, Spain, and Hawaii, where the species are not native but are doing what it takes to survive. In Australia, monarchs migrate in response to drought, not temperature change, and monarchs in Hawaii don't migrate at all. So, if parts of their traditional overwintering and breeding grounds in the United States become inhospitable, Karen Oberhauser, monarch expert and director of the University of Wisconsin–Madison Arboretum, believes the butterflies will move and a percentage of the population will survive. But environmental conditions could strip monarchs of one of their most iconic traits. "I don't think we're in danger of losing monarchs," she says, "but we are in danger of losing the migratory phenomenon, which is a pretty amazing thing."

Species that reproduce quickly and have a lot of genetic diversity tend to be the most resilient to a changing climate. But for most species, natural selection is slow and adaptation will take too long to be a plausible response to climate change. "Over the course of the evolution of our planet, organisms have always adapted, right? But most of the changes they came up against were gradual, and when they haven't been gradual, we've seen mass extinctions," Oberhauser adds.

Climate change is, perhaps, the most complex issue facing pollinators. We have the ability to establish new habitat, remove invasive species, and stop applying pesticides. Each option presents challenges and would trigger a series of domino effects, but all are possible. And while it's not possible to turn down the thermostat on the planet to reset bloom times, hold migration patterns steady, or keep pollinators in their cur-

Figure 5-2: A monarch butterfly lands on a colorful—and nectar-rich—lantana plant.

rent ranges, current research is exploring how to mitigate some of the effects. A 2017 study published in *Climatic Change* found that maintaining or restoring habitat helped retain bee diversity and guarded against the damage caused by climate events such as drought.

From her post at the Rocky Mountain Biological Laboratory, Ogilvie notes, "It's important for us to understand, at the very least, what effect climate change is having on populations so that we don't lose them. We don't know if pollinators are keeping pace with the changing climate . . . and it's a ticking time bomb."

CHAPTER 6

Helping without Hurting

THREE ROWS OF CHILDREN SAT ON THE STEPS in front of Davidson College Presbyterian Church, all eyes focused on two mesh cages. The preschoolers, some with handmade crowns perched on their heads, others wearing butterfly masks that made them look like lepidopterist superheroes, had been waiting for this moment. Their teacher held up a stuffed creature and asked, "What is this?"

Their voices rose in unison. "A CATERPILLAR!"

"And what is it after it's a caterpillar?"

"A CHRYSALIS!"

"And what is it after it's a chrysalis?"

"A BUTTERFLY!"

The annual spring butterfly release capped off a curriculum on pollinators. Preschool director Kristin Clark explained that the children had learned about the lifecycle of the fragile creatures. This was the finish line to their pollinator marathon. They had been training for this day. Literally. The children practiced the program, which included songs like "Fly, Fly Butterfly" (sung to the tune of "Twinkle, Twinkle Little Star") and learned what to do if one of the 300 released butterflies landed on them. The advice: stay still.

Residents of the North Carolina college town fluttered in to witness the event. A towheaded toddler wearing glittery butterfly wings over her sundress raced toward the mesh cage, her arms outstretched, shouting, "Come here, butterfly! Land on me!" before her mom could pull her back.

Associate Pastor John Ryan recited a prayer that included the lines, "*Oh little butterfly, messenger of God, fly away as high as you can go; fly, fly, little wings, fly where the angels sing; go now, find the light and keep the joy in your sight.*" Then a teacher from each of the nine classes opened an envelope or unzipped the mesh habitats. The colorful monarchs, giant swallowtails, and painted ladies took flight and all of the children, squealing with delight, tipped their faces toward the sky. A butterfly landed on the shoulder of a little boy wearing a superhero T-shirt and a butterfly mask and, just as he practiced, he stood still while his classmates gathered around in awe.

Davidson College Presbyterian Church has included monarch releases in its preschool curriculum since 2003. Clark orders both butterflies and caterpillars from Insect Lore, a butterfly breeder that has mailed more than 50 million caterpillars to be used in educational settings. Preschoolers watch the transformation from caterpillars to butterflies and help raise the colorful winged creatures, feeding them citrus fruits and plants from their nectar garden.

"We believe that children learn by doing, seeing, touching, and being part of things, so our curriculum is based around hands-on experiences," Clark explains. "I think that to teach them about butterflies and get them excited about the lessons, we need to get them up close and personal."

Clark is aware that there is some controversy around butterfly releases but says the preschool hasn't received any criticism about the program. Instead, she believes parents appreciate that their children are not

Figure 6-1: A monarch butterfly alights on a student at Davidson College Presbyterian Preschool in Davidson, North Carolina.

only learning about the transformation from caterpillar to chrysalis to butterfly but they are actually *witnessing* those changes and developing a deeper understanding of the lifecycle. "Deep down, I hope that taking care of the butterflies before we let them go creates special memories and builds that foundation that makes them want to care for other creatures," she says. "We're doing our part to give back to nature by creating more butterflies."

Despite the educational potential, a group of monarch researchers and conservationists have decried the practice of purchasing mass-reared butterflies from commercial breeders and releasing them, expressing fears it could harm wild monarch populations and disrupt important research that is critical to their conservation.

Box 6-1
Retailers Help Keep Gardens Neonic-Free

Much of the research on neonicotinoids has focused on commercial agriculture (where their use is most prevalent), but there is some data on the presence of the pesticide in garden plants. In 2014, Friends of the Earth and the Pesticide Research Institute purchased seventy-one "bee-friendly" plants such as daisies, lavender, marigolds, asters, and primrose at big-box retailers in eighteen cities across the United States and Canada. Their testing showed that neonics were present on 51 percent of the nectar-producing plants, with levels ranging from two to 748 parts per billion. A dose of 192 parts per billion is enough to kill a honeybee; as little as four parts per billion is enough to impair navigation, memory, and foraging ability. Landscape plants are actually treated at higher levels than agricultural crops. A single corn plant grown from a neonic-treated seed has access to about 1.34 milligrams of the common pesticide imidacloprid; the recommended label application rate for a perennial garden plant is 300 mg—220 times more of the chemical *per plant*.

A 2016 state-of-the-industry survey conducted by *Greenhouse Grower* magazine reported that 74 percent of growers that supply landscape plants to retail garden centers would no longer be applying neonicotinoids. The shift appeared

Box 6-1 *continued*

to have an impact on the levels of the pesticide found on plants: when Friends of the Earth and Pesticide Research Institute repeated their research in 2016, lab tests found that just 23 percent of plants contained neonics. The reduction was attributed to retailers like Home Depot, Whole Foods Markets, BJ's Wholesale Club, and Lowe's making public commitments to phase out the pesticides.

When you're walking through the garden departments at big-box retailers like Lowe's and Home Depot, it might not be obvious that pollinator protection is in action, but a closer look at the tags highlights efforts to make customers aware of which plants were treated with neonicotinoids. Plastic tags tucked into the moist soil read, "The plant is protected from problematic aphids, white flies, beetles, mealy bugs, and other unwanted pests by neonicotinoids," to help customers easily identify plants that have been sprayed.

Home Depot started labeling plants in 2014 to help customers concerned about the effects of the pesticide on pollinators make informed purchasing decisions and promised to phase out the use of neonics in 2018. In its statement about the decision, Home Depot noted that it was "deeply engaged" in understanding the connection between the pesticides and bee populations and remained in contact with the EPA, scientists, suppliers, and the pesticide industry to monitor the research. The statement also noted, "In total, we've now spent three years searching for clarity on the possible harm flowering plants have on pollinators. Although we haven't found any clear science that confirms what levels in plants are unsafe for pollinators, we will continue to offer natural and organic alternatives for plants and continue to work with our suppliers to phase out plants treated with neonics in our garden centers. Our contribution to the total neonics exposure is extremely small. In fact, more than 80 percent of our flowering plants are neonic-free."

Ecotoxicologist Vera Krischik researches neonicotinoids and believes the shift toward bee-friendly plants will benefit retailers. "[Retailers] can charge a premium, fifty cents more, a dollar more, on the plants that are labeled bee-friendly," she says. "It's come out that [phasing out the use of neonics] hasn't had a huge economic impact on the industry [because] it can be used as a marketing tool."

Krischik credits consumer demand for shaping the industry, explaining, "I think the consumers should get a pat on their backs for making this issue more obvious, bringing this issue to the forefront, and having the industry change to meet their needs. It's a really good example of how democracy works."

Populations in Peril

In a 2015 statement *Captive Breeding and Releasing Monarchs*, researchers argued that the conditions in mass-breeding facilities promote the spread of disease that can be transmitted among larvae. Despite the relative ease with which the common monarch pathogen *Ophyrocystis elektroscirrha* (OE) takes hold, commercial breeders are not required to test captive stock for diseases. (The USDA does regulate the interstate transport of butterflies, but the permits do not require disease screening.) OE, a protozoan (single-celled organism) parasite first discovered in 1966, spreads when monarch larvae consume spores that infected butterflies have shed onto eggs or milkweed leaves. The parasite can cause shorter wingspans and lower body mass; smaller butterflies have shorter lifespans and smaller females lay fewer eggs. OE is also linked with impaired flight, which could hinder migration. In fact, captive-bred monarchs are less apt to be recovered in Mexican overwintering grounds. In the wild, the OE infection rate among the breeding populations of monarchs was around 40 percent; peer-reviewed data on the rates of OE infections on commercial farms is lacking, but authors of the report noted that several mass-reared monarchs purchased from commercial breeders were infected with the disease. Experts fear that higher levels of pathogens in commercial breeding facilities will spread to wild populations; that the pathogens in commercial facilities will evolve to be more virulent; and that novel strains of pathogens will be introduced into new environments where the butterflies are shipped. There are also concerns that monarchs raised in commercial breeding facilities could lack the biological drive to migrate as a result of being raised with artificial lighting and constant temperatures. Monarchs reared in high densities are also at higher risk of becoming stressed and injured, and migration could exacerbate that.

An online article in *Discover* questioned whether we were "loving monarchs to death," noting that the mass rearing of butterflies was more about profit than bolstering pollinator populations. Commercial breeders sell one dozen monarchs for around $100, but charities charge up to $50 per monarch to participate in mass releases. The article claimed that "the monarchs themselves may be paying a higher price." But the International Butterfly Breeders Association claims that no damage to monarch populations or the environment have been reported as a result of 250,000-plus monarch larvae raised, sold, and released over the last decade and called concerns about releasing mass-reared butterflies "unsubstantiated by scientific data." The pushback did not stop both the Xerces Society and the North American Butterfly Association from calling for bans on releases of mass-reared monarchs. The experts who collaborated on the 2015 report struggled to reach a consensus; monarch expert Oberhauser told *Discover* that "there were some [conservationists] who thought people shouldn't be rearing *any* [monarchs indoors]. Well-meaning and smart people are going to disagree on a lot of things. . . ."

Elizabeth Howard, director of Journey North, an organization dedicated to tracking and preserving migratory animals, understands the desire to participate in monarch releases but thought the consensus statement released by organizations that included Journey North and the Xerces Society could have taken a stronger stand, explaining, "It's such a balancing act, because all of us recognize how important the experience of raising monarchs is from a public education standpoint. . . . Where it gets complicated is when you get into the question of how many [butterflies] is enough. It's the mass rearing that really raises concern."

The potential for captive-bred monarchs to interfere with ongoing research has been cited as another area of concern: monarch releases could skew the understanding of what is happening with wild populations.

Sarina Jepsen, director of endangered species and aquatic programs for the Xerces Society, explains that releasing monarchs "disrupts our ability to understand the natural movements of monarchs. In the western US, the Xerces Society and other researchers are currently trying to understand where and when monarchs breed so that we can best focus conservation efforts. Mass releases of monarchs could really interfere with this research."

Researchers started surveying monarch populations in 1993. Some of the highest population numbers were recorded during that time—an estimated 682 million monarchs were counted in 1997—but the number of butterflies continued plummeting. Thanks to factors like habitat loss, climate change, and pesticides, populations of the beleaguered butterflies have been in freefall, with just 25 million monarchs recorded in 2014. The population showed a rebound to 150 million in 2016, but the numbers are still down 78 percent from the population highs in the 1990s. The lowest overwintering populations have been recorded in the last decade, including an all-time low of 0.67 hectares in 2014. Experts warn that the population is still too small to be resilient to threats.

News that monarch populations are in peril has led some enthusiasts to take their devotion to the extreme, setting up their own miniature monarch nurseries and raising the butterflies at home. Monarch Joint Venture published a guide called *Rearing Monarchs Responsibly* on its website to help those passionate about conserving monarchs or rearing them for science and education. It advised collecting eggs from milkweed and raising them indoors (but argued against captive breeding, purchasing monarchs from commercial breeding facilities, and using captive breeding to supplement the natural monarch population). Even with instructions for cleaning and sterilizing containers and testing adult butterflies for OE parasites, the guide warned that captive-bred species adjust to their captive settings within a few generations. Some conservationists get in over their heads, often to the detriment of the butterflies.

Leslie Uppinghouse, horticulturalist at Lady Bird Johnson Wildflower Center, will never forget receiving a call from the front gate that two unexpected packages were waiting for her. She tore into the boxes and found egg cartons filled with chrysalises; each one had been hot-glued to a piece of dental floss so it would hang in the cartons. A few of the monarchs had hatched in transit and died. The pre-emergent monarchs came with a note explaining that the caterpillars were raised on tropical milkweed in a northern climate and the novice breeder shipped them to Texas in the hopes the temperate climate and knowledgeable staff at the Wildflower Center could help the monarchs survive. The staff managed to save a few of the monarchs but most perished.

"This was someone who really cared about monarchs and spent a ton of time and energy raising and shipping them to us, and it all went very wrong," Uppinghouse says.

The Problem with Planting Habitat

Raising and shipping monarchs might seem like an obvious gaffe, but even planting habitat is fraught. Loss of habitat is one of the major threats to monarch populations. Milkweed is disappearing fast. Mature monarchs lay their eggs exclusively on milkweed, and the plants are the primary food source for monarch caterpillars. Milkweed used to spring up on farmland, pushing its way through the soil between rows of corn, soybeans, wheat, and other commercial crops. Thanks to herbicide-resistant seeds for crops grown in herbicide-treated fields, milkweed declined 21 percent between 1995 and 2013. The rapid declines—amounting to about 6,000 acres of potential monarch habitat per day, or 2.2 million acres per year—make the situation for monarchs dire.

Of the 108 species of milkweed, 73 are native to the United States. Each species has a specialized habitat; most prefer open areas, but a few species will thrive in dense woodlands or on the edges of forests and agricultural fields. Their super-specific growing conditions makes it hard for wind-blown seeds to take root. The same is true for seed mixes, so restoration projects often plants plugs rather than seeds.

News of plummeting monarch populations and their dependence on disappearing milkweed triggered a "plant milkweed" message that spread far and wide. During its annual Spring Plant Fundraiser and Open House, Monarch Watch at the University of Kansas sells upwards of 4,000 milkweed plants in a single seven-hour event. Lady Bird Johnson Wildflower Center also hosts semi-annual plant sales, and milkweed is among the first species to sell out. Uppinghouse has noticed an increase in the number of members interested in planting pollinator habitat, including several gardeners she describes as "hell-bent" on purchasing milkweed; they get mad when it's sold out. "We'll start talking and I'll realize that they have no idea why they want to plant milkweed; they just know it's for butterflies [and will say], 'The butterflies need flowers,' not realizing that milkweed is grown as a larval food," Uppinghouse says. "You can tell them that milkweed is good for caterpillars, but they want 'the one with the flowers' and don't understand that all of the plants [we sell at the plant sale] are good for pollinators. It's this thing where they're trying to do something good and they chose monarchs as this signifier of pollinators, but the whole education piece is missing."

Conservationists are working to spread information about planting the right species of milkweed. Too often, well-meaning gardeners plant tropical milkweed (*Asclepias curassavica*). The nonnative perennial produces attractive red and orange flowers, is simple to grow, and is available at most retail nurseries. Unlike native milkweed, which dies each winter, tropical milkweed grows all year long; in temperate climates like the southern United States and California, it continues flowering and producing new leaves. Continuous growth leads monarchs to continue breeding during fall and winter, remaining in northern ranges instead of migrating to Mexico. "We think monarchs flying south encounter good-condition milkweed and are more likely to remain there without migrating all the way to their overwintering grounds," explains monarch expert Oberhauser. "So having tropical milkweed in the garden is changing their behavior."

A 2015 study confirmed that the presence of tropical milkweed kept the monarchs from migrating. Volunteers with the Monarch Larva Monitoring Project have reported larval sightings during the winter in the southern United States. During the winter, thousands of monarch eggs and larvae can be found in a garden planted with tropical milkweed. While it's unclear whether these eggs and larvae are from resident monarchs or migratory monarchs that did not migrate, winter larvae feeding on tropical milkweed are at higher risk of OE. Native milkweed plants die off during the winter, killing off the contaminated plants; the parasite thrives on the tropical varieties year-round. Almost half of winter-breeding monarchs were infected with the parasite (compared to 9 percent of the population that migrated to Mexico). Higher infection rates are believed to be related to monarchs using the same plants for multiple generations, allowing the parasite to take hold in both the monarch populations and tropical milkweed plants. Higher densities of monarch larvae on tropical milkweed during the winter months also increases competition for food and could lead to shortages—assuming freeze events don't kill the milkweed plants and the monarchs depending on them. Migrating also weeds out sick monarchs, preventing them from passing along the parasite to their offspring.

Researcher Dara Satterfield explains, "Many animal migrations are changing in response to human activities, whether climate change, habitat destruction, or barriers to migration. Some migrations are changing in terms of timing or distance traveled. Some animals have stopped migrating altogether. So in these animals, some pathogens that have been historically kept in check by migration might now become a problem."

"We're getting a change in behavior, but we also get a less healthy population because pathogens build up for many species when they use the same breeding locations generation after generation," adds Oberhauser.

Organizations like Monarch Joint Venture, a partnership of federal and state agencies, nongovernmental programs, and academic programs dedicated to conserving the monarch, encourage gardeners to prioritize native milkweed, choosing species native to their regions—but that isn't as simple as it seems. Native milkweed seeds are scarce. A collaboration of government agencies and nonprofit conservation organizations that included the USDA Natural Resources Conservation Service and the Xerces Society launched Project Milkweed to increase the sources of milkweed seed in priority regions such as California, Arizona, New Mexico, Texas, and Florida. The Lady Bird Johnson Wildflower Center launched a similar initiative, also called Project Milkweed. The goal was to increase the abundance of milkweeds native to Texas, providing appropriate places for monarchs to lay their eggs during their northward spring migration through the Lone Star State. The goal was to collect and distribute Texas milkweed seeds to local growers who would, in turn, grow the seeds and sell the native milkweed to their customers.

The Wildflower Center hosted a Monarch Symposium that featured a speaker from the Native American Seed Company (a grower specializing in native seeds), who acknowledged the shortage of native milkweed seed had coincided with a spike in demand. Director of horticulture DeLong-Amaya recalls, "He told us, 'You can say we need to grow a million milkweeds . . . but I don't have the seed; there isn't that amount of seed being produced or left in the wild that I can collect.' So everyone wants to plant milkweed and can't find [native] milkweed, so they're panicking and planting tropical milkweed, and that's causing issues."

Hummingbirds are another species being loved to death. Thanks to the abundance of feeders in temperate climates like Louisiana and Texas, the Audubon Society is seeing more hummingbirds spending the winter in these areas instead of migrating farther south; even hummingbirds in more northern climates are staying put for the winter.

"It's a lack of nectar, a lack of food resources, that cause hummingbirds [to migrate]. One of the big questions hummingbird lovers need to ask, especially if they are feeding hummingbirds in the northern part of their ranges, is: 'Should we keep supplying nectar feeders late into the

Box 6-2
The Unexpected Consequence of Your Favorite Drink

Consumers are nuts about almond milk. Sales of the popular plant-based "milk" increased 25 percent between 2010 and 2015, making it the most popular milk substitute in the dairy case. During the same period, the market for traditional dairy milk decreased by more than $1 billion. But almond milk, made by grinding the nuts with water and straining out the pulp, has come under fire for potential harm to pollinators.

Fungicides used on almond trees appear to be fatal to honeybees. Research published in the *Journal of Economic Entomology* found that the chemicals, designed to fight fungi that attack almond trees, showed up in high levels in pollen. The researchers conducted three separate trials, in September, October, and November 2015. In the latter two trials, bees exposed to the doses of the fungicide iprodione recommended on the labels died at up to three times the rate of unexposed bees after ten days. The researchers are unclear on the mechanism and recommend longer trials.

The number of acres of almond orchards continues expanding alongside the growing demand for almond milk. The 1.3 million acres of almond orchards in California rely almost exclusively on honeybees for pollination, and some 60 percent of managed colonies spend at least some time on California almond farms. Given the intimate connection between honeybees and almonds, could drinking almond milk put additional strain on the pollinators? It depends.

Almond milk might not use a significant number of almonds. A 2015 lawsuit against Blue Diamond Growers, manufacturers of the popular Almond Breeze milk, alleged that the milk was made with just 2 percent almonds; the main ingredients were water, sugar, carrageenan, and sunflower lecithin, according to the lawsuit. The suit was later dismissed.

It might not be necessary to give up the plant-based beverage, especially if organic options are available to help protect bees from pesticide exposures.

fall when the hummingbirds should be gone?'" says LeBaron of the National Audubon Society. "They are incredibly adept at knowing the location and temporal availability of their food resources so they know where the nectar is, and they are going to keep going to those areas in their territories for as long as they live—and if you're not there next year and the hummingbirds come back, what then?"

The Buzz about Beekeeping

In the race to save pollinators, even the ancient hobby of beekeeping has come under fire. Critics warn that domesticated honeybees are detrimental to wild pollinators. In fact, a 2018 study published in the journal *Science* was titled "Conserving Honeybees Does Not Help Wildlife"; the study suggested that widespread efforts to tend hives of European honeybees were misguided. A growing number of researchers have suggested that, instead of treating honeybees like pollinators, beekeepers should see them as livestock, since managed colonies face issues similar to those faced by cows, pigs, and chickens raised in cramped conditions: overcrowding and homogenous diets depress their immune systems and increase the presence of pathogens. In one meta-analysis, more than half of studies found that competition for resources had negative effects on wild bees. (The research did not measure the direct effects of honeybees on wild bee fitness, abundance, or diversity; managed hives located in their native ranges had a lower impact on wild bees than those in hives situated in nonnative ranges.)

Says Lee-Mader of the Xerces Society, "Much of the discussion and the debate around pollinators and pollinator health over the last ten years has really been driven and fueled by the honeybee. . . . I think those of us who have worked on pollinator ecology for a long time, we feel a certain amount of affinity for the honeybee. But out of the whole range of pollinator issues, the honeybee is doing fairly well compared to some species. The honeybee is not going extinct anytime soon."

Thanks to the focus on honeybees, Lee-Mader believes that native pollinators might not get enough credit for their role in crop pollination. He cites squash and pumpkins as examples of crops where native bees outperform honeybees. But farmers, often failing to realize this, pay for hive rentals to ensure pollination takes place, even though native bees are more than equipped to do the work.

Lee-Mader notes that the native bees tend to be active early in the morning, often before the sun has fully risen, so farmers don't realize they're getting a free service. He hopes that beekeeping can evolve so people understand that honeybees are not the answer to every pollination challenge. We can't keep ignoring the larger health of the natural environment. "Unfortunately, when we look at beekeeping, especially large-scale beekeeping, there tend to be a lot of problematic and troubling questions that arise," he adds. "The honeybee, unfortunately, suffers from the challenges that have arisen from within the beekeeping industry, like the long-distance movement of bees . . . that has facilitated the spread of bee diseases."

One serious concern is the spread of pathogens between managed bees and wild bees. The majority of studies on the topic have found potential harm to wild species. The possibility that honeybees could be contributing to the decline of their wild brethren led researchers to test 169 bees from four families and eight genera for five common honeybee viruses: deformed wing virus, black queen cell virus, Israeli acute paralysis virus, Kashmir bee virus, and sacbrood virus. More than 80 of the wild bees were diagnosed with at least one virus, but virus levels were minimal—and significantly lower than the viral loads found in honeybees raised in hives. In at least two bee species, the alfalfa leafcutter bee (*Megachile rotundata*) and polyester bee (*Colletes inaequalis*), there appeared to be no threats to short-term survival despite being diagnosed with a mixture of common viruses that are lethal to honeybees. The researchers pointed out that their 2016 paper was the first to assess viral load in a broad spectrum of wild bees, and more data is needed to understand how common honeybee viruses affect additional native bee species at different stages of life.

The spread of viruses between honeybees and wild bees is not surprising. Farmers rent hives to pollinate their fields, but flowering crops, from almonds and apples to oilseed rape, bloom for a few weeks; honeybees need to forage for much longer periods (up to a full year in temperate climates) and can travel several miles to access nectar and pollinate crops, providing a service—and using resources—normally reserved for wild pollinators. In Spain, hive densities were almost four times higher in landscapes with large numbers of orange groves; after agricultural crops stopped blooming, the number of honeybees in the groves increased eight-fold, showing that there is a consistent spillover of managed honeybees from agricultural crops to natural habitats, which could hurt wild bees. Viruses can be spread when both species visit the same flowers. Moving hives between pollination sites is equivalent to bringing new, nonnative species to different areas. These dangers led the study authors to suggest that honeybee declines should be seen as an agricultural issue, not a threat to biodiversity. They also argued for policies such as hive size limits, location restrictions, and greater controls of managed hives in protective areas. The authors offered a firm directive, noting, "Honeybees may be necessary for crop pollination, but beekeeping is an agrarian activity that should not be confused with wildlife conservation."

Penn State's Grozinger embraces a less hard-core stance on the issue, noting that while it's currently popular to say that honeybees are destroying landscapes, she doesn't think that the data back up that view. "I don't think it's a zero-sum game where you have honeybees in the landscape, and therefore the wild bees go down," she says.

Novice beekeepers might be making life harder for honeybees. As the "save the bees" message spreads, the number of new beekeepers has increased. In 2015, the Florida Department of Agriculture reported a record number of registered beekeepers in the state, with 3,856 beekeepers maintaining 460,000 new colonies (up from 150,000 hives in 2007). Illinois has also reported a surge in new beekeepers, with 700 new beekeepers registering with the state Department of Agriculture in a single year, bringing the number to the highest level since 2005. Meanwhile, 300 new beekeepers have joined the Backyard Beekeepers Association in Spokane, Washington, since 2015.

Even though one of the Back Yard Beekeepers Association cofounders called uneducated beekeepers "one of the largest killers of local bee populations," most beginners lack adequate support to succeed. Even the most enthusiastic new beekeepers might struggle to maintain their hives without education and mentoring. According to some estimates, 70 percent of new beekeepers quit within the first two years.

Inexperienced beekeepers might not be equipped to recognize and treat pathogens like varroa mites. Bees from infected colonies could abandon their hives and merge with other colonies. Or when they die off, bees from other colonies will "rob" the honey from infected hives and bring it back to their colonies, spreading disease. Whether or not a colony is healthy can depend on the beekeeper's background and apicultural practices. Unfortunately, those practices are currently trending away from good science and management. An article in *American Bee Journal* notes a "strong mood shift" among aspiring beekeepers. Some want zero interaction with their bees, believing that feeding bees or smoking the hive (to keep bees calm during routine inspections) are acts against nature. The author explains that "some of these people do not want to have a discussion about the facts-of-life of bee management or the results of scientific research. Beekeepers help bees by the simple acts of feeding starving colonies, of adding frames of honey or brood when the bees need food, or of providing young larvae to create a new queen. . . ."

Given the hands-off approach that some new and "natural" beekeepers take to maintaining hives, it might not be surprising that beginning beekeepers experienced double the winter losses of professional beekeepers; beginners also had more signs of bacterial infections and heavier varroa infestations. Pesticides are the sole treatment option for varroa mites.

Novice beekeepers often want to steer clear of chemical treatments, which puts other hives at risk. Because small-scale beekeepers have hives spread across the landscape—as opposed to concentrated in agricultural areas—starting a hive without understanding how to maintain it increases the risk that viruses will spread. Hobbyist beekeepers have exacerbated the spread of pathogens and resistance to miticides and antibiotics, according to a recent study published in the *Journal of Economic Entomology*. After a few years of repeated losses, many beekeepers quit altogether.

Just as monarch releases have the potential to skew research, data collected from beginning beekeepers could be making the status of honeybee populations appear more dire than is warranted. Reports of abandoned hives have led to widespread concerns about Colony Collapse Disorder, but information about losses comes from voluntary surveys from beekeepers; beginning beekeepers—whose inexperience leads to greater losses—contributed to those surveys, and their die-offs became part of the scientific record. During the 2017–2018 season, for example, backyard beekeepers lost 46.3 percent of their colonies over the winter, compared with just 26.4 percent for commercial beekeepers.

Box 6-3
A Desire to Help the Bees Drives Honey Demand

The awareness of honeybee declines could be increasing honey sales as consumers look for opportunities to support pollinators. *Bee Culture* magazine reports that per capita honey consumption has experienced steady increases.

2010: 1.20 pounds per person
2011: 1.27 pounds per person
2012: 1.26 pounds per person
2013: 1.44 pounds per person
2014: 1.55 pounds per person
2015: 1.51 pounds per person
2016: 1.60 pounds per person

Prices have increased, too, from $1.60 per pound in 2010 to $2.07 per pound in 2016.

The demand for honey has led to some unscrupulous practices. Laboratory tests showed that more than 75 percent of the honey sold in US supermarkets was not fresh-from-the-hive at all. High-tech "ultra-filtering" procedures heat honey to high temperatures, filtering out all the pollen and making it impossible to determine whether honey came from legitimate sources.

The US Food and Drug Administration guidelines are lax. Manufacturers are not

Box 6-3 *continued*

allowed to add water or high-fructose corn syrup to products labeled as honey, but there are no restrictions about removing pollen. Vaughn Bryant, director of the Palynology Laboratory at Texas A&M University cites a lack of truth in labeling as the main reason consumers might be duped at the supermarket.

Bryant tested sixty jars, jugs, and plastic bears of honey purchased in ten states and the District of Columbia in 2011. The results showed that 100 percent of the honey purchased at drugstores, 77 percent of honey sold at big-box stores like Costco and Target, and 76 percent of the honey purchased at supermarkets contained no pollen. Manufacturers claim that pollen is removed before honey is bottled because consumers want crystal-clear honey (and unfiltered pollen particles can crystallize); supermarkets also prefer filtered honey because it has a longer shelf life. Pollen removal can have more sinister motivations, too. Without pollen, it's almost impossible to identify the region where it was produced; masking its geographic origin allows honey producers from certain countries, like China, to avoid additional tariffs. In a practice known as "honey laundering," manufacturers mask the countries of origin, sending honey through intermediary countries where it's relabeled.

Filtering pollen also makes it impossible to tell the floral source, according to Bryant. That means, for example, that clover honey can be labeled as sourwood honey and sold for $16 per eight-ounce jar rather than the typical price for clover honey, under $4 per eight-ounce jar. "Without pollen, the consumer has no idea what they're buying," he explains, "and there's no easy way to verify it."

Small-scale beekeepers argue that removing pollen is not necessary; traditional filtering (used when honey is extracted from the hive) removes most bee parts, waste, and debris from the honey without affecting the pollen content. Truly local honey retains pollen: 100 percent of the tested samples purchased at farmer's markets, food co-ops, and "natural" markets like Trader Joe's contained full amounts of pollen—which ensures that both the flavor and nutritional value of the sweet stuff is retained.

After the study came out, Mark Jensen, past president of the American Honey Producers Association, remarked, "Elimination of all pollen can only be achieved by ultra-filtering, and this filtration process does nothing but cost money and diminish the quality of the honey. In my judgment, it is pretty safe to assume that any ultra-filtered honey on store shelves is Chinese honey, and it's even safer to assume that it entered the country uninspected and in violation of federal law."

To avoid being a victim of "honey laundering," buy honey from local beekeepers who are willing to answer questions about their hives and their honey-extraction and processing practices.

Box 6-4

Beekeepers Feel the Sting of Stolen Hives

Between December and March, beekeepers send millions of hives to California to pollinate almond trees. Not all of the hives make it back home.

"The number of beehive thefts is increasing," explains Jay Freeman, a detective with the Butte County (California) Sheriff's Office. In California, 1,734 hives were stolen during peak almond pollination season in 2016. In Butte County alone, the number of stolen hives jumped from 200 in 2015 to 400 in 2016, according to Freeman.

Denise Qualls, a California bee broker who arranges contracts between beekeepers and almond growers, isn't surprised that beehive thefts are on the rise. It takes more than 2 million beehives to pollinate California almonds. Currently, beekeepers are paid $200 per hive for pollination services (compared with $130 per hive in 2010). To complicate matters, bee brokers who arrange contracts between beekeepers and almond growers are discovering that there are not enough beehives to go around, driving up demand, rental costs—and thefts. Because of the expertise required to steal hives, the general consensus is that beekeepers are behind the heists. "Beekeepers have the knowledge and equipment to go in and take the hives, and [they have] the market to profit from them," Qualls says.

Thieves targeting hives to rent during pollination season are not making off with one or two hives. Butte County reported several large-scale hive thefts ranging from 64 to 200 hives swiped at a time. The locations of almond orchards—rural areas with acres of trees, few homesteads and almost no surveillance—make it harder for growers to monitor hives and easier for thieves to target them.

Most hives are unmarked, making it impossible to identify hives that might be stolen. Beekeepers who do brand each of their hives with the names and numbers of their apiaries often fall victim to creative thieves who remove the frames (the guts of the hive that are covered with bees and laden with honey) and put them in new, unmarked hive bodies. "Thieves are going after easily accessible hives and unmarked hives," says Freeman. "Someone who knows how to handle them can move 200 hives in a matter of minutes."

Because stolen hives are hard to detect, it's difficult for law enforcement to catch and prosecute thieves and return hives to beekeepers. When thieves are caught, the penalties are harsh. A beekeeper who stood trial for the theft of sixty-four hives that he pilfered from Butte County was convicted of grand theft of an animal—a felony in California—and sentenced to ninety days in county jail and three years' probation.

Insurance policies are cost prohibitive, according to Freeman, and few beekeepers are reimbursed for their losses. To combat bee theft, some beekeepers are putting

Box 6-4 *continued*

GPS units in their hives and some growers are hiring guards to patrol almond orchards overnight.

"For the growers, this is their entire livelihood," Qualls says. "If someone steals their bees, it hurts their crops."

Box 6-5
Are Bee Hotels Bad for Bees?

Bee hotels are generating a lot of buzz. Fashioned from a combination of reeds, hollow flower stems, cardboard rolls, and wood blocks with drilled holes, bee hotels provide nesting habitat for solitary bees and other pollinators. When bees cover the entrance to the entrance hole, it's a sign that an egg was laid inside.

Of the 5,000 native bee species in North America, about 30 percent build their nests in aboveground cavities and tunnels. Blue orchard bees (*Osmia lignaria*), small mason bees (*Osmia pumila*), unarmed leafcutter bees (*Megachile inermis*), and giant resin bees (*Megachile sculpturalis*) are among the natives that might check into bee hotels.

Increased awareness of the plight of pollinators has led to a bee hotel construction boom. But as nest boxes pop up in parks, college campuses, businesses, and backyards, their effectiveness has been called into question. In one study of 600 bee hotels in Toronto, researchers found more than 27,000 bees and wasps had "checked in" to the bee hotels. Nonnative (introduced) bees nested at almost 33 percent of sites, and native wasps were guests in almost three-quarters of bee hotels. So, the "bee hotels" attracted far more wasps than bees. Parasites were also a problem: The thin walls and densely-packed populations made it easier for diseases to spread, which could lead to the demise of all hotel residents. The problems ranged from pollen mites to chalkbrood.

Although bee hotels might not be a panacea for native bee populations and might, in fact, lead to the spread of disease, the artificial nesting sites could offer an unexpected benefit: the hotels can help shed light on wild pollinator behavior. Researchers in the United Kingdom collected leaf scraps left behind by leafcutter bees to learn which plants the bees preferred for nesting; and Australian scientists collected pollen bread (bee food) from nests and then used genetics to figure out where the pollen came from in order to gather data about which plants bees are most reliant on.

Researchers warn against falling for misleading claims about the potential for bee hotels to bolster wild bee populations, warning that this kind of "bee-washing" can mask the real issues and make it seem like putting a nesting site in the garden is sufficient to overcome pollinator decline.

Figure 6-2: Brightly painted beehive supers were used to create a colorful bee hotel that attracts solitary bee species.

Making Amends

Highlighting the possible downsides of good intentions is not meant to dissuade public efforts to help pollinators. Rather, letting concerned citizens know what could go wrong—and providing education and resources to minimize those unintended consequences—can help pollinator populations bounce back. Experts support pollinator-protection initiatives, including even some of the "harmful" practices such as releasing monarchs, maintaining gardens of tropical milkweed, and beekeeping.

Jepsen, director of endangered species and aquatic programs at the Xerces Society, acknowledges that hands-on experience with wildlife, including monarchs, can be valuable to children, helping them understand the fragility of the species and the need to be good stewards of the environment in order to save them. Rather than ordering the butterflies online from commercial farms, Jepsen advocates finding monarch caterpillars or caterpillars of other locally common butterflies or moths and bringing them into the classroom to observe, which minimizes the potential downsides of releasing mass-reared butterflies. "It's really important to understand the species that you're trying to protect," she says. "Often, we need to act before we fully understand why a species is declining, and it's really important to continue to do research to answer the most relevant questions and to continually adjust conservation strategies as new research becomes available."

Planting habitat is one of the most important conservation strategies. A 2017 study by the US Geological Survey estimates that 1.8 billion new stems of milkweed must be planted before monarchs will rebound to sustainable population sizes. It takes 28.5 milkweed stems to produce a single monarch overwintering in Mexico. To increase the population to 127 million monarchs will require 3.62 billion milkweed stems; the current population is just 1.34 billion stems. The goal of planting additional milkweed is to almost double the population of monarchs before 2020. Native milkweed is best, but gardens with tropical milkweed need not be ripped up. Gardeners in USDA plant hardiness zones 8–11 can cut their milkweed to the ground two to three times per season to remove diseased parts of the plant and allow new, healthy foliage to grow to support the next generations of monarchs. According to some estimates, planting tropical milkweed has helped increase the number of monarchs overwintering in Mexico from 57 million butterflies to 200 million.

While milkweed is essential for monarchs, planting it to the exclusion of other nectar-rich plants is a mistake. A diverse collection of native plants supports the largest number of pollinator species. Planting native species helps increase pollinator density and diversity—and the larger the patches of native plants, the better. One study found that greater densities of wild bees were observed in patches over 30 square meters

(323 square feet) compared to smaller patches. Even at small scales, wild bees are sensitive to the richness of floral resources, and planting gardens with more-diverse native plant species helps conserve wild pollinators.

Lee-Mader believes that filling gardens with native plants will be far more effective than beekeeping. "There's now more and more media about this," he points out, "highlighting the fact that pollinators seem to be faring worse, and the solution is not to go out and keep honeybees, but the solution is really to go out and [create] habitat."

Still, beekeeping is still a worthwhile hobby, and committed beekeepers need not abandon their hives, says Penn State's Grozinger. "In

Box 6-6
Don't Forget about Trees

When it comes to pollinator habitat, milkweed and flowering (nectar-producing) plants get all the attention—but trees are also essential in pollinator landscapes. Windbreaks (rows of trees and shrubs on the edges of farm fields) planted between neonicotinoid-treated crops and pollinator-friendly plants can help prevent pesticide drift; the roots of the trees help filter pesticides in the soil. Windbreaks also reduce wind speeds, thus boosting pollinator efficiency (bees often stop pollinating when it gets too windy).

Trees used in windbreaks should not be attractive to pollinators. Using evergreens such as Colorado blue spruce (*Picea pungens*), Black Hills spruce (*Picea glauca*), and Norway spruce (*Picea abies*) for windbreaks ensures that pollinators will not be on the plants when adjacent crops are sprayed.

Farmers often remove windbreaks to accommodate irrigation. As the number of acres under center-pivot systems has increased, so too has the number of trees removed or topped. (Farmers are currently adding an estimated 26,000 acres under center-pivot irrigation every year.) Removing trees could hurt yields. Research shows that cropland bordered by windbreaks increases winter wheat yield by 23 percent, soybean yield by 15 percent, and corn yield by 13 percent.

Establishing pollinator habitat without incorporating trees is only an incomplete solution, particularly if the habitat is near fields where pesticides are sprayed or coated seeds are planted. All habitat should also include hedgerows, especially if a lot of pesticide is being applied close by.

many ways, I love that people are wanting to keep bees and, through the bees, are learning more about the environment around them. It's a great way to understand the phenology of flowering plants in your area . . . and a great window into the natural world," she says. "I do deal with a lot of people who are like, 'I want to help the bees. I'm going to get a honeybee colony.' Unless you really want to have a pet that requires a lot of care, you should set up wild bee nesting boxes or plant pollinator gardens; that will be more beneficial in the long run—even for the honeybees in your neighborhood—than setting up a hive. Ultimately, I think it will probably be more satisfying for people, too."

CHAPTER 7

Stand Up and Be Counted

Elaine Tucker learned how to spot monarch eggs on milkweed plants during summer camp. She recalls going in search of eggs when no one was looking, checking the undersides of the bright green leaves for the telltale oval white or off-white eggs with small vertical ridges on their edges, plucking four eggs from the leaves of the milkweed plants and taking them home. Two monarchs hatched, delighting the curious child and triggering a self-described "obsession" with the butterflies, which has followed her into adulthood.

In 1998, concerned over reports of declining monarch populations, Tucker signed up as a citizen scientist with the Monarch Larva Monitoring Project. "I'm never going to be a lobbyist," she says. "I don't write letters to my legislators . . . but I do care about a lot of issues, about the environment and the impact on the monarchs, and I see [the Monarch Larva Monitoring Project] as a way that I can help those who are helping the things I care about."

Monarch expert Karen Oberhauser started MLMP in 1991 at the University of Minnesota as a grassroots effort. Her goal was to collect long-term data from citizen scientists to learn about monarch populations and milkweed habitat at breeding grounds across North America. Citizen scientists commit to observing a specific patch of milkweed and reporting when the plant emerges, when the first egg appears, stages of larval development, and sightings of migrating monarchs.

Tucker signed on to observe a patch of milkweed plants at the Eastman Nature Center in Minneapolis. Each week, she walks a trail to a sheltered patch of milkweed, moving the stems on each plant to and fro to check for eggs and larvae beneath the bright green leaves and recording her observations. She repeats the process each week between May and September—the peak times for monarch sightings in Minnesota—and uploads her findings through the MLMP website.

Tucker notes that good policy requires hard data and that is what citizen scientists provide. "I'm seeing the help I want to give to the monarch being spread farther than I could reach myself," she says, "and that's what citizen science is about."

Although researchers coined the term "citizen science" in the 1990s, it is not a new concept. The first examples of the practice, also called community science, crowd science, crowdsourced science, participatory science, and volunteer monitoring, date back centuries. In the 1700s, a Danish bishop enlisted his clergy to collect natural objects and record observations to describe species in different regions of Europe. Naturalist Henry David Thoreau collected flowering dates, leaf-out dates, and arrival dates of migrating birds in Concord, Massachusetts, between 1851 and 1858—information that is still used to assess shifts in these annual events. And the Cayuga Bird Club in Ithaca, New York, started recording arrival dates of migrating birds in 1903. Data collected through these amateur efforts provides valuable historical information about long-term environmental changes and how they're affecting migration patterns, flowering dates, pollinator populations, and more.

The number of citizen-science projects has exploded, thanks to technologies like the Internet, GPS, and advanced monitoring devices that make it easier for the public to collect and contribute information and for scientists to manage data. Projects can range from recording flowering dates and counting the number of hummingbirds visiting feeders to using high-tech equipment to map bat echolocation. Private citizens can often offer more data and more-diverse observations than conventional research.

Two categories of citizen-science projects are growing the fastest. The first is developing large-scale data sets over longer periods of time than would be possible for professional scientists to gather on their own. The second involves projects too regional or limited in scope for research scientists to want to tackle.

Although we don't know the total number of citizen scientists engaged in either one-time or ongoing research projects, the level of participation in pollinator projects is staggering. Western Monarch Milkweed Mapper invites citizen scientists to take photos of monarchs and milkweed to help researchers understand breeding behaviors and population distribution of both species. Bumble Bee Watch takes a similar approach, gathering photos and data to create a virtual bumblebee collection so that scientists can better understand the conservation needs of the species. The Great Sunflower Project, the largest citizen-science project in the nation, engages 150,000 volunteers to collect data about the number of pollinators visiting plants. (It takes its name from an original focus on pollinators visiting Lemon Queen sunflowers.) Since 2012, three citizen-science organizations—the [United States] Citizen Science Association, the Australian Citizen Science Association, and the European Citizen Science Association—have popped up to support projects, fostering collaborations between organizations.

"Citizen science has increased a lot in the last few years, [and] hav-

Figure 7-1: A bumblebee covered with small grains of pollen lands on a hibiscus flower in search of nectar.

ing these associations shows that we've reached a point where there is a need," explains Meg Domroese, land-trust program director at Gathering Waters: Wisconsin's Alliance for Land Trusts.

The authors of a study on crowdsourced data called citizen science "a powerful force for scientific inquiry" that has "transformed the practice of science." Involving the general public in field research is essential to understanding—and protecting—pollinators.

Citizen scientists provided the data that demonstrated sharp declines in monarch populations. Thanks to data collected from multiple sites over thirty-six years, researchers learned that the abundance of monarch butterflies plummeted 95 percent from the 1980s to the 2000s and faced an 86 percent risk of extinction within fifty years. Projects like Monarch Watch, Monarch Joint Venture, Journey North, and the Monarch Larva Monitoring Project at the University of Minnesota also engage citizen science in data collection to better understand breeding, migration, and populations.

"One of the reasons that we know what we need to do to preserve monarch populations is that so many citizen scientists have been involved in collecting data on monarchs over, in some cases, decades," notes Oberhauser.

Digging for More Data

Counting the number of hummingbirds visiting a feeder, logging the dates when monarchs appear (and disappear) from a garden, or recording the bee species that alight on a specific flower might not seem like a big deal, but without citizen scientists, the data sets would be too limited for biologists to assess potential patterns or tease out trends. Scientists are ill-equipped to conduct extensive fieldwork solo. Large-scale data collection wouldn't be possible without the help of volunteer citizen scientists. "We've been working diligently to pull together data from all of these projects, [and] it's amazing how much we've learned about

Box 7-1

Putting Milkweed on the Map

Helping monarchs is as simple as taking photos of the butterflies or milkweed plants, uploading photos to MonarchMilkweedMapper.org, compiling basic details about the sightings, and submitting the information to a long-term citizen-science project. The project, a partnership between the Xerces Society, the Idaho Department of Fish and Game, the Washington [State] Department of Fish and Wildlife, and the National Fish and Wildlife Foundation, launched in 2017.

Prior to launching the website, the partners used records from a number of sources, including museums, online herbaria, botanists, and land managers to compile a significant database of monarch and milkweed occurrences, but they still lacked sufficient data to create conservation plans. Citizen scientists were identified as the best method for gathering additional data.

Loss of milkweed was identified as the most significant threat to monarch populations in the eastern United States, but less is known about what could be causing declines in the western region of the country. As its name suggests, Western Monarch Milkweed Mapper focuses on monarchs and milkweeds in eleven Western states: Washington, Oregon, California, Nevada, Idaho, Montana, Wyoming, Colorado, Utah, Arizona, and New Mexico.

The project relies on citizen scientists to collect data to help researchers better understand geographic distributions of monarchs and their host plants. The data will be used to map populations, pinpoint important breeding areas, and provide information about where milkweed is abundant (and in what kinds of habitats), so that researchers can better understand conservation needs, including where planting milkweed and nectar plants would be most effective. The website and corresponding smartphone app provide a color-coded map of monarch and milkweed sightings and monarch breeding areas; it also includes data on more than 40,000 monarch and milkweed records dating back to the 1900s.

Mark Klym, information specialist and coordinator of the Texas Wildscapes program at Texas Parks and Wildlife, explained that the department fielded multiple questions per week from concerned citizens asking what was happening to the monarch population and why TPWD wasn't treating them as priorities in its conservation plan. Western Monarch Milkweed Mapper was created, in part, to showcase a commitment to making a difference.

Citizen scientists stepped up to help. In the first ten months after the Milkweed Mapper launched, 660 participants registered with the site and submitted 450 new records. A total of 128 monarch sightings and 211 milkweed records were generated. The greatest number of sightings were reported in Washington, Oregon, and California.

what we need to do. The data is really helping us set population goals, understand the kinds of habitat that are good for [pollinators], and understand what drives behavior," Oberhauser says. "It's hugely important in understanding and preserving our pollinator populations."

Gathering the kind of long-term data that scientists need in order to observe patterns and make recommendations takes time. Gretchen LeBuhn, professor of biology at San Francisco State University and director of the Great Sunflower Project, launched the citizen-science initiative in 2008.

LeBuhn was conducting research in the California wine regions when she discovered that several specialist pollinators had disappeared in Napa and Sonoma Counties. She came up with a project that required sending a graduate student into the field to track species. Before it launched, she decided that asking a solo researcher to gather data was not the best approach. "I realized the important metric was pollination service [or the number of visits a plant received in an hour] for different landscapes," she recalls, "and once we had that insight, we realized that almost anyone could count how many bees visited a flower over a period of time."

LeBuhn reached out to master gardeners in several states in the southeastern United States to recruit citizen scientists for the inaugural season of the Great Sunflower Project and hoped that 1,500 gardeners would sign up. To her great surprise, word spread fast and 25,000 eager citizen scientists registered for the project. LeBuhn mailed Lemon Queen sunflower seeds to all participants, along with instructions for their participation: plant the seeds, count pollinator visits, record and submit the data. The first season was lackluster: only a small percentage of the sunflower seeds germinated, leaving eager citizen scientists without plants for their pollinator observations. But the project marched on. "I didn't have any idea how it was going to go that first year. I didn't even know if we'd get anybody signing up. Once we had such broad interest,

Figure 7-2: As pollinator habitat disappears, establishing natural areas with a diversity of plant species is more important than ever.

my vision for what could happen with the project changed," LeBuhn recalls. "People were really worried [about pollinators], and I had a lot of people write to me with questions and notes to express that they were so happy that I had started the Great Sunflower Project. I realized that it was a way for me to give out information based on science about what we knew while also getting information."

Data started trickling in. The original protocol had citizen scientists counting all of the pollinators that landed on Lemon Queen sunflowers in a one-hour period and reporting their data. In 2010, the project expanded to include a wider range of garden plants, from bee balm (*monarda*) and purple coneflower (*Echinacea purpurea*) to cosmos and coreopsis; counts were reduced to five minutes. More than 150,000 citizen scientists from all fifty states have signed on to participate in the Great Sunflower Project over the last decade, making it the largest pollinator-specific citizen-science project in the world. Between 5 and 10 percent of participants submit pollinator data (others plant sunflowers and establish habitat but never turn in their observations). The project releases annual reports with raw data and highlights from the research, but despite gathering millions of data points, no large-scale, peer-reviewed paper has been published to report the findings—yet. LeBuhn believes it takes a significant data set to begin to make broad statements about pollinators, and that work is just beginning. "If we can maintain participation at reasonable levels, it means we can start to see patterns," she says. "It gives us the potential to track, over time, how things are changing, and it might even provide some sort of warning system if we see year-over-year national declines."

The data have already revealed some patterns. Pollination service in the northeastern United States is strong, perhaps owing to the expansive swaths of green in New England. The Upper Midwest has lower-than-expected pollination service. Most of the West Coast, including the Pacific Northwest, has good pollinator service with some exceptions:

pollinator populations are far less robust in California's Central Valley, which LeBuhn attributes to persistent use of pesticides on local farms. The Great Sunflower Project has too few citizen scientists in Colorado and some of the major agricultural states to justify making statements about their pollination services. LeBuhn is attempting to recruit more volunteers in those areas. "We're just getting to the point where we have enough data to start speaking to these things," LeBuhn says. "Every year that we [continue the project] and that people are willing to contribute data, we get closer to spotting those trends. It's an extraordinary gift that people have given to us through their participation."

Citizen scientists involved with the Great Sunflower Project started collecting data after a problem was identified. In Wisconsin, the Department of Natural Resources wanted help gathering information about bat populations before there was a problem. Recognizing that it was just a matter of time before the first cases of white-nose syndrome were diagnosed in the state, the Wisconsin DNR wanted to assess local bat colonies before the disease hit. With just two biologists on staff, monitoring bats across the entire state would have been impossible without research support. The department partnered with the Urban Ecology Center to engage citizen scientists. "Community scientists can help expand the amount of data we were out there collecting and the number of surveys we could do per year, and really expand our efforts," says Jennifer Callaghan, research and community science coordinator for the Milwaukee-based nonprofit.

In 2007, the Urban Ecology Center mounted a stationary acoustic device at its Riverside Park location. The microphone and recorder can pick up the frequencies of passing bats, providing biologists with important information about migration patterns and the times bats were most active. The technology, while valuable, was limited to recording bats in a single location that represented only a small fraction of bats in the area. To gather a wider swatch of information, a team of citizen scientists were given mobile acoustic devices to gather data at their own locations. The nonprofit also established driving and paddling routes along roads and waterways that were known bat habitat so that citizen scientists could collect additional population data.

When the first cases of WNS were detected in Wisconsin in 2015, researchers had amassed eight years of data and were able to compare populations pre- and post-disease to learn how it affected local bats. Thanks to citizen scientists, researchers determined that bat populations had dropped up to 75 percent in certain caves. The acoustic monitoring devices also recorded decreased bat populations in a fast-growing neighborhood, which Callaghan attributes to light pollution. Scientists might not have fully appreciated how WNS and urban development were harming bats without the contributions of citizen scientists. "Our goal [at the Urban Ecology Center] is not just to use volunteers in a data-collection role but to engage them in the entire scientific process and to make them realize that the can contribute to science meaningfully," Callaghan says.

Finding volunteers can be as simple as putting out a call on social media. The Audubon Society has engaged volunteers to gather data for its annual Christmas Bird Count and Breeding Bird Survey, generating the two largest bird-specific data sets available to researchers. In 2017, citizen scientists counted 58,478,151 birds during the Christmas Bird Count. Federal agencies have used the citizen-scientist-generated data to help inform decisions about birds; citizen scientists have also laid the foundation for hundreds of peer-reviewed articles. The Audubon Society used community-generated data collected over three decades to create the Audubon Birds and Climate Report, which used temperature, precipitation, seasonal changes, and greenhouse-gas-emission scenarios to map how birds might shift their ranges to adapt. The future projections—for 2020, 2050, and 2080—showed that 314 species, including 126 classified as "climate endangered," are expected to lose more than 50 percent of their ranges by 2080.

The rufous hummingbird is the sole pollinator on the list. The long-distance migrants, with ranges from Alaska to Mexico, follows flowers. Its southbound migration starts in June, as the hummingbirds pass through high mountain meadows and feed on abundant wildflowers. In February, March, and April the hummingbirds return north, traveling from Mexico through the southwestern states, where desert flowers are blooming. Based on citizen-science data, ecologists have projected that rufous hummingbirds will lose 100 percent of their non-breeding range in the United States by 2080.

The bird counts were so popular and the observations were so valuable to scientists that the National Audubon Society decided to establish a pollinator-specific citizen-science project: Hummingbirds at Home, launched in 2013. Since then, more than 34,000 citizen scientists have signed on to collect data about where hummingbirds gather nectar, how often hummingbirds are feeding, and which species are showing up in their yards. LeBaron of the Audubon Society says the project is "still in its early stages," but he hopes that the nonprofit will release a report that summarizes some of the findings soon. "Hummingbirds have a tremendous and passionate following, and the people who get involved with Hummingbirds at Home develop attachments, not just to the birds but to their locations. You develop attachments and, over time, recognize changes, which makes you worry and want to do something to address those worries and encourage others to think about addressing those issues," explains LeBaron.

The Reliability of Community-Sourced Data

Despite the potential benefits of engaging citizens in pollinator research, critics warn that data gathered from nonscientists might not be accurate and that relying on it for research could impact results. While some studies, including 2012 research published in *Wildlife Society Bulletin* and the *Journal of Wildlife Management,* found citizen-science data to be comparable to data collected from scientists, other studies paint a murkier picture.

Box 7-2
Ten Principles of Citizen Science

The European Citizen Science Association has developed ten key principles that provide the foundation for the best practices in citizen science.

1. Citizen-science projects involve citizens in scientific endeavors to generate new knowledge or understanding. Citizens can participate in projects as contributors, collaborators, or project leaders.
2. Citizen-science projects have genuine science outcomes.
3. Both professional scientists and citizen scientists benefit from participating in these projects.
4. Citizen scientists can participate in multiple stages of a project: developing research questions, designing methods, gathering data, and communicating the results.
5. Citizen scientists should receive feedback on the project, including information about how the data is being used.
6. Citizen science is a research approach, and variables should be considered and controlled.
7. The meta-data and results of citizen science projects should be made available to the public in open-source formats.
8. The contributions of citizen scientists must be acknowledged in project results and publications.
9. Citizen-science projects should be evaluated for their scientific output, data quality, participant experience, and societal and policy impacts.
10. Leaders of citizen-science projects should consider legal and ethical issues surrounding copyright, intellectual property, data-sharing agreements, confidentiality, attribution, and environmental impacts of their activities.

A study published in *Conservation Biology* trained thirteen citizen scientists to observe and record the visits of pollinator superfamilies (bees, wasps, flies) to flowers in seventeen specific locations; the volunteers were asked to further classify specific species such as members of the *Apoidea* superfamily. The researchers compared reports from citizen scientists and professionals. There was significant overlap in certain data, including the abundance of honeybees and non-honeybees at different sites, but professional scientists observed twice as many bee groups as the citizen scientists did. The study's authors concluded that citizen-sci-

Box 7-3
Pollinators Seek Out Urban Addresses

How do pollinators fare among skyscrapers, freeways, and urban sprawl? Quite well, it turns out. One study showed that there were as many bees in urban landscapes as in farmland and nature reserves—and bee diversity was actually higher in cities than on farms. A separate study found that native bees provided adequate pollination services in San Francisco despite the urban setting. The amount of pollination a plant received was more strongly associated with the density of flowers than the size of the garden, the researchers noted.

To test pollinator service in urban areas, researchers put three tomato plants in gardens across San Francisco; each plant was divided into a set of floral clusters that received a different pollination treatment: one cluster was covered to prevent bee visits (and tomatoes were limited to self-pollination); another cluster was left open for native bee pollination; and two sets were covered and artificially pollinated. At the end of the two-week study period, the plants were moved to the university greenhouse and allowed to grow under uniform conditions. The tomato plants available for bee pollination outperformed the plants in other clusters, growing larger tomatoes in greater numbers.

Researcher Gretchen LeBuhn, a professor of biology at San Francisco State University, was "surprised" by the results, saying, "We expected to find that there was not adequate pollinator service in the city, but in fact we actually found bees do quite well. . . . What this shows is that just because you're in an urban setting doesn't mean that bees aren't providing important pollinator service, and not just honeybees. Our wild bees here are providing all the service you might need."

While this seems like good news, LeBuhn cautioned that if native bee populations are not sustained, it could lead to significant declines in urban agriculture.

Multiple efforts have been undertaken to explore the health, abundance, and diversity of pollinators in urban areas. The Urban Pollinator Project at the University of Washington is investigating how to increase the number of pollinators buzzing around cities. The effort includes a citizen-science project to quantify the pollination services provided by native bumblebees in community gardens across Seattle. Citizen scientists are collecting data on cherry tomato yield.

Cherry tomatoes can self-pollinate, but the size of fruit and overall yield increases when bees pollinate the plants. Tomatoes are among a small group of plants that includes blueberries and kiwi that cannot be pollinated by honeybees because the pollen is packed so tightly into the anther that it's difficult to access. These fruits rely on

Box 7-3 *continued*

"buzz pollination" via native bees. The bees contract their flight muscles, causing a vibration that is directed toward the anther, which explodes and coats the bees in pollen.

The Urban Pollination Project recruited citizen scientists to grow three tomato plants (using a protocol similar to the one used in San Francisco): yield was assessed for an "open" plant available to bees for buzz pollination, a covered (self-pollinated) plant, and a plant that received both bee pollination and hand-pollination. The goal is to run the project through the end of 2019 and use the citizen-scientist-generated data to estimate the number of native bees and how efficiently they're pollinating. Ultimately, researchers want to understand how features of the urban landscape such as land use and pesticide applications affect the numbers of bees and urban crop yields.

These kinds of studies lead to a greater understanding of how the environment affects pollinators. While cities might not be thought of as havens for biodiversity, pollinators are found in abundance in some urban areas; as urbanization expands, preserving pollinator populations becomes more important than ever.

ence observations have limited utility and "may not reliably reflect the abundance or frequency of occurrence of specific pollinator species or groups." In a separate analysis, researchers reviewed sixty-three studies, comparing the data collected from citizen scientists versus data collected from professional researchers, and found that less than 62 percent of the data met minimum thresholds for scientific accuracy. This was despite the fact that most (73 percent) of the abstracts in individual studies used terms like *accurate*, *reliable*, and *statistically similar* to describe the data collected from citizen scientists; just 8 percent of researchers used terms like *overestimated*, *contradictions*, or *no significant correlations* to describe data from laypeople.

Domroese, the land trust program director, acknowledges criticisms about the reliability of community-generated data but contends that the right protocols and appropriate use of technology can help overcome the issues, noting, "Where there are good projects and good protocols and quality checks, citizen scientists do every bit as well as scientists."

Volunteers often receive some degree of training as part of their participation in citizen-science projects. In the Great Pollinator Project, for example, organizers created online quizzes to allow volunteers to test their knowledge of different bee species. The protocol also called for basic data collection, asking citizen scientists to identify whether the floral visitors were bumblebees or not (rather than requesting specifics on the species); volunteers were also encouraged to submit photographs of their observations so that scientists could confirm their identifications. To add another layer of education for citizen scientists—while improving the accuracy of their data collection—researchers from the American Museum of Natural History hosted field days that served as mini training sessions and boosted volunteer confidence, according to Domroese.

Though three decades of data collection have turned Tucker, the citizen scientist, into a skilled observer, she admits that recognizing the different stages of monarch development is difficult to learn. Monarch larvae develop in stages called *instars* that refer to the number of times

Box 7-4
Three Ways the Public Participates in Citizen Science

There is no one-size-fits-all citizen-science project. The Center for Advancement of Information Science Education has established three basic models for public participation in scientific research.

- *Contributory projects*: Scientists design these projects and ask citizen scientists to contribute data. The data included in these projects might come from historical records, journals, and other public observations.
- *Collaborative projects*: Scientists might be responsible for the initial design of collaborative projects, but the citizen scientists, in addition to gathering data, might also help refine the design, analyze data, and share the findings.
- *Co-created projects*: As the name suggests, citizen scientists work hand in hand with scientists to develop co-created projects, taking a role in all aspects of the research. Citizen scientists come up with the ideas and implement the protocols for some of the projects in this category.

they have shed their larval skin: a first-instar larva has a small black head capsule; a second-instar larva starts to show striping; in the final stage of development before a larva becomes a chrysalis—the fifth instar—the caterpillar will be 3,000 times larger than the day it hatched. The entire process takes two weeks. MLMP used to provide printouts to citizen scientists to help them compare their field observations with black-and-white pictures of different stages of development. The project now provides videos to improve the odds of accurate identifications. At the nature center where Tucker collects data, specimens are on hand so that citizen scientists can review them before going out into the field to do their counts.

"These are programs that have been designed by scientists, but they have been designed with protocols that are accessible so that people can get as involved as they want in the science," adds Oberhauser.

Overcoming Stigmas

As citizen science gains traction and the public becomes more aware of pollinators' struggles, public participation grows. Projects that involve "attractive" species like sunflowers and butterflies tend to get more volunteers than ones with less-charismatic pollinators. Callaghan admits it was challenging for the Urban Ecology Center to recruit volunteers when the bat-monitoring project began. "Back when we first started, we had a very small group," she says. "There are still a lot of old stereotypes [that bats will] swoop down and start sucking your blood . . . or get tangled in your hair . . . or that they carry rabies. I think as people start to recognize the importance of [bats] and their role in the ecosystem . . . they're able to get past the initial stigma. Last year, we had the most attendees of any bat project in all the years we've been doing it."

Participating in citizen-science projects can help overcome phobias about bats. A study published in the journal *Human Ecology Review* explored whether citizen science could change hearts, minds, and behaviors. Scientists from the Center for Biodiversity and Conservation at the American Museum of Natural History and the New York City Department of Parks and Recreation partnered with the Great Pollinator Project to identify urban areas with good pollinator habitat, to better understand bee activity in the city, and to improve park management to the benefit of native bees. Beginning in 2007, the team recruited volunteer "Bee Watchers" to collect data about the number of bees visiting flowers at predetermined sites throughout New York City. Over the next four seasons, 125 Bee Watchers submitted 1,500 observations from all five boroughs. Domroese, one of the researchers involved in the study, notes that "data brings to light the active role we've taken in impacting our environment and leading to solutions to what we need to do about it."

Data gathered by citizen scientists also helped guide decisions about which areas should be left alone to allow ground-nesting bees to thrive.

The citizen scientists who planted pollinator habitat for the North Carolina Butterfly Highway were initially worried about attracting certain pollinators to their gardens. Hjarding of the North Carolina Wildlife Federation recalls a conversation with one resident who confessed to being afraid of bees before planting the gardens, explaining, "It helped people care. Instead of thinking, 'Oh, I'm afraid of it,' it helps break down some of those barriers and becomes a curiosity, an awakening and an interest. One woman told me, 'Before I met you, every time I saw a bee, I'd swat at the thing or take something and kill it; but now that I've been part of the [North Carolina] Butterfly Highway, I think twice about it and think, 'Maybe that bee's actually doing something in this yard and it doesn't care about me.'"

The North Carolina Butterfly Highway created some good-natured competition between neighbors who compared the number of butterflies and bees visiting their gardens. It also helped participants move past their fears and misconceptions, allowing them to develop an appreciation for the fragile creatures.

Box 7-5
Citizen Scientists Honor the Stars

What do Leonardo DiCaprio, Kate Winslet, Donald Trump, and Arnold Schwarzenegger have in common? All of these celebrities have creatures named in their honor.

The Donald Trump moth (*Neopalpa donaldtrumpi*), named for the "blond" coif of scales on its head, was discovered just before the forty-fifth president took office; the moth makes its home on the West Coast of North America between California and Mexico. Kate Winslet has a beetle named in her honor (*Agra katewinsletae*). In 2018, a new water beetle was discovered during a field trip to Borneo. Scientists at Ateneo de Manila University in the Philippines led a field trip for citizen scientists to share information about capturing, studying, and identifying new species. Citizen scientists were allowed to name the new beetle and voted to call it Leonardo DiCaprio—*Grouvellinus leonardodicaprioi*—to honor the actor's environmental activism.

To date, citizen scientists haven't discovered a new pollinator species, but that shouldn't stop citizen scientists from thinking about potential names. A bat named after *Batman* actor Christian Bale? A beetle named for John Lennon? A butterfly called Giacomo Puccini in honor of the composer of *Madame Butterfly*?

Participation Pays Off

Getting nonexperts involved in research combines science with education, allowing people to experience the scientific method firsthand. Citizen science has also been hailed for democratizing science, encouraging scientific literacy, and engaging the next generation of scientists. Although citizen scientists volunteer their time, the goal is not to acquire data on the cheap. Instead, scientists leverage diverse groups to access data across great spans of space and time; nonscientists provide novel perspectives on research and help scientists translate their findings into policies and action.

Data collected through these endeavors aren't just valuable to those involved in the projects. Most data are open-source and available to all researchers. Citizen Science Central, a project of the Cornell Lab of Ornithology, estimates that hundreds of peer-reviewed articles have been published that draw significant conclusions based on data from volunteers. These studies not only present data but offer strategies to guide management and decision making. "The promise of citizen science is that it's a shared endeavor that we both create data sets that we use to learn more about what's happening but through participation people gain knowledge and learn about their environment," says LeBuhn, director of the Great Sunflower Project.

In the process of gathering data, citizen scientists develop closer connections to the natural world and a deep sense of satisfaction that their contributions are making a difference. "Climate change feels so big and, as individuals, people start thinking, 'What can we do?" Domroese says. "Bearing witness to the change through [citizen-science] projects . . . people can feel a sense of empowerment to contribute to the understanding of what's happening in the world."

Pollinators also benefit from all of the attention. Organizers surveyed Great Pollinator Project volunteers about their participation and found that 90 percent reported an increased appreciation for bees and the natural world; 77 percent started planting pollinator-friendly gardens with 73 percent of the participating gardeners planting native plants. Bee Watchers also expressed interest in contributing to pollinator-protection campaigns. In 2010, as part of the Great Pollinator Project, 82 citizen scientists submitted 709 bee observations and indicated their motivations for participating. They wanted to learn about bees, attract pollinators to their gardens, and help with a science or conservation project. Returning volunteers were especially motivated by the idea of contributing to scientific research. The volunteer Bee Watchers also noted that they were taking their own action because of the project. Their feedback included comments like: "I used to garden for vegetables or pretty flowers, and now I garden for the bees," and "I've let my herbs to go down to seeds . . . ever since I let everything flower it has been like a little bee city out there."

Citizen scientists take ownership of their projects and spur others to get involved. Volunteers for the North Carolina Butterfly Highway helped select plants, choosing from a list of native nectar and host plants known to be drought-tolerant and low-maintenance; volunteers also provided feedback on garden designs, requesting raised beds and signs to make their neighbors aware that the gardens were part of a special project. The installation of fifty-one gardens at single-family homes and apartment complexes created a ripple effect, and residents of the six Charlotte neighborhoods planted their own small gardens to attract pollinators. Hjarding recalls a conversation with another participant who told her, "There were individuals that I asked to be a part of [the Butterfly Highway] and they politely declined, but after they saw the beautiful gardens throughout the [neighborhood] and the city, then they were most definitely [interested in being part of it]."

Callaghan believes that citizen scientists become unofficial public-relations reps for pollinators when they tell other people about the plight of these delicate creatures and what can be done to protect them.

Tucker started counting monarch larvae on milkweed plants because it allowed her to spend time outdoors interacting with a species she's loved since childhood. During weekly treks to monitor the patch of milkweed at Eastman Nature Center in Minneapolis, she looks for opportunities to talk to others about her role as a citizen scientist. "I like it when someone walks by and says, 'What are you doing?' and I get to show off what I know. It makes you feel like you're really helping out and doing something," she says. "I think it's really cool the way citizen science helps scientists make a difference in the world and gets everyday people involved in that process."

Box 7-6

Twenty-Nine Ways You Can Help Protect Pollinators

Do you want to give bees (and other pollinators) a chance? Lending a helping hand for pollinator protection is simple. Here are twenty-nine ideas to help you get started.

1. *Garden with native plants.* Native plants are adapted to certain geographic regions and they thrive in those specific climates. Unlike nonnative species, which might lack sufficient nectar or pollen or might lack adequate nutrition to support pollinators, native plants often co-evolved with pollinators to provide the perfect resources for their health and survival.
2. *Plan for multi-season blooming.* Pollinators require food all year long. Instead of filling the garden with plants that only burst into bloom in the summer, select a diversity of species that provide continuous bloom during winter, spring, summer, and fall. Don't have a green thumb? Ask your local nursery professional for advice.
3. *Choose plants with different colors, shapes, and scents.* Different pollinators are attracted to different flowers: hummingbirds prefer tubular-shaped orange and red flowers; bees are attracted to white, yellow, and blue flowers, especially if they have a mild scent; and bats like green and purple flowers with a strong fragrance. The more diversity of colors, shapes, and scents in your garden, the more pollinators you'll attract.
4. *Embrace organic pest control.* Organic methods of pest control range from beneficial insects to products proven to have minimal impact on pollinators. For minor infestations, consider removing pests by hand.
5. *Provide clean water.* Pollinating your favorite foods and flowers is hard work. When pollinators work up a thirst, make sure they have a place to get a cool drink of water. A shallow dish or a birdbath are both great options. Place a half-submerged stone in the water to give insect pollinators a place to perch so they don't drown.
6. *Spray with care.* If you must spray, apply pesticides only to the plants with pest issues. By targeting specific plants—rather than spraying the entire garden, including plants with no pest issues—you'll limit the amount of the chemical you use and lessen the impact on pollinators.
7. *Switch to evening applications.* If pesticide or herbicide applications are a must, avoid spraying plants during daylight hours. Most pollinators are not active at night, so switching to nighttime applications lessens the likelihood that pollinators will be sprayed or affected by pesticide drift.
8. *Arrange flowering plants in clumps.* Planting several of the same flowers in one area of the garden (rather than scattering single plants all around) makes the patch easier for pollinators to spot. Pollinators are more apt to visit a garden where species are in abundance.

Box 7-6 *continued*

9. *Plant milkweed.* Monarchs depend on milkweed: their caterpillars feast exclusively on the leaves of milkweed plants, and adult butterflies lay their eggs on milkweed leaves. Planting milkweed in the garden, especially if you live in an area along their migratory route, provides essential habitat for the beleaguered butterflies.
10. *Provide nesting spots.* Small stacks of twigs and bare patches of lawn are ideal nesting spots for pollinators; dead tree trunks, called *snags*, are excellent nesting sites for wood-nesting bees and beetles. Adding these features to your garden gives pollinators suitable places to reproduce. Bee hotels are another option. You can make these small structures as DIY projects to offer pollinators a series of nesting spots, or you can purchase one from an online vendor and watch pollinators move in.
11. *Adopt a monarch.* The National Wildlife Federation offers an "adopt a monarch" program that allows the public to adopt the iconic pollinators symbolically. The adoption fees start at $25 and include a certificate of adoption. NWF uses the funds to restore monarch habitats. You can also adopt a bat or a ruby-throated hummingbird through the conservation organization.
12. *Create a monarch way station.* Monarch Watch provides specific guidelines for gardeners to have their sites certified as monarch way stations. To be certified, a site must include a minimum of ten native milkweed plants made up of at least two different varieties as well as nectar plants; sustainable gardening practices, including elimination of pesticides, removing dead stalks, and thinning, watering, and mulching to ensure that monarchs have access to the healthiest plants. The organization sends a sign designating a site a Certified Monarch Way Station with all completed applications.
13. *Take the Million Pollinator Garden Challenge.* The Million Pollinator Garden Challenge is a nationwide effort to register one million pollinator gardens on public and private lands. To date, 695,542 gardens have been registered through the Pollinator Partnership. Registration is free.
14. *Leave "mulch-free" zones.* Most native bees nest in the ground. A thick layer of mulch makes it impossible for them to dig a nest to raise their babies. Leaving areas of bare soil in the garden ensures that these essential pollinators have access to nesting spots.
15. *Get involved in a citizen-science project.* Without the help of citizen scientists, researchers can't gather the volume of data they need to understand current pollinator populations and assess threats facing their survival. There are citizen-science projects available for all interests and skill levels. Check out the Great Sunflower Project, the Monarch Larvae Monitoring Project, or the Western Monarch Milkweed Mapper to get started, or check local universities for opportunities to help with data collection.

continued

Box 7-6 *continued*

16. *Support pollinator-friendly businesses.* A growing number of companies are stepping up to support pollinators by planting pollinator habitats, avoiding the use of pesticides, and donating funds to nonprofit organizations working to protect the fragile species. Some companies, including General Mills and Bayer CropScience, also provide free seed packets to help gardeners plant their own pollinator gardens.
17. *Be a lazy lawnmower.* Letting clover grow before mowing it down gives the bees access to an abundant nectar source. Clover is one of the first pollen- and nectar-producing plants to emerge in the spring and can provide important nourishment for bees on their first spring foraging journeys. Waiting a little longer between mowing gives them a chance to take advantage of the clover.
18. *Get certified.* The National Wildlife Federation has a certified wildlife-habitat program. While the criteria to have your garden certified focus on all wildlife, those requirements, which include providing food, water, and cover, also benefit pollinators. Certified wildlife habitats are recognized with a personalized certificate, NWF membership, and, for an extra fee, garden signs designating the site a wildlife habitat. The fee supports the work the nonprofit does to protect wildlife.
19. *Shop at a native-plant sale.* Not all nurseries stock native plants; the annual or semiannual sales held at botanical gardens, arboretums, native-plant societies, and universities cater to native-plant enthusiasts and stock many species that will thrive in specific regions. Most have knowledgeable staff on hand to answer questions about the benefits of each plant species for pollinators.
20. *Welcome all pollinators.* Do not discriminate. Your garden should be welcoming to *all* pollinators. You cannot aim to attract birds but not bees or bats. A healthy ecosystem has a diversity of pollinators, and some of the less appreciated species are the ones that need the most help.
21. *Install a bat house.* Bats need love, too. A bat house provides a safe place for bats to roost during daylight hours. At night, bats will emerge and feast on nectar and provide pest control, feasting on insects in the garden. Mount a bat house at least twelve feet above ground and twenty-plus feet from obstacles like tree branches to provide a clear flight path.
22. *Clean hummingbird feeders.* Mold and fungus can form in hummingbird feeders, causing hummingbirds to get sick or die. Drinking from a mold- or fungus-filled feeder could give the pint-sized pollinators a fungal infection that causes their tongues to swell, making it impossible to eat; mama hummingbirds can pass the infection to their babies, sometimes fatally. Cleaning the feeder is as simple as washing it in hot water and mild detergent and using a bottle brush to scrub the jar. Rinse out all soapy residue before refilling the feeder.

Box 7-6 *continued*

23. *Give weeds a chance.* Some of the wild plants that pop up in the grass are important nectar sources for pollinators. Instead of plucking dandelions and clover or giving them a dose of weed killer, embrace their role in the ecosystem and let them grow.
24. *Remove invasive species from the garden.* It's tempting to take a live-and-let-live approach to invasive species, especially when plants like Japanese honeysuckle and butterfly bush grow so well. But pollinators don't get the resources they need from these nonnative plants. Rather than letting them grow unchecked, banish invasive species from the garden and replace them with native plants to provide a more appropriate diet for pollinators.
25. *Shop for sustainably grown foods.* Agriculture has a major impact on pollinator health, abundance, and diversity. Shop local and ask farmers about their practices: cover crops, pollinator strips, and reduced pesticide use (or the use of approved organic methods) can all help pollinators.
26. *Research what is native in your area.* Before heading to the garden center, research popular native plants in your area. There are likely to be a large number of pretty, easy-to-grow natives that thrive in your specific climate. You'll discover new plants, and pollinators will benefit from the resources they need. The Lady Bird Johnson Wildflower Center has an excellent native-plant database on its website, www.wildflower.org/plants, to help you search for native species in your area.
27. *Volunteer.* Sign up for an invasive species removal event, join a native-plant society, or raise funds on behalf of environmental organizations that want to protect habitat. There are plenty of opportunities to pitch in for pollinators. Find one that speaks to you, recruit friends, and create a buzz over protecting pollinators.
28. *Shop smart.* Check the labels before purchasing plants. Several retailers have started adding tags to plants sprayed with neonicotinoids to let gardeners know that the plant could harm pollinators. The word "protected" on the label is a red flag that the plant has been chemically treated. More stores are stocking neonicotinoid-free plants, but it's always a good idea to double-check before making a purchase.
29. *Spread the word.* Let your friends and neighbors know about the plight of pollinators. Share information about what you're doing to protect essential pollinator populations and encourage others to do the same.

Acknowledgments

Just as we benefit from the pollinators that devote their lives to ensuring we have bountiful foods and flowers, I benefited from the support of an incredible team to help this idea blossom.

Thanks to Emily Turner at Island Press for championing this project and allowing me to turn a passion for the environment into a book.

Without the amazing group of experts who shared their stories, explained their research, and welcomed me into their worlds, there would be no book. I'm so grateful to: Christine Bishop, Amy Boyd, Vaughn Bryant, Ana Cabrera, Jennifer Callaghan, Kristin Clark, Kathy Dale, Andrea DeLong-Amaya, Meg Domroese, Guillermo Fernandez, Wayne Fredericks, Christina Grozinger, Angel Hjarding, Scott Horn, Elizabeth Howard, Kim Huntzinger, Sarina Jepsen, Reed Johnson, Christopher Kaiser-Bunbury, Lynn Kimsey, Vera Krischik, Jesse Lasky, Geoffrey LeBaron, Gretchen LeBuhn, Eric Lee-Mader, Joe Milone, Ashley Minnerath, Lora Morandin, Sarah Myers, Jane Ogilvie, Karen Oberhauser, Beth Robinson-Martin, Dara Satterfield, Clyde Sorenson, Philip Stepanian, Barb Svenson, Elaine Tucker, Leslie Uppinghouse, David Wilcove, and Amy Witt.

Without Rosie Molinary to provide feedback on chapters, reassure me that an idea and piles of notes could be turned into a book, and entertain me along the way, I would never have reached the finish line.

My dear friends Megan Bame, Heather Rice Books, Polly Campbell, Kym Goins, Kylie Hall, Kate Hanley, Wendy Helfenbaum, Beth Howard, Kelly James, Judi Ketteler, and Makeda Pennycooke were indefatigable cheerleaders.

My most heartfelt gratitude goes to my family—Jerry Porter, Hank and Dianne Helmer, and Shannon and Charlotte McKinnon: y'all are my world. Thank you for all you do.

Selected Bibliography

Aceves-Bueno, Eréndira, Adeyemi S. Adeleye, Yuxiong Huang, Mengya Tao, Yi Yang, and Sarah E. Anderson. "The Accuracy of Citizen Science Data: A Quantitative Review." Ecological Society of America. *ESA Bulletin* 98, no. 4 (September 29, 2017). https://esajournals.onlinelibrary.wiley.com/doi/full/10.1002/bes2.1336#bes21336-bib-0002.

Alaback, Paul. "A True Partnership." Ecological Society of America, *Frontiers in Ecology and the Environment* 10, no. 6 (August 1, 2012). https://esajournals.onlinelibrary.wiley.com/doi/10.1890/1540-9295-10.6.284a.

Altizer, Sonia, Lincoln Brower, Elizabeth Howard, David James, Sarina Jepsen, Eva Lewandowski, Gail Morris, Kelly Nail, Karen Oberhauser, and Robert Pyle. "Joint Statement Regarding Captive Breeding and Releasing of Monarchs." Xerces Society. Accessed October 15, 2018. https://xerces.org/joint-statement-against-captive-breeding-and-releasing-of-monarchs/.

Altizer, Sonia, and Japp De Roode. "When Butterflies Get Bugs—The ABCs of Lepidopteran Disease." *American Butterflies*, 2010. http://www.biology.emory.edu/research/deRoode/PDFs/Altizer and De Roode 2010-Butterfly diseases.pdf.

Altizer, Sonia M., and Karen S. Oberhouser. "Effects of the Protozoan Parasite *Ophryocystis Elektroscirrha* on the Fitness of Monarch Butterflies (*Danaus Plexippus*)." *Journal of Invertebrate Pathology* 74, no. 1 (July 1999): 76–88. https://www.sciencedirect.com/science/article/pii/S002220119994853X.

American Veterinarian Medical Association. "White-Nose Syndrome." Accessed October 10, 2018. https://www.avma.org/KB/Resources/Reference/wildlife/Pages/White-Nose-Syndrome.aspx.

Appalachian Mountain Club. "Adopt-a-Trail." Accessed October 10, 2018. https://www.outdoors.org/volunteer/volunteer-trails/adopt-a-trail.

Appalachian Mountains Joint Venture. "2014 Farm Bill Field Guide." Accessed October 10, 2018. https://www.fws.gov/greatersagegrouse/documents/Landowners/2014_Farm_Bill_Guide%20to%20Fish%20and%20Wildlife%20Conservation.pdf.

Arita, Hector T., and Don E. Wilson. "Long-Nosed Bats and Agaves: The Tequila Connection." Bat Conservation International. *BATS Magazine* 5, no. 4 (Winter 1987). http://www.batcon.org/resources/media-education/bats-magazine/bat_article/299.

Arrington, Debbie. "In Our Busy Farming Region, These Five Crops Are Tops." *Sacramento* Bee, February 17, 2014. http://www.sacbee.com/food-drink/article2590463.html.

Aubrey, Allison. "As Beekeepers Lose More Hives, Time for New Rules on Pesticides?" National Public Radio, November 24, 2015. https://www.npr.org/sections/thesalt/2015/11/24/457130929/as-beekeepers-lose-more-hives-time-for-new-rules-on-pesticides.

Avaaz. "Hours to Save the Bees." Accessed October 10, 2018. https://secure.avaaz.org/campaign/en/save_the_bees_neonics_loc_ns/.

Bailey, Wayne, Chris DiFonzo, Eric Hodgson, Thomas Hunt, Keith Jarvi, Bryan Jansen, Janet Knodel, Robert Koch, Christian Krupke, Brian McCornack, Andrew Michel, Julie Peterson, Bruce Potter, Ada Szczepaniec, Kelley Tilmon, John Tooker, and Sarah Zukoff. "The Effectiveness of Neonicotinoid Seed Treatments in Soybeans." Purdue University Extension, December 2015. http://ento.psu.edu/extension/field-crops/fact-sheet-Effectiveness-of-Neonicotinoid-Seed-Treatments-in-Soybean.

Baldock, Katherine C. R., Mark A. Goddard, Damien M. Hicks, William E. Kunin, Nadine Mitschunas, Lynne M. Osgathorpe, Simon G. Potts, Kirsty M. Robertson, Anna V. Scott, Graham N. Stone, Ian P. Vaughan, and Jane Memmott. "Where Is the UK's Pollinator Biodiversity? The Importance of Urban Areas for Flower-Visiting Insects." *Proceedings of the Royal Society of London B: Biological Sciences* 282, no. 1803 (March 22, 2015). http://rspb.royalsocietypublishing.org/content/282/1803/20142849.

Barkham, Patrick. "Endangered Butterfly Defies Climate Change with New Diet and Habitat." *The Guardian*, April 07, 2014. https://www.theguardian.com/environment/2014/apr/07/endangered-butterfly-species-defies-climate-change-quino-checkerspot.

Bat Conservation Trust. "Are UK Bats Immune to White-Nose Syndrome Which Is Killing Millions of North American Bats?" Accessed October 10, 2018. http://

www.bats.org.uk/news.php/200/are_uk_bats_immune_to_white_nose_syndrome_which_is_killing_millions_of_north_american_bats.

Bayer. "Bayer North American Bee Care Center Celebrates 10,000 Visitors." Press release, April 20, 2017. https://www.prnewswire.com/news-releases/bayer-north-american-bee-care-center-celebrates-10000-visitors-300442985.html.

———. "Bee Care—Neonicotinoids." Accessed October 12, 2018. https://beecare.bayer.com/what-to-know/pesticides/neonicotinoids.

———. "Feed a Bee Kicks Off 2018 by Funding 20 New Projects in 50-State Forage Initiative." *Bayer Global*, March 7, 2018. https://www.cropscience.bayer.us/news/press-r releases/2018/feed-a-bee-kicks-off-2018-by-funding-20-new-projects-in-50-state-forage-initiative.

———. "A New Way of Protecting Bees against Varroa Mites." Accessed October 12, 2018. https://beecare.bayer.com/media-center/news/detail/a-new-way-of-protecting-bees-against-varroa-mites.

Baylor College of Medicine. "Honey Bee Genome Project." BCM-HGSC, January 30, 2018. https://www.hgsc.bcm.edu/arthropods/honey-bee-genome-project.

Beaty, Colleen. "Keeping Fireflies from Blinking Out for Good." Wildlife Habitat Council, July 12, 2017. http://www.wildlifehc.org/keeping-fireflies-from-blinking-out-for-good/.

Bee Better Certified. "Getting Started." Accessed October 10, 2018. https://beebettercertified.org/.

Bee City USA. Accessed October 10, 2018. http://www.beecityusa.org/.

Bee Informed Partnership. "Colony Loss 2016–2017: Preliminary Results." August 28, 2017. https://beeinformed.org/results/colony-loss-2016-2017-preliminary-results/.

———. "Honey Bee Colony Losses 2017–2018: Preliminary Results." May 23, 2018. https://beeinformed.org/results/honey-bee-colony-losses-2017-2018 - preliminary-results.

Bell, Adam. "Robust Growth Continues for Most—but Not All—Places in Charlotte Region." *Charlotte* (North Carolina) *Observer*, May 25, 2017. http://www.charlotteobserver.com/news/local/article152427944.html.

Belt, Jami J., and Paul R. Krausman. "Evaluating Population Estimates of Mountain Goats Based on Citizen Science." *Wildlife Society Bulletin* 36, no. 2 (May 11, 2012). https://onlinelibrary.wiley.com/doi/10.1002/wsb.139.

Bessin, Ric. "Varroa Mites Infesting Honey Bee Colonies." University of Kentucky, College of Agriculture. Accessed October 11, 2018. https://entomology.ca.uky.edu/ef608.

Bishop, Christine A., Alison J. Moran, Michelle C. Toshack, Elizabeth Elle, France Maisonneuve, and John E. Elliott. "Hummingbirds and Bumble Bees Exposed to Neonicotinoid and Organophosphate Insecticides in the Fraser Valley, British Columbia, Canada." *Environmental Toxicology and Chemistry* 37, no. 8 (August 2018): 2143–52. https://setac.onlinelibrary.wiley.com/doi/pdf/10.1002/etc.4174.

Blaauw, Brett R., and Rufus Isaacs. "Larger Patches of Diverse Floral Resources Increase Insect Pollinator Density, Diversity, and Their Pollination of Native Wildflowers." *Basic and Applied Ecology* 15 (October 12, 2014): 701–11. http://www.isaacslab.ent.msu.edu/Images/Blaauw and Isaacs 2014 Larger patches of diverse floral resources increase insect pollinator density diversity and their pollination of native wildflowers.pdf.

Black, Scott Hoffman. and Mace Vaughan. "Checkerspots: Quino Checkerspot (*Euphydryas editha quino*)." Accessed October 15, 2018. https://xerces.org/quino-checkerspot/.

Blue Ridge Partnership for Regional Invasive Species Management. "Prolific and Menacing Invasive Japanese Honeysuckle." *Blue Ridge Prism*, May 2017. http://blueridgeprism.org/wp-content/uploads/2017/06/Japanese-Honeysuckle-factsheet-5-24-17-VDOF-w-Box-FINAL.pdf.

Boeing. "2014 Environment Report—Remediation." 2014. http://www.boeing.com/aboutus/environment/environment_report_14/3.2_remediation.html.

Bond, Jennifer, Kristy Plattner, and Kevin Hunt. "Fruit and Tree Nuts Outlook: Economic Insight." US Department of Agriculture, September 26, 2014. http://docplayer.net/16188476-Fruit-and-tree-nuts-outlook-economic-insight-u-s-pollination-services-market.html.

Bonney, Rick, Heidi Ballard, Rebecca Jordan, Ellen McCallie, Tina Phillips, Jennifer Shirk, and Candie C. Wilderman. "Public Participation in Scientific Research: Defining the Field and Assessing Its Potential for Informal Science Education." Cornell University, Center for Advancement of Informal Science Education, July 2009. http://www.birds.cornell.edu/citscitoolkit/publications/CAISE-PPSR-report-2009.pdf.

Bourne, Val. "Everything You Need to Know about Red Mason Bees." *The Telegraph*, February 15, 2016. https://www.telegraph.co.uk/gardening/how-to-grow/everything-you-need-to-know-about-red-mason-bees/.

Brackney, Susan. "Are We Loving Monarchs to Death?" *Discovery Magazine—The Crux*, June 28, 2016. http://blogs.discovermagazine.com/crux/2016/06/21/are-we-loving-monarchs-to death/#.WwihD2WlfBJ.

Brasher, Philip. "CRP Expansion Set for Fight in Farm Bill." *AgriPulse*, March

7, 2018. AgriPulse Communications, Inc. https://www.agri-pulse.com/articles/10686-crp-expansion-set-for-fight-in-farm-bill.

Brenna, B. "Clergymen Abiding in the Fields: The Making of the Naturalist Observer in Eighteenth-Century Norwegian Natural History." National Institutes of Health. *Science in Context* 24, no. 2 (June 2011): 143–66. https://www.ncbi.nlm.nih.gov/pubmed/21797077?dopt=Abstract.

Brocious, Ariana. "Protect Pollinators, Plant Trees? Nebraska Researchers Look to Land for Answers." Harvest Public Media, October 25, 2017. http://harvestpublicmedia.org/post/protect-pollinators-plant-trees-nebraska-researchers-look-land-answers.

———. "UNL Research Examines How to Make Farms More Pollinator-Friendly." NET Nebraska, October 12, 2017. http://netnebraska.org/article/news/1099104/unl-research-examines-how-make-farms-more-pollinator-friendly.

Brokaw, Julia, and Rufus Isaacs. "Building and Managing Bee Hotels for Wild Bees," Extension Bulletin E-3337. Michigan State University, Department of Entomology, June 2017. https://pollinators.msu.edu/publications/building-and-managing-bee-hotels-for-wild-bees/.

Brown, Timothy, Susan Kegley, Lisa Archer, and Tiffany Finck-Haynes. "Toxic Pesticides Found in 'Bee-Friendly' Plants Sold at Garden Centers across the United States and Canada." Friends of the Earth, Canada. *Gardeners Beware*, 2014. http://foecanada.org/en/files/2014/06/GardenersBewareReport2014.pdf.

Buchman, Steve. "Hawk Moths or Sphinx Moths (Sphingidae)." US Department of Agriculture, US Forest Service. Accessed October 17, 2018. https://www.fs.fed.us/wildflowers/pollinators/pollinator-of-the-month/hawk_moths.shtml.

Budburst. "About Budburst." Accessed October 17, 2018. http://www.budburst.org/aboutus.

Bumblebee Conservation Trust. "What Makes Bumblebees Such Good Pollinators?" Bumblebeeconservation.org, 2018. https://www.bumblebeeconservation.org/bee-faqs/buzz-pollination/.

"Burt's Bees Foundation." Burt's Bees. Accessed August 27, 2018. https://www.burtsbees.com.

Business Wire. "Global Tequila Market to Witness Growth Through 2021, Owing to the Introduction of New Flavors: Technavio." March 9, 2017. https://www.businesswire.com/news/home/20170309005955/en/Global-Tequila-Market-Witness-Growth-2021-Owing.

Butterflies and Moths of North America. "Pipevine Swallowtail *Battus philenor* (Linnaeus, 1771)." Butterfliesandmoths.org. Accessed August 25, 2018. https://www.butterfliesandmoths.org/species/Battus-philenor.

Canadian Press. "Insecticide Found in Same B.C. Hummingbirds That Are in Decline." *CBC News*, July 10, 2017. http://www.cbc.ca/news/canada/british-columbia/insecticide-found-in-same-b-c-hummingbirds-that-are-in-decline-1.4196876.

CaraDonna, Paul J., Amy M. Iler, and David W. Inouye. "Shifts in Flowering Phenology Reshape a Subalpine Plant Community." *Proceedings of the National Academy of Sciences* (March 13, 2014). http://www.pnas.org/content/early/2014/03/12/1323073111.

Carpenter, Les. "Wildcats, Butterflies, Tortoises: All Are Endangered by Trump's Border Wall." *The Guardian*, December 12, 2017. https://www.theguardian.com/us-news/2017/dec/12/butterflies-trump-wall-mexico-border-wildlife.

Carrington, Damian. "Climate Change Is Disrupting Flower Pollination, Research Shows." *The Guardian*, November 06, 2014. https://www.theguardian.com/environment/2014/nov/06/climate-change-is-disrupting-flower-pollination-research-shows.

CBS News. "Trump Admin. Delays Protection for 'Endangered' Bumblebees." CBSNews.com, February 10, 2017. https://www.cbsnews.com/news/bumblebees-endangered-species-protection-delayed-by-trump-administration/.

Center for Biological Diversity. "Landmark Report: Hundreds of Native Bee Species Sliding Toward Extinction." Press release, March 1, 2017. https://www.biologicaldiversity.org/news/press_releases/2017/bees-03-01-2017.php.

———. "Lawsuit Launched to Protect Endangered Rusty Patched Bumblebee." Press release, October 16, 2017. https://www.biologicaldiversity.org/news/press_releases/2017/rusty-patched-bumblebee-10-16-2017.php.

———. "Monarch Butterfly." Accessed October 15, 2018. https://www.biologicaldiversity.org/species/invertebrates/monarch_butterfly/.

———. "Monarch Butterfly Population Rebounds to 68 Percent of 22-year Average." Press release, February 26, 2016. https://www.biologicaldiversity.org/news/press_releases/2016/monarch-butterfly-02-26-2016.html.

———. "White-Nose Syndrome: Questions and Answers." Accessed October 15, 2018. https://www.biologicaldiversity.org/campaigns/bat_crisis_white-nose_syndrome/Q_and_A.html.

Center for Food Safety. "Hidden Costs of Toxic Seed Coatings." Centerforfoodsafety.org, June 2015. https://www.centerforfoodsafety.org/files/neonic-factsheet_75083.pdf.

Checketka, Svetlana, Yue Yu, Masayoshi Tange, and Eijiro Miyako. "Materially Engineered Artificial Pollinators." *Chem*, no. 2 (February 9, 2017): P224–39. http://www.cell.com/chem/fulltext/S2451-9294(17)30032-3.

City of Columbia (Missouri). "Adopt-a-Trail Program." 2018. https://www.como.gov/volunteer/volunteer-opportunities/adopt-trail-program/.

City of Portland (Oregon). "The Problem with Invasive Plants." February 17, 2016. https://www.portlandoregon.gov/bes/article/330681.

Clayton, Chris. "Crop Insurance Won't Rescue Farmers from Dicamba Drift." *DTN Progressive Farmer*, July 6, 2017. https://www.dtnpf.com/agriculture/web/ag/perspectives/blogs/ag-policy-blog/blog-post/2017/07/06/crop-insurance-rescue-farmers-drift.

CNN Wires. "Bumblebee Is First Bee in Continental US to Be Listed as Endangered." Fox2now.com, January 10, 2017. https://fox2now.com/2017/01/10/bumblebee-is-first-bee-in-continental-us-to-be-listed-as-endangered/.

Cohen, Elyse. "Spring Has Sprung: The Sixth-Annual White House Garden Planting." The White House, April 3, 2014. https://obamawhitehouse.archives.gov/blog/2014/04/03/spring-has-sprung-sixth-annual-white-house-garden-planting.

Comba, Livio, Sarah A. Corbet, A. Barron, A. Bird, S. Collinge, N. Miyazaki, and M. Powell. "Garden Flowers: Insect Visits and the Floral Reward of Horticulturally Modified Variants." Macquarie University (Australia), January 16, 2017. https://researchers.mq.edu.au/en/publications/garden-flowers-insect-visits-and-the-floral-reward-of-horticultur.

Connor, Larry. "Beekeeping by the Numbers." *American Bee Journal*, December 10, 2015. https://americanbeejournal.com/beekeeping-by-the-numbers-2/.

Cornell Lab of Ornithology. "Anna's Hummingbird." Cornell University. *All About Birds*, 2017. https://www.allaboutbirds.org/guide/Annas_Hummingbird.

———. "Ruby-Throated Hummingbird." Cornell University. *All About Birds*, 2017. https://www.allaboutbirds.org/guide/Ruby-throated_Hummingbird/id.

———. "Rufous Hummingbird." Cornell University. *All About Birds*, 2017. https://www.allaboutbirds.org/guide/Rufous_Hummingbird/overview.

———."What Is Citizen Science and PPSR?" Cornell University. *Citizen Science Central*, 2018. http://www.birds.cornell.edu/citscitoolkit/about/defining-citizen-science/.

Costin, Kevin J., and April M. Boulton. "A Field Experiment on the Effect of Introduced Light Pollution on Fireflies (Coleoptera: Lampyridae) in the Piedmont Region of Maryland." *Coleopterists' Bulletin* 70, no. 1 (March 2016): 84–86. http://www.bioone.org/doi/full/10.1649/072.070.0110.

Courter, Jason R., Ron J. Johnson, William C. Bridges, and Kenneth G. Hubbard. "Assessing Migration of Ruby-Throated Hummingbirds (*Archilochus colubris*) at Broad Spatial and Temporal Scales." American Ornithological Society. *The Auk* 135, no. 4 (January 2013): 107–17. http://www.bioone.org/doi/abs/10.1525/auk.2012.12058.

Crawford, Elizabeth. "Almond Milk Sales Continue to Surge, as Dairy Milk Contracts, Nielsen Data Shows." Foodnavigator-usa.com, April 15, 2016. https://www.foodnavigator-usa.com/Article/2016/04/15/Almond-milk-sales-continue-to-surge-as-dairy-milk-contracts-Nielsen.

CropLife America. "CropLife America Responds to Today's Pollinator Health Task Force Report." Croplifeamerica.org, May 19, 2015. http://www.croplifeamerica.org/news/2015/5/19/croplife-america-responds-to-todays-pollinator-health-task-force-report.

Cusser, Sarah, John L. Neff, and Shalene Jha. "Natural Land Cover Drives Pollinator Abundance and Richness, Leading to Reductions in Pollen Limitation in Cotton Agroecosystems." *Agriculture, Ecosystems, & Environment* 226 (June 16, 2016): 33–42. https://www.sciencedirect.com/science/article/pii/S0167880916302237.

Danielle (no last name indicated—grade-12 Young Naturalist Award winner). "The Prevalence of *Ophryocystis elektroscirrha* Infections in the Monarch Butterfly (*Danaus plexippus*): A Study of the Protozoan Parasite in a Wild Population of Western Monarchs." American Museum of Natural History, 2012. https://www.amnh.org/learn-teach/young-naturalist-awards/winning-essays2/2012-winning-essays/the-prevalence-of-ophryocystis-elektroscirrha-infections-in-the-monarch-butterfly-danaus-plexippus-a-study-of-the-protozoan-parasite-in-a-wild-population-of-western-monarchs/.

Davidson-Lowe, Elizabeth, Bahodir Eshchanov, Sara Hermann, Andrew Myers, Saisi Xue, and Christie A. Bahlai. "Thermally Moderated Firefly Activity Is Delayed by Precipitation Extremes." Cold Spring Harbor Laboratory. *BioRxiv*, January 1, 2016. https://www.biorxiv.org/content/early/2016/09/11/074633.

Dayton, Mark (Governor of Minnesota). "Directing Steps to Reverse Pollinator Decline and Restore Pollinator Health in Minnesota. State of Minnesota, August 25, 2016. https://mn.gov/governor/assets/2016_08_25_EO_16-07_tcm1055-253931.pdf.

DeGrandi-Hoffman, Gloria, Fabiana Ahumada, Danka, Mona Chambers, Emily Watkins DeJong, and Geoffrey Hidalgo. "Population Growth of Varroa destructor (Acari: Varroidae) in Colonies of Russian and Unselected Honey Bee (Hymenoptera: Apidae) Stocks as Related to Numbers of Foragers with Mites." *Journal of Economic Entomology* 110, no. 3 (June 1, 2017): 809–15. https://academic.oup.com/jee/article-abstract/110/3/809/3072898?redirectedFrom=PDF.

de la Peña-Domene, Marinés, Cristina Martínez-Garza, Sebastián Palmas-Pérez, Edith Rivas-Alonso, and Henry F. Howe. "Roles of Birds and Bats in Early Tropical-Forest Restoration." *PLOS One* (August 13, 2014). http://journals.plos.org/plosone/article?id=10.1371/journal.pone.0104656.

del Bosque, Melissa. "National Butterfly Center Sues Trump Administration over Border Wall." *Texas Observer*, December 12, 2017. https://www.texasobserver.org/national-butterfly-center-sues-trump-administration-border-wall/.

Dignan, Clare. "Goats Are Taking a Bite out of Edgewood Park in New Haven." *New Haven Register*, May 21, 2018. https://www.nhregister.com/news/article/Goats-are-taking-a-bite-out-of-Edgewood-Park-in-12931550.php.

Dininny, Shannon. "A Better Bee? Blue Orchard Bees Show Promise as Pollinators." *Good Fruit Grower*, March 26, 2018. http://www.goodfruit.com/a-better-bee-blue-orchard-bees-show-promise-as-pollinators/.

Dolezal, Adam G., Stephen D. Hendrix, Nicole A. Scavo, Jimena Carrillo-Tripp, Mary A. Harris, M. Joseph Wheelock, Matthew E. O'Neal, and Amy L. Toth. "Honey Bee Viruses in Wild Bees: Viral Prevalence, Loads, and Experimental Inoculation." *PLOS One* (November 10, 2016). http://journals.plos.org/plosone/article?id=10.1371/journal.pone.0166190.

Domroese, Meg, and Elizabeth Johnson. "Great Pollinator Project: Native Bees and Their NYC Watchers." Center for Biodiversity and Conservation, American Museum of Natural History, 2011. http://www.birds.cornell.edu/citscitoolkit/conference/ppsr2011/workshop-posters/Domroese and Johnson 2011 Great Pollinator Project Native Bees and their NYC Watchers.pdf.

Donaldson, John. "Effects of Habitat Fragmentation on Pollinator Diversity and Plant Reproductive Success in Renosterveld Shrublands of South Africa." *Conservation Biology* 16, no. 5 (October 2002): 1267–76. https://www.jstor.org/stable/3095322?seq=1#page_scan_tab_contents.

Donley, Nathan. "A Menace to Monarchs—Drift Prone Dicamba Poses a Dangerous New Threat to Monarch Butterflies." Center for Biological Diversity, March 2018. http://www.biologicaldiversity.org/species/invertebrates/monarch_butterfly/pdfs/Menace-to-Monarchs.pdf.

Douglas, Margaret R., Jason R. Rohr, and John F. Tooker. "Neonicotinoid Insecticide Travels through a Soil Food Chain, Disrupting Biological Control of Non-target Pests and Decreasing Soya Bean Yield." *Journal of Applied Ecology* 52, no. 1 (December 4, 2014): 250–60. https://besjournals.onlinelibrary.wiley.com/doi/full/10.1111/1365-2664.12372.

Drossart, Maxime, Denis Michez, and Maryse Vanderplanck. "Invasive Plants as Potential Food Resource for Native Pollinators: A Case Study with Two Invasive Species and a Generalist Bumble Bee." *Nature News* (November 24, 2017). https://www.nature.com/articles/s41598-017-16054-5.

Eat the Invaders. "Fighting Invasive Species, One Bite at a Time!" Accessed October 15, 2018. http://eattheinvaders.org/.

Ellis, James D., and C. M. Zettel Nalen. "Varroa Mite." University of Florida. *Featured Creatures*, May 2016. http://entnemdept.ufl.edu/creatures/misc/bees/varroa_mite.htm.

Ellis, Jamie. "Colony Collapse Disorder (CCD) in Honey Bees." University of Florida Extension. EDIS New Publications, April 2, 2018. http://edis.ifas.ufl.edu/in720.

Embry, Paige. "A Promising Backup to the Honeybee Is Shut Down." *Scientific American*, March 5, 2018. https://www.scientificamerican.com/article/a-promising-backup-to-the-honeybee-is-shut-down/.

Emerson, Sarah. "Honey Bee Extinction Will Change Life As We Know It." *Motherboard*, June 7, 2016. https://motherboard.vice.com/en_us/article/mg77z3/honey-bee-extinction-will-change-life-as-we-know-it.

Ericson, Jenny A., Tani Hubbard, Marilyn Hanson, Dave Barnett, and Giselle Block. "Engaging Volunteers in Invasive Species Management." US Fish & Wildlife Service. Accessed October 12, 2018. https://www.fws.gov/invasives/staffTrainingModule/pdfs/planning/WAB06-paper-Ericson et al-volunteers and invasive species-TRVDec06FINAL.pdf.

Erwin, Terry. "The Beetle Family Carabide of Costa Rica: Twenty-Nine New Species of *Agra* Fabricius." *ZooTaxa* 119, no. 1 (2002). https://biotaxa.org/Zootaxa/article/view/zootaxa.119.1.1.

European Citizen Science Association. "Ten Principles of Citizen Science." Accessed October 12, 2018. https://www.wilsoncenter.org/sites/default/files/ten_principles_of_citizen_science_english.pdf.

European Commission. "Neonicotinoids." Last modified May 2018. https://ec.europa.eu/food/plant/pesticides/approval_active_substances/approval_renewal/neonicotinoids_en.

Faldyn, Matthew J., Mark D. Hunter, and Bret D. Elderd. "Climate Change and an Invasive, Tropical Milkweed: An Ecological Trap for Monarch Butterflies." Ecological Society of America. *Ecology* 99, no. 5 (April 4, 2018): 1031–38. https://esajournals.onlinelibrary.wiley.com/doi/abs/10.1002/ecy.2198.

Fallon, Candace. "Help Researchers Track Milkweeds and Monarchs across the West." Xerces Society, February 16, 2017. https://xerces.org/2017/02/16/help-researchers-track-milkweeds-and-monarchs-across-the-west.

Firefly. "Bioluminescent Insects." Accessed October 12, 2018. http://www.firefly.org/bioluminescent-insects.html.

Fisher, Adrian, Chet Coleman, Clint Hoffmann, Brad Fritz, and Juliana Rangel. "The Synergistic Effects of Almond Protection Fungicides on Honey Bee (Hymenoptera: Apidae) Forager Survival." *Journal of Economic Entomology* 110, no. 3 (March 21, 2017): 802–8. https://academic.oup.com/jee/article-abstract/110/3/802/3074380.

Flacher, Floriane, Xavier Raynaud, Amandine Hansart, Eric Motard, and Isabelle Dajoz. "Competition with Wind-Pollinated Plant Species Alters Floral Traits of Insect-Pollinated Plant Species." *Scientific Reports* 5 (2015). https://www.nature.com/articles/srep13345.

Flottum, Kim. "U.S. Honey Industry Report—2016." Bee Culture. *Bee Culture*, April 24, 2017. http://www.beeculture.com/u-s-honey-industry-report-2016/.

Food and Agriculture Organization of the United Nations. "Climate Change and Crop Pollination." Accessed October 12, 2018. http://www.fao.org/docrep/014/i2242e/i2242e01.pdf.

———. "Pollinators Vital to Our Food Supply under Threat." Accessed October 12, 2018. http://www.fao.org/news/story/en/item/384726/icode/.

Frick, W. F., D. S. Reynolds, and T. H. Kunz. "Influence of Climate and Reproductive Timing on Demography of Little Brown Myotis Myotis Lucifugus." National Institutes of Health. *Journal of Animal Ecology* 79, no. (January 2010): 128–36. https://www.ncbi.nlm.nih.gov/pubmed/19747346.

Friends of the Earth. "New Tests Find Bee-Killing Pesticides in 51% of Bee-Friendly Plants from Garden Centers across U.S. and Canada." Accessed October 12, 2018. https://foe.org/news/2014-06-new-tests-find-bee-killing-pesticides-in-51-percent-of-bee-friendly-plants/.

Furlan, Lorenzo, and David Kreutzweiser. "Alternatives to Neonicotinoid Insecticides for Pest Control: Case Studies in Agriculture and Forestry." National Institutes of Health. *Environmental Science and Pollution Research* 22 (2015): 135–47. https://www.ncbi.nlm.nih.gov/pmc/articles/PMC4284368/.

Gannon, Michael R., and Michael R. Willig. "The Effects of Hurricane Hugo on Bats of the Luquillo Experimental Forest of Puerto Rico." *Biotropica* 26, no. 3 (1994): 320–31. https://www.jstor.org/stable/2388854?seq=1#page_scan_tab_contents.

Garbarino, Jeanne, and Christopher E. Mason. "The Power of Engaging Citizen Scientists for Scientific Progress." National Institutes of Health. *Journal of Mi-*

crobiology and Biology Education 17, no. 1 (March 2016): 7–12. https://www.ncbi.nlm.nih.gov/pmc/articles/PMC4798819/.

Gardner, Kianna. "Hundreds of New Beekeepers Help Spokane Honeybees Rebound." *Spokesman-Review* (Spokane, WA), August 14, 2017. http://www.spokesman.com/stories/2017/aug/15/hundreds-of-new-beekeepers-help-spokane-honeybees-/#/0.

Gavrilles, Beth. "Canceled Flights: For Monarch Butterflies, Loss of Migration Means More Disease." University of Georgia, Odum School of Ecology. Accessed October 15, 2018. http://www.ecology.uga.edu/canceled-flights-for-monarch-butterflies-loss-of-migration-means-more-disease/.

Geldmann, Jonas, and Juan P. González-Varo. "Conserving Honey Bees Does Not Help Wildlife." *Science*, January 26, 2018. http://science.sciencemag.org/content/359/6374/392.

General Assembly of Maryland. GAM-HB1536 2018 Regular Session. http://mgaleg.maryland.gov/webmga/frmMain.aspx?pid=billpage&stab=03&id=hb1536&tab=subject3&ys=2018RS.

General Mills. "Pollinators and Biodiversity." 2018. https://www.generalmills.com/en/Responsibility/OurPlanet/Sustainable-sourcing/pollinators-ecosystems.

Giannini, Tereza Cristina, Wilian França Costa, Guaraci Duran Cordeiro, Vera Lucia Imperatriz-Fonseca, Antonio Mauro Saraiva, Jacobus Biesmeijer, and Lucas Alejandro Garibaldi. "Projected Climate Change Threatens Pollinators and Crop Production in Brazil." *PLOS One* (August 9, 2017). http://journals.plos.org/plosone/article?id=10.1371/journal.pone.0182274#pone.0182274.ref026.

Gillespie Museum. "In Our Catalogue . . . Late Winter/Early Spring, 2016–17: Herbs, Greens, and Veggies." Stetson University. Accessed October 15, 2018. http://www.stetson.edu/other/gillespie-museum/seed-information.php.

Gomez, Tony. "Is Tropical Milkweed Killing Monarch Butterflies?" *Monarch Butterfly Garden*, June 15, 2018. https://monarchbutterflygarden.net/is-tropical-milkweed-killing-monarch-butterflies/.

González-Varo, Juan P., and Montserrat Vilà. "Spillover of Managed Honeybees from Mass-Flowering Crops into Natural Habitats." *Biological Conservation* 212, Part A (August 2017): 376–82. https://www.sciencedirect.com/science/article/pii/S000632071730040X.

Goulson, Dave. "Decline of Bees Forces China's Apple Farmers to Pollinate by Hand." *Chinadialogue*, October 2, 2012. https://www.chinadialogue.net/article/show/single/en/5193-Decline-of-bees-forces-China-s-apple-farmers-to-pollinate-by-hand.

Graham, Kelsey K. "Bee Battles: Why Our Native Pollinators Are Losing the War." *The Conversation*, May 6, 2015. https://theconversation.com/bee-battles-why-our-native-pollinators-are-losing-the-war-40620.

Gratas, Sofi. "Goats Wanted: UGA Office of Sustainability Seeks New Chew Crew Herd to Manage Invasive Species on Campus." *The Red and Black*, May 2, 2018. https://www.redandblack.com/uganews/goats-wanted-uga-office-of-sustainability-seeks-new-chew-crew/article_020c4f10-4dab-11e8-aa1c-3be5b563fc9c.html.

Greif. "Study of Pollinator Habitat in Managed Forests Receives SFI Conservation Leadership Award for Greif and Partners." September 24, 2013. https://www.greif.com/about-greif/news/news/article/study-of-pollinator-habitat-in-managed-forests-receives-sfi-conservation-leadership-award-for-greif-and-partners.

Häagen-Dazs. "Häagen-Dazs Loves Honey Bees." Accessed October 12, 2018. https://www.haagendazs.us/about/news/haagen-dazs-loves-honey-bees/.

Hadley, A. S., and M. G. Betts. "The Effects of Landscape Fragmentation on Pollination Dynamics: Absence of Evidence Not Evidence of Absence." National Institutes of Health. *Biological Reviews of the Cambridge Philosophical Society* 87, no. 3 (August 2012): 526–44. https://www.ncbi.nlm.nih.gov/pubmed/22098594.

Hakim, Danny. "Accused of Harming Bees, Bayer Researches a Different Culprit." *New York Times*, December 11, 2013. https://www.nytimes.com/2013/12/12/business/energy-environment/accused-of-harming-bees-bayer-researches-a-different-culprit.html.

Hanna, David Foote, and Claire Kremen. "Invasive Species Management Restores a Plant–Pollinator Mutualism in Hawaii." *Journal of Applied Ecology* 50, no. 1 (February 2013): 147–55. https://www.researchgate.net/publication/260104476_Invasive_species_management_restores_a_plant-pollinator_mutualism_in_Hawaii.

Hannah, Lee, Marc Steele, Emily Fung, Pablo Imbach, and Alan Flint. "Climate Change Influences on Pollinator, Forest, and Farm Interactions across a Climate Gradient." *Climate Change* 141, no. 1 (March 2017): 63–75. https://link.springer.com/article/10.1007/s10584-016-1868-x.

Hanula, James, Scott Horn, and John W. Taylor. "Chinese Privet (Ligustrum Sinense) Removal and Its Effect on Native Plant Communities of Riparian Forests." *Plant Science and Management* 2 (2010): 292–300. https://www.srs.fs.usda.gov/pubs/34542.

Harris, Jeffrey W., and Audrey B. Sheridan. "Managing Varroa Mites in Honey Bee Colonies." Mississippi State University Extension Service. Publication

n. P2826, June 3, 2016. http://extension.msstate.edu/publications/publications/managing-varroa-mites-honey-bee-colonies.

Harris, Kathleen, and Susan Lunn. "Environmentalists Say Partial Pesticide Ban Not Enough to Protect Bees." *CBC News*, December 21, 2017. http://www.cbc.ca/news/politics/bees-environment-pesticides-1.4456011.

Hegland, Stein Joar, Anders Nielsen, Amparo Lázaro, and Ørjan Totland. "How Does Climate Warming Affect Plant–Pollinator Interactions?" *Ecology Letters* 12, no. 2 (February 2009): 184–95. https://onlinelibrary.wiley.com/doi/full/10.1111/j.1461-0248.2008.01269.x.

Henderson, Sandra. "Citizen Science Comes of Age." Ecological Society of America. *Frontiers in Ecology and the Environment* 10, no. 6 (August 1, 2012): 283. https://esajournals.onlinelibrary.wiley.com/doi/10.1890/1540-9295-10.6.283.

Henry, Mickaël, Maxime Béguin, Fabrice Requier, Pierrick Aupinel, Jean Aptel, Sylvie Tchamitchian, and Axel Decourtye. "A Common Pesticide Decreases Foraging Success and Survival in Honey Bees." *Science* 336, no. 6079 (April 20, 2012): 348–50. http://science.sciencemag.org/content/336/6079/348.

Holland, Jennifer S. "The Plight of the Honeybee." *National Geographic*, May 10, 2013. https://news.nationalgeographic.com/news/2013/13/130510-honeybee-bee-science-european-union-pesticides-colony-collapse-epa-science/.

Home Depot. "How Home Depot's Addressing 'Neonic' Concerns." Press release, May 4, 2016. https://corporate.homedepot.com/newsroom/how-home-depot-addresses-neonicotinoid-concerns.

Honeybee Conservancy. "5 Reasons to Sponsor-A-Hive Today." Accessed October 15, 2018. https://thehoneybeeconservancy.org/sponsor-a-hive/.

———. "BeeVillage Bee Sanctuary." Accessed October 15, 2018. https://thehoneybeeconservancy.org/beevillage/.

Hudson, Jacob R., James Hanula, and Scott Horn. "Removing Chinese Privet from Riparian Forests Still Benefits Pollinators Five Years Later." US Department of Agriculture, US Forest Service. *Biological Conservation* 167 (2014): 355–62. https://www.fs.usda.gov/treesearch/pubs/45489.

Hutchings, Michael J., David L. Roberts, and Anthony J. Davy. "Vulnerability of a Specialized Pollination Mechanism to Climate Change Revealed by a 356-year Analysis." *Botanical Journal of the Linnean Society* 186, no. 4 (March 27, 2018): 498–509. https://academic.oup.com/botlinnean/article-abstract/186/4/498/4937553?redirectedFrom=fulltext.

Ingels, Chuck, Mark Van Horn, Robert Bugg, and P. Rick Miller. "Selecting the Right Cover Crop Gives Multiple Benefits." University of California. *Califor-*

nia Agriculture 48, no. 5 (September 1, 1994): 43–48. http://calag.ucanr.edu/Archive/?article=ca.v048n05p43.

Insectlore. "Insect Lore Company History." 2018. http://www.insectlore.com/our-story/.

Integrated Pest Management, University of Missouri. "A Final Report on Dicamba-Injured Soybean Acres." University of Missouri, Division of Plant Sciences, October 30, 2017. https://ipm.missouri.edu/IPCM/2017/10/final_report_dicamba_injured_soybean/.

Intergovernmental Panel on Climate Change. "Climate Change 2014: Synthesis Report." IPCC, 2014. http://www.ipcc.ch/report/ar5/syr/.

Glassberg, Dr. Jeffrey. "IBBA's Response to NABA Statements and Opinions." International Butterfly Breeders Association, 2018. https://www.internationalbutterflybreeders.org/nabaresponse/.

International Union for Conservation of Nature. "Bat-Friendly Tequila." Accessed October 12, 2018. https://www.iucn.org/sites/dev/files/bat-friendly_tequila_factsheet.pdf.

Invasive Species Compendium. "Diseases Caused by Phages: American Foulbrood of Honey Bees." CAB International. Last modified, July 14, 2017. https://www.cabi.org/isc/datasheet/78183.

Jacques, Antoine, Marion Laurent, Magali Ribière-Chabert, Mathilde Saussac, Stéphanie Bougeard, Giles E. Budge, Pascal Hendrikx, and Marie-Pierre Chauzat. "A Pan-European Epidemiological Study Reveals Honey Bee Colony Survival Depends on Beekeeper Education and Disease Control." *PLOS One* (March 9, 2017). http://journals.plos.org/plosone/article?id=10.1371/journal.pone.0172591.

Johnson, Lady Bird. "She Was an Ispiration: Quotes from Lady Bird Johnson." University of Texas at Austin, Lady Bird Johnson Wildflower Center. Accessed October 12, 2018. http://www.ladybirdjohnson.org/quotes/.

Johnson, Renée, and Jim Monke. "What Is the Farm Bill?" Congressional Research Service, April 26, 2018. https://fas.org/sgp/crs/misc/RS22131.pdf.

Journey North. "Answers from the Monarch Butterfly Expert: Spring 2014." Accessed October 12, 2018. http://www.learner.org/jnorth/tm/monarch/ExpertAnswer14.html.

Kaiser-Bunbury, Christopher N., James Mougal, Andrew E. Whittington, Terence Valentin, Ronny Gabriel, Jens M. Olesen, and Nico Blüthgen. "Ecosystem Restoration Strengthens Pollination Network Resilience and Function." *Nature* 542 (February 9, 2017): 223–27. http://www.nature.com/articles/nature21071.

Keim, Brandon. "How Your Bee-Friendly Garden May Actually Be Killing Bees." *Wired*, June 25, 2014. https://www.wired.com/2014/06/garden-center-neo nicotinoids/.

Kelm, Detlev H., Kerstin R. Wiesner, and Otto von Helversen. "Effects of Artificial Roosts for Frugivorous Bats on Seed Dispersal in a Neotropical Forest Pasture Mosaic." *Conservation Biology* 22, no. 3 (June 28, 2008): 733–41. https://on linelibrary.wiley.com/doi/abs/10.1111/j.1523-1739.2008.00925.x.

Kerr, J. T., A. Pindar, P. Galpern, L. Packer, S. G. Potts, S. M. Roberts, P. Rasmont, O. Schweiger, S. R. Colla, L. L. Richardson, D. L. Wagner, L. F. Gall, D. S. Sikes, and A. Pantoja. "Climate Change Impacts on Bumblebees Converge across Continents." National Institutes of Health. *Science* 349, no. 6244 (July 10, 2015): 177–80. https://www.ncbi.nlm.nih.gov/pubmed/26160945.

Kessler, Sébastien, Erin Jo Tiedeken, Kerry L. Simcock, Sophie Derveau, Jessica Mitchell, Samantha Softley, Amy Radcliffe, Jane C. Stout, and Geraldine A. Wright. "Bees Prefer Foods Containing Neonicotinoid Pesticides." *Nature* 521 (May 7, 2015): 74–76. https://www.nature.com/articles/nature14414.

Keystone Policy Center. "Monarch Collaborative." 2017. https://www.keystone.org/our-work/agriculture/monarch-collaborative/.

Kiesel, Laura. "Invasive Plants May Adapt to Climate Change Better than Native Species." *BioScience* 64, no. 7 (July 1, 2014): 640. https://academic.oup.com /bioscience/article/64/7/640/2754158.

Klein, Betsy. "Melania Trump Visits Japanese Garden with Akie Abe." CNN, February 11, 2017. https://www.cnn.com/2017/02/11/politics/melania-trump -akie-abe-garden-tour-florida/index.html.

Koh, Insu, Eric V. Lonsdorf, Neil M. Williams, Claire Brittain, Rufus Isaacs, Jason Gibbs, and Taylor H. Ricketts. "Modeling the Status, Trends, and Impacts of Wild Bee Abundance in the United States." *PNAS* 113, no. 1 (January 5, 2016): 140–45. http://www.pnas.org/content/113/1/140.

Kopec, Kelsey, and Lori Ann Burd. "Pollinators in Peril—A Systematic Status Review of North American and Hawaiian Native Bees." Center for Biological Diversity, February 2017. https://www.biologicaldiversity.org/campaigns/na tive_pollinators/pdfs/Pollinators_in_Peril.pdf.

Kremen, C., K. S. Ullman, and R. W. Thorp. "Evaluating the Quality of Citizen-Scientist Data on Pollinator Communities." *Conservation Biology* 25, no. 3 (April 20, 2011): 607–17. https://onlinelibrary.wiley.com/doi/full/10.1111 /j.1523-1739.2011.01657.x.

Krupke, C. H., J. D. Holland, E. Y. Long, and B. D. Eitzer. "Planting of Neonicotinoid-Treated Maize Poses Risks for Honey Bees and Other Non-target Organisms over a Wide Area without Consistent Crop Yield Benefit." *Journal of Applied Ecology* 54, no. 5 (May 22, 2017): 1449–58. https://besjournals.onlinelibrary.wiley.com/doi/full/10.1111/1365-2664.12924.

Kudo, Gaku, Yoko Nishikawa, Tetsuya Kasagi, and Shoji Kosuge. "Does Seed Production of Spring Ephemerals Decrease When Spring Comes Early?" *Ecological Research* 19, no. 2 (March 25, 2004): 255–59. https://onlinelibrary.wiley.com/doi/10.1111/j.1440-1703.2003.00630.x.

La Jeunesse, Sara. "Dicamba Drift Affects Non-Target Plants and Pollinators." Penn State University, December 3, 2013. http://news.psu.edu/story/383449/2015/12/03/research/dicamba-drift-affects-non-target-plants-and-pollinators.

Landis, Tim. "Number of Registered Beekeepers Surges in Illinois." *State Journal Register* (Springfield, IL), June 16, 2014. http://www.sj-r.com/article/20140615/News/140619589.

Lasky, Jesse R., Walter Jetz, and Timothy H. Keitt. "Conservation Biogeography of the US-Mexico Border: A Transcontinental Risk Assessment of Barriers to Animal Dispersal." *Diversity and Distributions* 17, no. 4 (July 2011): 673–87. https://onlinelibrary.wiley.com/doi/abs/10.1111/j.1472-4642.2011.00765.x.

Leurck, Jeanna Childers. "Agroforestry Helps Pollinators Help You." Colorado State Forest Service, 2018. https://csfs.colostate.edu/agroforestry-helps-pollinators/.

Living Lands and Waters. "Invasive Species Removal Project." Accessed October 12, 2018. http://livinglandsandwaters.org/volunteer/invasive-species-removal-project/.

Loria, Keith. "The World's Food Supply Could Feel the Sting of Declining Bee Populations." *Food Dive*, March 7, 2017. https://www.fooddive.com/news/declining-bee-population-food/436497/.

Lucchesi, Nick. "Good News for Honeybees: 2016 Population Results Are Not 'Horrible.'" *Inverse*, May 28, 2017. https://www.inverse.com/article/32107-why-are-bees-dying.

Luiggi, Cristina. "Honey Bee Killer." *The Scientist*, June 11, 2012. https://www.the-scientist.com/?articles.view/articleNo/32205/title/Honey-Bee-Killer.

Lund University. "Sowing Strips of Flowering Plants Has Limited Effect on Pollination." May 15, 2018. https://www.lunduniversity.lu.se/article/sowing-strips-of-flowering-plants-has-limited-effect-on-pollination.

Lundin, Ola, Maj Rundlöf, Henrik G. Smith, Ingemar Fries, and Riccardo Bommarco. "Neonicotinoid Insecticides and Their Impacts on Bees: A Systematic Review of Research Approaches and Identification of Knowledge Gaps." *PLOS One*, August 27, 2015. http://journals.plos.org/plosone/article?id=10.1371/journal.pone.0136928.

MacIvor, J. Scott, and Laurence Packer. "'Bee Hotels' as Tools for Native Pollinator Conservation: A Premature Verdict?" *PLOS One*, March 18, 2015. http://journals.plos.org/plosone/article?id=10.1371/journal.pone.0122126.

MacIvor, J. Scott. "DNA Barcoding to Identify Leaf Preference of Leafcutting Bees." *Royal Society Open Science*, March 1, 2016. http://rsos.royalsocietypublishing.org/content/3/3/150623.

Maeckle, Monika. "First Lady Michelle Obama Gets Milkweed as White House Adds First Pollinator Garden." Texas Butterfly Ranch, April 6, 2014. https://texasbutterflyranch.com/2014/04/06/first-lady-michelle-obama-gets-milkweed-as-white-house-adds-first-pollinator-garden/.

———. "Texas Parks and Wildlife Launches Milkweed Monitoring Project." Texas Butterfly Ranch, December 12, 2014. https://texasbutterflyranch.com/2014/12/12/texas-parks-and-wildlife-launches-milkweed-monitoring-project/.

Main, Douglas. "The Ineffective, Expensive, and Dangerous Idea of Replacing Bees with Drones." *Newsweek*, February 15, 2017. http://www.newsweek.com/drone-bees-comically-ineffective-expensive-dangerous-real-bees-554881.

Mallinger, Rachel E., Hannah R. Gaines-Day, and Claudio Gratton. "Do Managed Bees Have Negative Effects on Wild Bees?: A Systematic Review of the Literature." *PLOS One*, December 8, 2017. http://journals.plos.org/plosone/article?id=10.1371/journal.pone.0189268.

Mason, Rosemary, Henk Tennekes, Francisco Sanchez-Bayo, and Pelle Und-Jepsen. "Immune Suppression by Neonicotinoid Insecticides at the Root of Global Wildlife Declines." *Journal of Immunology and Toxicology* 1, no. 1 (April 2013): 3–12. https://www.boerenlandvogels.nl/sites/default/files/JEIT Immune Suppression pdf_6.pdf.

May, Buddy. "Hands-On Mentoring—After the Classes There's Very Little Formal Education for New Beekeepers." Bee Culture. *Bee Culture*, November 27, 2017. http://www.beeculture.com/hands-mentoring-classes-theres-little-formal-education-new-beekeepers/.

May, Emily, Rufus Isaacs, Katharina Ullmann, Julianna Wilson, Julia Brokaw, Sarah Foltz Jordan, Jason Gibbs, Jennifer Hopwood, Nikki Rothwell, Mace Vaughan, Kimiora Ward, and Neal Williams. "Established Wildflower Habitat to Support Pollinators of Michigan Fruit Crops," Extension Bulletin E-3360. Michigan State University and the Xerces Society, July 2017. http://msue.anr.msu.edu/uploads/resources/pdfs/Establishing_Wildflower_Habitat_to_Support_Pollinators_of_Michigan_Fruit_Crops_-_E3360.pdf.

McIver, James S., Robbin Thorpe, and Karen Erichsen. "Pollinators of the Invasive Plant, Yellow Starthistle (*Centaturca solstitialis*), in Northeastern Oregon,

USA." *Weed Biology and Management* 9 (2009): 137–45. https://www.fs.fed.us/pnw/pubs/journals/pnw_2009_mciver002.pdf.

McKinney, Amy M., Paul J. CaraDonna, David W. Inouye, Billy Barr, C. David Bertelsen, and Nickolas M. Waser. "Asynchronous Changes in Phenology of Migrating Broad-tailed Hummingbirds and Their Early-Season Nectar Resources." *Ecology* 93, no. 9 (September 1, 2012): 1987–93. https://esajournals.onlinelibrary.wiley.com/doi/abs/10.1890/12-0255.1.

Memmott, Jane, Paul G. Craze, Nickolas M. Waser, and Mary V. Price. "Global Warming and the Disruption of Plant–Pollinator Interactions." *Ecology Letters* 10, no. 8 (August 2007): 710–17. https://onlinelibrary.wiley.com/doi/full/10.1111/j.1461-0248.2007.01061.x.

Merry, Mitch. "Climate Change Will Leave Edith's Checkerspot Butterflies out of Sync." Endangered Species Coalition, November 20, 2009. http://www.endangered.org/climate-change-will-leave-ediths-checkerspot-butterflies-out-of-sync.

Meyer, Christoph F. J., Matthew J. Struebig, and Michael R. Willig. "Responses of Tropical Bats to Habitat Fragmentation, Logging, and Deforestation." Pp. 63–103 in *Bats in the Anthropocene: Conservation of Bats in a Changing World*, ed. Christian C. Voigt and Tigga Kingston. Berlin: Springer, December 8, 2015. https://link.springer.com/chapter/10.1007/978-3-319-25220-9_4.

Midwest Center for Investigative Reporting. "EPA Eased Dicamba Regulations Following Monsanto Research, Records Show." *Successful Farming*, March 13, 2018. https://www.agriculture.com/crops/soybeans/epa-eased-dicamba-regulations-following-monsanto-research-records-show.

Miller-Rushing, Abraham, Richard Primack, and Rick Bonney. "The History of Public Participation in Ecological Research." *Frontiers in Ecology and the Environment* 10, no. 6 (August 2012): 285–90. https://esajournals.onlinelibrary.wiley.com/doi/10.1890/110278.

Minnesota Department of Natural Resources. "Purple Loosestrife (*Lythrum salicardia*)." 2018. https://www.dnr.state.mn.us/invasives/aquaticplants/purpleloosestrife/index.html.

Mission 2015: Biodiversity. "Bee Pollination and Technology." Accessed October 12, 2018. http://web.mit.edu/12.000/www/m2015/2015/bee_tech.html.

Mistry, Shahroukh, and Arnulfo Moreno-Valdez. "Climate Change and Bats: Vampire Bats Offer Clues to the Future." Bat Conservation International. *BATS Magazine* 26, no. 2 (Summer 2008). http://www.batcon.org/resources/media-education/bats-magazine/bat_article/1024.

Moisset, Beatriz, and Vicki Wojcik. "Blue Orchard Mason Bee (*Osmia lignaria*)."

USDA, US Forest Service. Accessed October 17, 2018. https://www.fs.fed.us/wildflowers/pollinators/pollinator-of-the-month/mason_bees.shtml.

Monarch Joint Venture. "Pesticides." MJV News RSS, 2018. https://monarchjointventure.org/threats/pesticides/.

———. "Potential Risks of Growing Exotic Milkweeds for Monarchs." Accessed October 15, 2018. https://www.fws.gov/southwest/es/Documents/R2ES/Pollinators/10-OE_fact_sheet_and_tropical_milkweed_Monarch_Watch_2014.pdf.

———. "Rearing Monarchs Responsibility." Accessed October 15, 2018. https://monarchjointventure.org/images/uploads/documents/Monarch_Rearing_Instructions.pdf.

Monarch Watch. "Bring Back the Monarchs." Accessed October 15, 2018. https://monarchwatch.org/bring-back-the-monarchs/.

Moore, Philip A., Michael E. Wilson, and John A. Skinner. "Honey Bee Viruses, the Deadly Varroa Mite Associates." *Extension*, November 29, 2016. https://articles.extension.org/pages/71172/honey-bee-viruses-the-deadly-varroa-mite-associates.

Morandin, Lora A., and Claire Kreman. "Bee Preference for Native versus Exotic Plants in Restored Agricultural Hedgerows." *Restoration Ecology* 21, no. 1 (January 2013): 26–32. https://food.berkeley.edu/wp-content/uploads/2014/09/Bee-Preference-Rest-Ecol.pdf.

Morrison, Sara. "Bayer Wants You to Know That It Does Not Kill Bees. Bayer Loves Bees." *The Atlantic*, December 13, 2013. https://www.theatlantic.com/international/archive/2013/12/bayer-wants-you-know-it-does-not-kill-bees-bayer-loves-bees/356104/.

Moyer-Horner, Lucas, Matthew M. Smith, and Jami Belt. "Citizen Science and Observer Variability during American Pika Surveys." *Wildlife Management* 76, no. 7 (March 6, 2012): 1472–79. https://onlinelibrary.wiley.com/doi/10.1002/jwmg.373.

Mullin, Christopher A., Maryann Frazier, James L. Frazier, Sara Ashcraft, Roger Simonds, Dennis VanEngelsdorp, and Jeffery S. Pettis. "High Levels of Miticides and Agrochemicals in North American Apiaries: Implications for Honey Bee Health." *PLOS One* (March 19, 2010). http://journals.plos.org/plosone/article?id=10.1371/journal.pone.0009754.

National Audubon Society. Audubon Christmas Bird Count. http://netapp.audubon.org/cbcobservation/.

———. "Christmas Bird Count Bibliography." *Audubon*, November 28, 2016. http://www.audubon.org/christmas-bird-count-bibliography.

———. "Rufous Hummingbird." Audubon Climate Report, 2014. http://climate.audubon.org/birds/rufhum/rufous-hummingbird.

———. "Why Native Plants Matter." *Audubon*, May 18, 2017. https://www.audubon.org/content/why-native-plants-matter.

National Invasive Species Council. "Management Plan: 2016–2018." US Department of the Interior, July 11, 2016. https://www.doi.gov/sites/doi.gov/files/uploads/2016-2018-nisc-management-plan.pdf.

National Invasive Species Information Center. "What Is an Invasive Species?" USDA, May 24, 2016. https://www.invasivespeciesinfo.gov/whatis.shtml.

National Pesticide Information Center. "Dicamba." Oregon State University, February 2012. http://npic.orst.edu/factsheets/dicamba_gen.html.

National Research Council. Status of Pollinators in North America. Washington, DC: National Academies Press, April 13, 2007.

Nature Conservancy. "Stories in Kentucky: Planting for Pollinators." Accessed October 15, 2018. https://www.nature.org/en-us/about-us/where-we-work/united-states/kentucky/stories-in-kentucky/planting-for-pollinators/.

North American Pollinator Protection Campaign. "Wildlife Fact Sheet: Invasive Species." Accessed October 15, 2018. http://pollinator.org/assets/generalFiles/NAPPC-Invasive-Species-Fact-Sheet.pdf.

Nunez, Martin A., Sara Kuebbing, Romina Dimario, and Daniel Simberloff. "Invasive Species: To Eat, or Not to Eat, That Is the Question." *Conservation Letters* 0 (April 5, 2012): 1–8. http://web.utk.edu/~mnunez/Nunez_etal_eating_invasives.pdf.

Ontario Ministry of the Environment, Conservation, and Parks. "Ontario Introducing New Rules to Protect Pollinators." Press release, June 9, 2015. https://news.ontario.ca/ene/en/2015/06/ontario-introducing-new-rules-to-protect-pollinators.html.

Rosetta, R. L. "European Wool Carder Bee." Oregon State University, Department of Horticulture. Last modified June 21, 2017. http://oregonstate.edu/dept/nurspest/European_wool_carder_bee.html.

Owen, Robert. "Role of Human Action in the Spread of Honey Bee (Hymenoptera: Apidae) Pathogens." *Journal of Economic Entomology* 110, no. 3 (June 2017): 797–801. https://academic.oup.com/jee/article-abstract/110/3/797/3105961?redirectedFrom=fulltext.

Pagad, Shyama, Piero Genovesi, Lucilla Carnevali, Dmitry Schigel, and Melodie A. McGeoch. "Introducing the Global Register of Introduced and Invasive Species." *Scientific Data* 5 (January 23, 2018). https://www.nature.com/articles/sdata2017202.

Pattemore, David E., and David S. Wilcove. "Invasive Rats and Recent Colonist Birds Partially Compensate for the Loss of Endemic New Zealand Pollinators." *Proceedings of the Royal Society of London B: Biological Sciences*

279, no. 1733 (April 22, 2012). http://rspb.royalsocietypublishing.org/content/279/1733/1597.

Pecenka, Jacob R., and Jonathan G. Lundgren. "Non-Target Effects of Clothianidin on Monarch Butterflies." *Science of Nature* 102 (April 2015): 18–19. https://bioscienceresource.org/wp-content/uploads/2015/04/Pecenka-and-Lundgren-2015-Early-On-line.pdf.

Pesticide Action Network UK. "About Neonicotinoids." Accessed October 15, 2018. http://www.pan-uk.org/about_neonicotinoids/.

Picchi, Malayka Samantha, Lerina Avolio, Laura Azzani, Orietta Brombin, and Giuseppe Camerini. "Fireflies and Land Use in an Urban Landscape: The Case of *Luciola italica* L. (Coleoptera: Lampyridae) in the City of Turin." *Journal of Insect Conservation* 17, no. 4 (August 2013): 797–805. https://link.springer.com/article/10.1007/s10841-013-9562-z.

Pimentel, David, Rodolfo Zuniga, and Doug Morrison. "Update on the Environmental and Economic Costs Associated with Alien-invasive Species in the United States." *Ecological Economics* 52, no. 3 (February 15, 2005): 273–88. https://www.sciencedirect.com/science/article/pii/S0921800904003027?via=ihub.

Pleasants, John M., and Karen S. Oberhauser. "Milkweed Loss in Agricultural Fields Because of Herbicide Use: Effect on the Monarch Butterfly Population." *Insect Conservation and Diversity* 6, no. 2 (March 2013): 135–44. https://onlinelibrary.wiley.com/doi/full/10.1111/j.1752-4598.2012.00196.x.

Portillo, Ely. "Are Developers Flooding Uptown with Too Many Luxury Apartments?" *Charlotte* (North Carolina) *Observer*, June 22, 2017. http://www.charlotteobserver.com/news/business/biz-columns-blogs/development/article157499064.html.

Potts, Simon G., Vera Imperatriz-Fonseca, Hien T. Ngo, Jacobus C. Biesmeijer, Thomas D. Breeze, Lynn V. Dicks, Lucas A. Garibaldi, Rosemary Hill, Josef Settele, and Adam J. Vanbergen. "Assessment Report on Pollinators, Pollination, and Food Production: Summary for Policymakers." IPBES, August 23, 2017. https://www.ipbes.net/assessment-reports/pollinators.

Powell, Kristen I., Kyra N. Krakos, and Tiffany M. Knight. "Comparing the Reproductive Success and Pollination Biology of an Invasive Plant to Its Rare and Common Native Congeners: A Case Study in the Genus *Cirsium* (Asteraceae)." *Biological Invasions* 13 (2011): 905–17. https://wubio.wustl.edu/files/biology/imce/powell_et_al_2011_biol_invasion.pdf.

Project *Apis m.* "Seeds for Bees." 2017. https://www.projectapism.org/seeds-for-bees-home.html.

Rader, Romina, Ignasi Bartomeus, Lucas A. Garibaldi, Michael P. D. Garratt, Brad G. Howlett, Rachael Winfree, Saul A. Cunningham, Margaret M. Mayfield, Anthony D. Arthur, Georg K. S. Andersson, Riccardo Bommarco, Claire Brittain, Luísa G. Carvalheiro, Natacha P. Chacoff, Martin H. Entling, Benjamin Foully, Breno M. Freitas, Barbara Gemmill-Herren, Jaboury Ghazoul, Sean R. Griffin, Caroline L. Gross, Lina Herbertsson, Felix Herzog, Juliana Hipólito, Sue Jaggar, Frank JaukerAlexandra-Maria Klein, David Kleijn, Smitha Krishnan, Camila Q. Lemos, Sandra A. M. Lindström, Yael Mandelik, Victor M. Monteiro, Warrick Nelson, Lovisa Nilsson, David E. Pattemore, Natália De O. Pereira, Gideon Pisanty, Simon G. Potts, Menno Reemer, Maj Rundlöf, Cory S. Sheffield, Jeroen Scheper, Christof Schüepp, Henrik G. Smith, Dara A. Stanley, Jane C. Stout, Hajnalka Szentgyörgyi, Hisatomo Taki, Carlos H. Vergara, Blandina F. Viana, and Michal Woyciechowski. "Non-Bee Insects Are Important Contributors to Global Crop Pollination." *PNAS* 113, no. 1 (January 5, 2016): 146–51. http://www.pnas.org/content/113/1/146.

Riesch, Hauke, and Clive Potter. "Citizen Science as Seen by Scientists: Methodological, Epistemological, and Ethical Dimensions." *Public Understanding of Science* 23, no. 1 (August 27, 2013): 107–20. http://journals.sagepub.com/doi/10.1177/0963662513497324.

Riley, Noelle. "Getting Garlic Mustard's Goat." *Traverse City* (Michigan) *Record-Eagle*, May 17, 2018. http://www.record-eagle.com/news/go/getting-garlic-mustard-s-goat/article_51d3ba0f-a3fe-5efa-b6ea-45c6c3e63d40.html.

Russo, Laura. "Positive and Negative Impacts of Non-Native Bee Species around the World." National Institutes of Health. *Insects* 7, no. 4 (December 2016): 69. https://www.ncbi.nlm.nih.gov/pmc/articles/PMC5198217/.

Ryabov, Eugene V., Anna K. Childers, Yanping Chen, Shayne Madella, Ashrafun Nessa, Dennis vanEngelsdorp, and Jay D. Evans. "Recent Spread of *Varroa destructor* Virus-1, a Honey Bee Pathogen, in the United States." *Scientific Reports* 7 (December 12, 2017). https://www.nature.com/articles/s41598-017-17802-3.pdf?origin=ppub.

Salisbury, Susan. "Love of Bees and Honey Draws Some to Beekeeping, Florida Numbers Up." *Palm Beach* (Florida) *Post*, July 18, 2015. https://www.mypalmbeachpost.com/business/love-bees-and-honey-draws-some-beekeeping-florida-numbers/2WgYxLCl2PqDmA6O3fZ4cN/.

Sample, Ian. "New Beetle Species Named after Leonardo DiCaprio." *The Guardian,* April 30, 2018. https://www.theguardian.com/science/2018/apr/30/new-beetle-species-named-after-leonardo-dicaprio.

San Francisco State University. "Urban Pollinators Get the Job Done." *ScienceDaily*, February 12, 2015. https://www.sciencedaily.com/releases/2015/02/150212154533.htm.

Sanz, Juan José, and Oscar Gordo. "Temporal Trends in Phenology of the Honey

Bee *Apis mellifera* (L.) and the Small White *Pieris rapae* (L.) in the Iberian Peninsula (1952–2004)." *Ecological Entomology* 31, no. 3 (June 2006): 261–68. https://onlinelibrary.wiley.com/doi/10.1111/j.1365-2311.2006.00787.x.

Satterfield, Dara A., Sonia Altizer, Mary-Kate Williams, and Richard J. Hall. "Environmental Persistence Influences Infection Dynamics for a Butterfly Pathogen." National Institutes of Health. *PLOS One* 12, no. 1 (January 18, 2017).https://www.ncbi.nlm.nih.gov/pmc/articles/PMC5242512/#pone.0169982.s001.

Satterfield, Dara A., John C. Maerz, and Sonia Altizer. "Loss of Migratory Behaviour Increases Infection Risk for a Butterfly Host." *Proceedings of the Royal Society of London B: Biological Sciences* 282, no. 1801 (February 22, 2015). http://rspb.royalsocietypublishing.org/content/282/1801/20141734.

Saunders, Sarah P., Leslie Ries, Karen S. Oberhauser, Wayne E. Thogmartin, and Elise F. Zipkin. "Local and Cross-Seasonal Associations of Climate and Land Use with Abundance of Monarch Butterflies *Danaus plexippus*." *Ecography* 41, no. 2 (February 2018): 278–90. https://onlinelibrary.wiley.com/doi/abs/10.1111/ecog.02719.

Schlaepfer, Martin A., Dov F. Sax, and Julian D. Olden. "The Potential Conservation Value of Non-Native Species." *Conservation Biology* 25, no. 3 (February 22, 2011): 428–37. https://onlinelibrary.wiley.com/doi/abs/10.1111/j.1523-1739.2010.01646.x.

Schneider, Andrew. "Tests Show Most Store Honey Isn't Honey." *Food Safety News*, November 7, 2011. http://www.foodsafetynews.com/2011/11/tests-show-most-store-honey-isnt-honey/#.WwtIDmWlfBI.

Schultz, Cheryl B., Leone M. Brown, Emma Pelton, and Elizabeth E. Crone. "Citizen Science Monitoring Demonstrates Dramatic Declines of Monarch Butterflies in Western North America." *Biological Conservation* 214 (October 2017): 343–46. https://www.sciencedirect.com/science/article/pii/S0006320717304809.

Scofield, Hailey N., and Heather R. Mattila. "Honey Bee Workers That Are Pollen Stressed as Larvae Become Poor Foragers and Waggle Dancers as Adults." *PLOS One*, April 8, 2015. http://journals.plos.org/plosone/article?id=10.1371/journal.pone.0121731.

Scotts Miracle-Gro. "Ortho Plans to Remove Neonics." Press release, April 12, 2016. https://scottsmiraclegro.com/ortho-announces-plan-to-eliminate-neonics-from-all-outdoor-products/.

Shulman, Seth. "Will Climate Change Hasten the Spread of Invasive Plants." *Grist*, January 5, 2011. https://www.ucsusa.org/global-warming/science-and-impacts/science/climate-scientist-bethany-bradley.html#.WwXOtmWlfBI.

Sidhu, C. Sheena, and Neelendra K. Joshi. National Institutes of Health. *Frontiers in Plant Science* 7 (March 24, 2016): 363. https://www.ncbi.nlm.nih.gov/pmc/articles/PMC4806296/.

Sinu, Palatty Allesh, V. C. Sibisha, M. V. Nikhila Reshmi, K. S. Reshmi, T. V. Jasna, K. Aswathi, and P. P. Megha. "Invasive Ant (*Anoplolepis gracilipes*) Disrupts Pollination in Pumpkin." *Biological Invasions* 19, no. 9 (September 2017): 2599–607. https://link.springer.com/article/10.1007/s10530-017-1470-9.

Smith, Lindsay N. "Monarch Butterfly's Reign Threatened by Milkweed Decline." *National Geographic*, August 20, 2014. https://news.nationalgeographic.com/news/2014/08/140819-monarch-butterfly-milkweed-environment-ecology-science/.

Southeast Farm Press. "Crop Insurance Acreage, Farmers' Expense for It Up in 2017." *Southeast FarmPress*, February 7, 2018. https://www.southeastfarmpress.com/insurance/crop-insurance-acreage-farmers-expense-it-2017.

Stanley, Dara A., Karen E. Smith, and Nigel E. Raine. "Bumblebee Learning and Memory Is Impaired by Chronic Exposure to a Neonicotinoid Pesticide." *Scientific Reports* 5 (November 16, 2015). http://www.nature.com/articles/srep16508.

Stepanian, Phillip M., and Charlotte E. Wainwright. "Ongoing Changes in Migration Phenology and Winter Residency at Bracken Bat Cave." *Global Change Biology* 24, no. 7 (July 2018): 3266–75. https://onlinelibrary.wiley.com/doi/abs/10.1111/gcb.14051.

Stokstad, Erik. "European Union Expands Ban of Three Neonicotinoid Pesticides." *Science*, April 27, 2018. http://www.sciencemag.org/news/2018/04/european-union-expands-ban-three-neonicotinoid-pesticides.

Strayer, Sarah Easter, Karen Everstine, and Shaun Kennedy. "Economically Motivated Adulteration of Honey: Quality Control Vulnerabilities in the International Honey Market." *Food Protection Trends* (January 2014). http://www.foodprotection.org/files/food-protection-trends/Jan-Feb-14-everstine.pdf.

Szyniszewska, Anna. "Invasive Species & Climate Change." Climate Institute, 2010. http://climate.org/archive/topics/ecosystems/invasivespecies.html.

Soper, J., and J. R. Beggs. "Assessing the Impact of an Introduced Bee, *Anthidium manicatum*, on Pollinator Communities in New Zealand." *New Zealand Journal of Botany* 51, no. 3 (2013): 213–28. https://www.tandfonline.com/doi/abs/10.1080/0028825X.2013.793202.

Tequila Interchange Project. "We Advocate the Preservation of Sustainable, Traditional, and Quality Practices in the Industries of Agave Distilled Spirits." Universidad Nacional Autónomo de México, 2018. http://www.tequilainterchangeproject.org/.

Tequila Ocho. "Rancho 'Las Aguilas.'" 2017. http://ochotequila.com/us/wp-content/uploads/sites/5/2017/08/Download-Las-Aguilas-Tasting-Notes-ilovepdf-compressed.pdf.

Texas A&M Agrilife Extension. "Insects in the City: What Is a Neonicotinoid?" Texas A&M University. Accessed October 15, 2018. https://citybugs.tamu.edu/factsheets/ipm/what-is-a-neonicotinoid/.

Texas Invasive Species Institute. "Japanese Honeysuckle." 2014. http://www.tsusinvasives.org/home/database/lonicera-japonica.

Thogmartin, Wayne E., Ruscena Wiederholt, Karen Oberhauser, Ryan G. Drum, Jay E. Diffendorfer, Sonia Altizer, Orley R. Taylor, John Pleasants, Darius Semmens, Brice Semmens, Richard Erickson, Kaitlin Libby, and Laura Lopez-Hoffman. "Monarch Butterfly Population Decline in North America: Identifying the Threatening Processes." Royal Society Open Science (September 2017). https://doi.org/10.1098/rsos.170760 Tinker, Dani. "A Visual Journey through the Monarch Life Cycle." *National Wildlife Federation Blog*, September 5, 2014. http://blog.nwf.org/2014/09/a-visual-journey-through-the-monarch-life-cycle/.

Toomey, Anne H., and Margret C. Domroese. "Can Citizen Science Lead to Positive Conservation Attitudes and Behaviors?" *Human Ecology Review* 20, no. 1 (2013): 50–62. http://marcus.ib.usp.br/biz0304/lib/exe/fetch.php?media=aulas:toomey_e_domroese_2013_can_citizen_science_lead_to_positive_conservation .pdf.

Toyota. "2016 North American Environmental Report." Accessed August 27, 2018. https://www.toyota.com/usa/environmentreport2016/biodiversity.html.

Unglesbee, Emily. "Neonic Seed Treatments: Yield Benefits vs. Potential Harm—Study Draws Conclusion—DTN." *AgFax*, May 23, 2017. https://agfax.com/2017/05/23/neonic-seed-treatments-yield-benefits-vs-potential-harm-study-draws-conclusion-dtn/.

United States Department of Agriculture. "2017 California Almond Acreage Report." April 25, 2018. https://www.nass.usda.gov/Statistics_by_State/California/Publications/Specialty_and_Other_Releases/Almond/Acreage/201804 almac.pdf.

———. "Conservation Reserve Program." US Department of Agriculture, Farm Service Agency, June 1, 2018. https://www.fsa.usda.gov/programs-and-services/conservation-programs/conservation-reserve-program/.

———. "Honey Bee Colonies Down Slightly for Operations with Five of More Colonies." National Agricultural Statistics Service, August 1, 2018. http://usda.mannlib.cornell.edu/usda/current/BeeColonies/BeeColonies-08-01-2018.pdf.

———. "Loss Adjustment Manual Standards Handbook 2017 and Succeeding Crop Years." US Department of Agriculture, Federal Crop Insurance Corporation FCIC-25010 (10-2016), 2017. https://vdocuments.site/2017-loss-adjustment-manual-fcic-25010-handbook-replaces-the-2016-loss-adjustment.html.

———. "Pollinators." US Department of Agriculture, Farm Service Agency. Accessed October 17, 2018. https://www.fsa.usda.gov/programs-and-services/economic-and-policy-analysis/natural-resources-analysis/pollinators/index.

———. "Report on the National Stakeholders Conference on Honey Bee Health: Key Findings." US Department of Agriculture, Agricultural Research Service, May 2, 2013. https://www.ars.usda.gov/oc/br/epabees/index/.

———. "USDA Launches New Conservation Effort to Aid Monarch Butterflies." US Department of Agriculture, Natural Resources Conservation Service press release, November 12, 2015. https://www.nrcs.usda.gov/wps/portal/nrcs/detail/national/newsroom/releases/?cid=nrcseprd414821.

———. "Washington State-Listed Noxious Weeds." US Department of Agriculture, Natural Resources Conservation Service. Accessed October 17, 2018. https://plants.usda.gov/java/noxious?rptType=State&statefips=53.

———. "Washington Tree Fruit Acreage Report." US Department of Agriculture, National Agriculture Statistics Service. Accessed November 8, 2017. https://www.nass.usda.gov/Statistics_by_State/Washington/Publications/Fruit/2017/FT2017.pdf.

———. "Working Trees Info—How Does Agroforestry Help Crop Pollination?" US Department of Agriculture, National Agroforestry Center, 2016. https://www.fs.usda.gov/nac/documents/workingtrees/infosheets/WTInfoSheetCropPollinationJune2016.pdf.

United States Department of Homeland Security. "Real ID." August 14, 2018. https://www.dhs.gov/real-id.

United States Department of the Interior. "National Invasive Species Council." August 2, 2018. https://www.doi.gov/invasivespecies.

United States Environmental Protection Agency. "Benefits of Neonicotinoid Seed Treatments to Soybean Production." Last modified April 7, 2016. https://www.epa.gov/pollinator-protection/benefits-neonicotinoid-seed-treatments-soybean-production.

———. "DDT—A Brief History and Status." Last modified August 11, 2017. https://www.epa.gov/ingredients-used-pesticide-products/ddt-brief-history-and-status.

———. "Endangered Species Facts: Bay Checkerspot Butterfly." February 2010.

https://www.epa.gov/sites/production/files/2013-08/documents/bay-checkerspot-butterfly.pdf.

———. "EPA Releases Four Neonicotinoid Risk Assessments for Public Comment." Press release, January 12, 2017. https://www.epa.gov/pesticides/epa-releases-four-neonicotinoid-risk-assessments-public-comment.

———. "Proposal to Mitigate Exposure to Bees from Acutely Toxic Pesticide Products; Extension of Comment Period." National Archives, Federal Register, July 27, 2015. https://www.federalregister.gov/documents/2015/07/27/2015-18413/proposal-to-mitigate-exposure-to-bees-from-acutely-toxic-pesticide-products-extension-of-comment.

United States Fish and Wildlife Service. "Attracting Pollinators to Your Garden." Item no. FW 7005. Accessed October 15, 2018. https://www.fws.gov/pollinators/pdfs/pollinatorbookletfinalrevweb.pdf.

———. "Birds: Santa Ana National Wildlife Refuge." July 2011. https://www.fws.gov/uploadedFiles/BirdList-2011_508.pdf.

———. "Butterflies of Santa Ana National Wildlife Refuge." October 2008. https://www.fws.gov/uploadedFiles/SA NWR Butterflies 2008-508.pdf.

———. "Collaborative Conservation Efforts Lead to Recovery, Proposed Delisting of Endangered Southwest Bat." Press release, January 5, 2017. https://www.fws.gov/news/ShowNews.cfm?ref=collaborative-conservation-efforts-lead-to-recovery-proposed-delisting-o&_ID=35998.

———. "Endangered Species Act: A History of the Endangered Species Act of 1973." Last modified November 1, 2017. https://www.fws.gov/endangered/laws-policies/esa-history.html.

———. "Fact Sheet: Rusty Patched Bumble Bee (*Bombus affinis*)." Last modified August 14, 2018. https://www.fws.gov/midwest/endangered/insects/rpbb/factsheetrpbb.html.

———. "Greater Sage-Grouse: (*Centrocercus urophasianus*)." Environmental Conservation Online System. Accessed October 12, 2018. https://ecos.fws.gov/ecp0/profile/speciesProfile?spcode=B06W.

———. "Pollinators." Last modified September 24, 2018. https://www.fws.gov/pollinators/.

———. "Pollinators: Endangered Species Program." Last modified November 13, 2017. https://www.fws.gov/pollinators/programs/endangered.html.

———. "Rusty Patched Bumble Bee: Archives." Last modified March 12, 2018. https://www.fws.gov/midwest/endangered/insects/rpbb/archives.html.

United States Geologic Survey. "Billions More Milkweeds Needed to Restore Monarchs." US Department of the Interior, USGS, April 27, 2017. https://www.usgs.gov/news/billions-more-milkweeds-needed-restore-monarchs.

———. "Learn About Pollination." US Department of the Interior. Last modified May 19, 2015. https://www2.usgs.gov/ecosystems/wildlife/pollinators/pollination.html.

———. "Patuxent Wildlife Research Center." Accessed October 17, 2018. https://www.pwrc.usgs.gov/prodabs/ab10070308/abs6920.htm.

United States Senate. Pollinator Habitat Protection Act of 2007 (Max Baucus, sponsor). S.1496, 110th Cong. Congress.gov, June 12, 2007. https://www.congress.gov/bill/110th-congress/senate-bill/1496/text.

———. Pollinator Protection Act of 2007 (Barbara Boxer, sponsor). S.1694, 110th Cong. Congress.gov, June 26, 2007. https://www.congress.gov/bill/110th-congress/senate-bill/1694.

University of California, Davis. "Honey Flavor and Aroma Wheel Is Complete!" UC Davis Honey and Pollination Center. Last modified January 17, 2018. https://honey.ucdavis.edu/news/honey-flavor-and-aroma-wheel-complete.

———. "Wool Carder Bee Not the Terrorist Some Folks Think It Is." UC Davis Department of Entomology and Nematology, January 27, 2011. http://entomology.ucdavis.edu/News/Wool_Carder_Bee_Not_the_Terrorist_Some_Folks_Think_It_Is/.

University of Cambridge. "Think of Honeybees as 'Livestock' Not Wildlife, Argue Experts." University of Cambridge Research, January 25, 2018. http://www.cam.ac.uk/research/news/think-of-honeybees-as-livestock-not-wildlife-argue-experts.

University of Florida, Institute of Food and Agricultural Sciences. "Blue Butterflies." UF/IFAS. Last modified December 7, 2017. http://gardeningsolutions.ifas.ufl.edu/design/gardening-with-wildlife/blue-butterflies.html.

———. "Coontie." UF/IFAS. Last modified February 19, 2018. http://gardeningsolutions.ifas.ufl.edu/plants/trees-and-shrubs/palms-and-cycads/coontie.html.

University of Kansas. "Habitat Destruction May Wipe Out Monarch Butterfly Migration." *ScienceDaily*, April 5, 2008. https://www.sciencedaily.com/releases/2008/04/080401230705.htm.

University of North Carolina Asheville, Ramsey Library. "Pollinator Seed Library: Seeding Ideas." 2018. http://library.unca.edu/seeds.

University of Texas at Austin. "Supporting Pollinators Could Have Big Payoff for Texas Cotton Farmers." *UT News*, January 24, 2017. https://news.utexas.edu/2016/06/13/an-eco-friendly-way-to-boost-texas-cotton-production.

Urban Pollination Project. "About UPP." 2014. https://urbanpollinationproject.org/about/.

Vail (Colorado) *Daily*. "Adopt a Trail Volunteer Trail-Maintenance and Education

Efforts Expand to More Public Lands." January 19, 2018. https://www.vaildaily.com/news/adopt-a-trail-volunteer-trail-maintenance-and-education-efforts-expand-to-more-public-lands/.

Vancouver (British Columbia) Public Library. "Seed Library." Accessed October 17, 2018. https://www.vpl.ca/collection/seed-library.

VanEngelsdorp, Dennis, Jay D. Evans, Claude Saegerman, Chris Mullin, Eric Haubruge, Bach Kim Nguyen, Maryann Frazier, Jim Frazier, Diana Cox-Foster, Yanping Chen, Robyn Underwood, David R. Tarpy, and Jeffery S. Pettis. "Colony Collapse Disorder: A Descriptive Study." *PLOS One* (August 3, 2009). http://journals.plos.org/plosone/article?id=10.1371/journal.pone.0006481.

Vishnani, Ayesha. "Adopt-a-Trail Helps the City Keep Trails Safe and Invasive Species Out." *Columbia Missourian*, February 17, 2018. https://www.columbiamissourian.com/news/local/adopt-a-trail-helps-the-city-keep-trails-safe-and/article_ffc1ae40-141f-11e8-8cdf-bbd9dd750bea.html.

Walker, Meredith Swett. "Mite-Resistant Russian Honey Bees Might Not Prevent Varroa Infestations." *Entomology Today*, May 3, 2017. https://entomologytoday.org/2017/04/11/mite-resistant-russian-honey-bees-might-not-prevent-varroa-infestations/.

Walter, Robin. "Popcorn's Dirty Little Secret." *Sierra*, November 12, 2015. https://www.sierraclub.org/sierra/2015-6-november-december/green-life/popcorns-dirty-little-secret.

Watson, Elaine. "Almond Breeze Almond Milk Only Contains 2% Almonds, Claims False Advertising Lawsuit." Foodnavigator-usa.com, July 30, 2015. https://www.foodnavigator-usa.com/Article/2015/07/22/Almond-milk-only-contains-2-almonds-claims-lawsuit-v-Blue-Diamond.

———. "Judge Takes Wind Out of Plaintiffs' Sails in '2% Almonds' False Advertising Class Action vs WhiteWave, Blue Diamond." Foodnavigator-usa.com, October 23, 2015. https://www.foodnavigator-usa.com/Article/2015/10/23/No-injunctive-relief-in-almond-milk-lawsuit-vs-WhiteWave-Blue-Diamond?utm_source=copyright&utm_medium=OnSite&utm_campaign=copyright.

Weber, Jeremy G., Nigel Key, and Erik J. O'Donoghue. "Does Federal Crop Insurance Encourage Farm Specialization and Fertilizer and Chemical Use?" Selected paper for presentation at 2015 AAEA and WAEA Annual Meetings in San Francisco, CA, July 26–28. https://ageconsearch.umn.edu/bitstream/204972/2/AAEA Paper.pdf.

Weener, Adrian M., Robbin W. Thorpe, and John F. Barthell. "Biological Control and Eradication of Feral Honey Bee Colonies on Santa Cruz Island, California: A Summary." Pp. 327–35 in *Proceedings of the 7th California Islands*

Symposium, C. C. Damiani and D. K. Garcelon, eds. 2009. http://iws.org/CISProceedings/7th_CIS_Proceedings/Wenner.pdf.

Weise, Elizabeth. "Robot Drone Bees? It's Not a Horror Movie, It's a Walmart Patent." *USA Today*, March 16, 2018. https://www.usatoday.com/story/tech/science/2018/03/15/walmart-robot-drone-bees-patent/428935002/.

Western Monarch Milkweed Mapper. "Frequently Asked Questions." 2018. https://www.monarchmilkweedmapper.org/frequently-asked-questions/#1.

Whitehorn, Penelope R., Stephanie O'Connor, Felix L. Wackers, and Dave Goulson. "Neonicotinoid Pesticide Reduces Bumble Bee Colony Growth and Queen Production." *Science* 336, no. 6079 (April 20, 2012): 351–52. http://science.sciencemag.org/content/336/6079/351.

White House. "Pollinator Partnership Action Plan." June 2016. www.whitehouse.gov.

———. "Presidential Proclamation Modifying the Bears Ears National Monument." December 4, 2017. https://www.whitehouse.gov/presidential-actions/presidential-proclamation-modifying-bears-ears-national-monument/.

———. "Second Lady Karen Pence, Secretary Perdue Unveil Beehive at Vice President's Residence, and Asks Public to Help Boost Pollinator Population." June 6, 2017. https://www.whitehouse.gov/briefings-statements/second-lady-karen-pence-secretary-perdue-unveil-beehive-vice-presidents-residence-asks-public-help-boost-pollinator-population/.

Wiedemann, Kenia. "The White-Nose Syndrome and the Rampant Use of Pesticides in North America: An Environmental Risk Management Challenge." LinkedIn, May 16, 2016. https://www.linkedin.com/pulse/pesticides-linked-white-nose-syndrome-environmental-kenia-wiedemann/.

Wildlife Trusts. "Buff-Tailed Bumblebee." Accessed October 15, 2018. https://www.wildlifetrusts.org/wildlife-explorer/invertebrates/bees-wasps-and-ants/buff-tailed-bumblebee.

Williams, Geoffrey R., Aline Troxler, Gina Retschnig, Kaspar Roth, Orlando Yañez, Dave Shutler, Peter Neumann, and Laurent Gauthier. "Neonicotinoid Pesticides Severely Affect Honey Bee Queens." *Scientific Reports* 5 (October 13, 2015). http://www.nature.com/articles/srep14621.

Wilson, Rachel Sarah, Sara Diana Leonhardt, Alison Shapcott, Alexander Keller, Tim Heard, Chris Fuller, Wiebke Sickle, Tobias Smith, and Helen M. Wallace. "Pollen Meta-Barcoding to Understand Australian Native Bee Foraging Patterns." ResearchGate. Last modified July 12, 2017. https://www.researchgate.net/project/Pollen-meta-barcoding-to-understand-Australian-native-bee-foraging-patterns.

Woodcock, B. A., J. M. Bullock, R. F. Shore, M. S. Heard, M. G. Pereira, J. Redhead, L. Ridding, H. Dean, D. Sleep, P. Henrys, J. Peyton, S. Hulmes, L. Hulmes, M. Sárospataki, C. Saure, M. Edwards, E. Genersch, S. Knäbe, and R. F. Pywell. "Country-Specific Effects of Neonicotinoid Pesticides on Honey Bees and Wild Bees." *Science* 356, no. 6345 (June 30, 2017): 1393–95. http://science.sciencemag.org/content/356/6345/1393.

World Bee Project. "IPBES: The Assessment Report on Pollinators, Pollination, and Food Production." August 23, 2017. http://worldbeeproject.org/latest-posts/2017/8/23/ipbes-the-assessment-report-on-pollinators-pollination-and-food-production.

Wyatt, Gary. "Windbreak and Crop Yield Study." University of Minnesota Extension. *Minnesota Crop News*, April 29, 2015. http://blog-crop-news.extension.umn.edu/2015/04/windbreak-and-crop-yield-study.html.

Xerces Society. "Calling All Western Monarch and Milkweed Observers!" October 3, 2017. https://xerces.org/2017/10/03/calling-all-western-monarch-and-milkweed-observers/.

———. "Native Bee Biology." Accessed October 15, 2018. https://xerces.org/pollinator-conservation/native-bees/.

———. "New Western Monarch and Milkweed Website Launched." Press release, February 16, 2017. https://xerces.org/2017/02/16/new-western-monarch-and-milkweed-website-launched/.

———. "Project Milkweed." Accessed October 15, 2018. https://xerces.org/milkweed/.

———. "Providing Wildflowers for Pollinators." Accessed October 15, 2018. http://xerces.org/providing-wildflowers-for-pollinators/.

———. "Releasing Monarch Butterflies Is Not a Good Conservation Strategy." October 8, 2015. https://xerces.org/2015/10/08/releasing-monarch-butterflies-is-not-a-good-conservation-strategy/.

Yates, Diana. "Report: Milkweed Losses May Not Fully Explain Monarch Butterfly Declines." University of Illinois. *Illinois News Bureau*, March 13, 2017. https://news.illinois.edu/view/6367/474116.

Yirka, Bob. "NASA Funds Project to Study Feasibility of Using Robot Bees to Study Mars from a New Perspective." Phys.org, April 3, 2018. https://phys.org/news/2018-04-nasa-funds-feasibility-robot-bees.html.

Youngsteadt, Elsa, Rebecca E. Irwin, Alison Fowler, Matthew A. Bertone, Sara June Giacomini, Michael Kunz, Dale Suiter, and Clyde E. Sorenson. "Venus Flytrap Rarely Traps Its Pollinators." *American Naturalist* 191, no. 4 (February 5, 2018). https://www.journals.uchicago.edu/doi/10.1086/696124.

Index

Island Press | Board of Directors